Down Your Street

Cambridge Past and Present

VOLUME III

West Cambridge

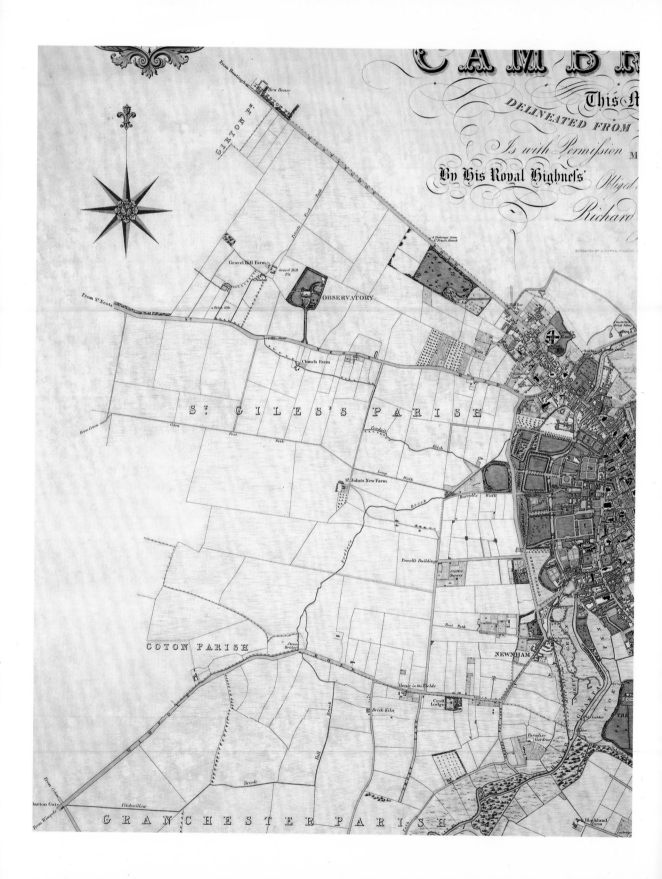

Down Your Street

Cambridge Past and Present

VOLUME III

West Cambridge

SARA PAYNE

Sara Payne

THE DALEGARTH PRESS

Published by The Dalegarth Press
Cambridge

© The Dalegarth Press 2014

ISBN 978-0-9930097-0-9

The major parts of the chapters in this book were originally published in the *Cambridge Weekly
News* between 1981 and 1985 and are copyright Cambridge Newspapers Ltd. The author wishes
to thank Cambridge Newspapers Ltd for their co-operation. More nostalgic stories about the
Cambridge area can be found in the Cambridge News and Weekly News series, and online at
www.cambridge-news.co.uk. The generous provision of information and illustrations by the
Cambridgeshire Collection, Cambridge Libraries is gratefully acknowledged.

Edited by Sarah Brierley
Proofreading by Richard Hall
Designed by Paul Barrett Book Production, Cambridge www.pbbp.co.uk
Printed in Northern Ireland by W.G. Baird

Front cover: Silver Street bridge in 2014
Back cover: Harraden's view of Queens' College in 1798 showing one of the old bridges
Frontispiece: Detail from Baker's New Map of the University and town of Cambridge 1830
Ref. R53/11*/2. *Copyright Cambridgeshire Archives and Local Studies*
Map on p.VIII by Jon Harris

Contents

Foreword

If you want to know about Cambridge start here. *Down Your Street Cambridge Past and Present Volume III West Cambridge* explores the streets of west Cambridge, and fills them with the stories and the people the author met when she first visited the area thirty years ago, and with those living there today.

Sara Payne's original *Down Your Street* articles are among the best written journalism ever published in the *Cambridge Weekly News*. Each week from 1981–87 she told the story of the streets, roads, avenues and terraces that together make up Cambridge. This was never dull history. In a lively and informative way she traced the origins of each street, told the story of past inhabitants and added contemporary interviews with present-day residents.

In a city where there are many books about the University and its famous staff and students, but few about the people who live here, the articles filled a void. They still do. The story of each street is a reminder of how Cambridge has always been changing, with old houses rebuilt, courtyards demolished and former open countryside absorbed into the urban fabric. Whether residents live in Newnham, Mill Road or Arbury, they live on what were fields not long ago. *Down Your Street* explored how this happened and took, as it were, a snapshot of the town in the late 20th century filling it with a huge variety of people, their different occupations and their memories.

The original articles captured Cambridge on the cusp of change. Published in the 1980s Arbury was still a new development, the M11 had only just been completed, and the University Departments were all in the City centre.

Thirty years ago no-one had heard of "Silicon Fen", and Clive Sinclair was an eccentric entrepreneur working in the new field of computers. When Sara Payne first visited it Cranmer Road was known as "Dons Alley", and was home to university professors. Today Clive Sinclair's successors in businesses associated with the growth of hi-tech industries have ousted the "Dons", as house prices soar towards £2 million. It is a change that has affected the whole city, and can be seen even more clearly in Newnham Croft where you can now find the university professors living in terraces built for college servants. This book meets old and new residents, and in the process chronicles the change that has affected the whole city.

Allan Brigham
Blue Badge Guide. Town Not Gown Tours of Cambridge
Honorary MA awarded by the University for Services to the City
Chair of Friends of the Folk Museum of Cambridge

Preface

Ever since the publication of the first two volumes of *Down Your Street* many people have been asking when I was going to publish another one.

So thirty years later, here is Volume III. It is a book about west Cambridge, the traditional fiefdom of Cambridge University and its colleges, and home from the late 1800s, to a line of outstanding scientists and other scholars, many of them Nobel prize winners. Go up to one of the hidden spots in west Cambridge, the Burial Ground of the Ascension, and you will find many of them buried there.

Eleven streets are included in the book. Each chapter, as in the previous volumes, consists of the original article as it appeared in the *Cambridge Weekly News* at the time, with some additional material added (the dates of those articles are given at the head of each chapter) but a new feature is a second part documenting some of the changes in the last thirty years.

The journey starts in Shelly Row, part of Roman Cambridge, and moves west down Storey's Way, Grange Road and adjoining roads, before visiting Silver Street, Newnham Road and heading south out of Cambridge down the Barton Road via adjacent streets in Newnham Croft.

I would like to thank Cambridge Newspapers Ltd for giving me the opportunity to write the original series of articles, collectively entitled *Down Your Street*.

The Cambridgeshire Collection has been an essential source of documents and records. Both the original articles and the first two books – *Down Your Street Volume I Central Cambridge* and *Volume II East Cambridge* published by the Pevensey Press, as well as this book would not have been published without the help of all its librarians.

I am indebted to Philomena Guillebaud for sharing her expert knowledge of the history of west Cambridge, to Jon Harris for drawing another fine map, to Professor Neboysha Ljepojevic for enlightening me about several of the giants of science and to the many college archivists, librarians and Fellows and west Cambridge residents who have helped me.

My thanks to my son, Julian Weigall for taking many of the photographs and for his advice on the design and production of the book, and to Diana Levy for her assistance with the production process. I am especially grateful to Sarah Brierley for editing the text so thoroughly and to Paul Barrett of Paul Barrett Book Production for designing the book that combines old and new in a subtle way – it has been a pleasure to work with a former "News" colleague.

I dedicate this book to Rodney Dale and Mike Petty who helped and encouraged me throughout. Without their help it would not have been written.

Sara Payne
Cambridge, 2014

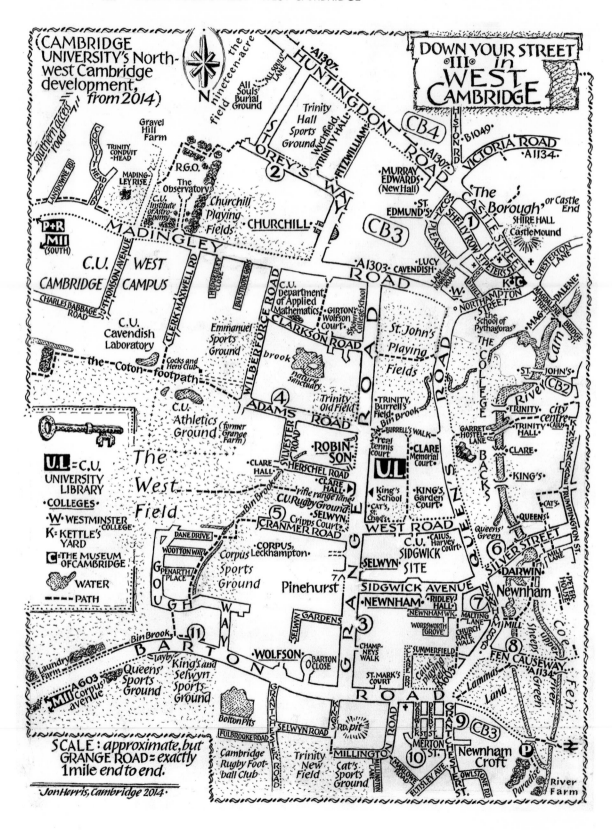

Historical introduction

The west side of Cambridge is an historically important part of the town, particularly in relation to the development of the University and colleges. It encompassed the West Fields, over 1,300 acres in extent, while on the east side were the slightly smaller East or Barnwell Fields, with the increasingly congested town itself hemmed in by these two open Fields. In 1800 both Fields were divided into hundreds of strips of different sizes and shapes, each with a specific owner, and any given owner's strips might be scattered anywhere in one of the Fields. The process of consolidating these strips into larger units suitable for modern agricultural practices was called Enclosure; in the West Fields it took place between 1800 and 1805 and in the East Fields five years later, in each case preceded by an Act of Parliament.

As was standard practice, in preparation for Enclosure of the West Fields a detailed ownership survey was made, which revealed that a handful of colleges owned more than half the land in question. The subsequent redrawing of boundaries reflected the previous ownership pattern – no-one who had not previously been a land- or tithe-owner received any land under the redistribution – and in the upshot St John's was entitled to 30 per cent of the land enclosed, or 410 acres, while other colleges with significant amounts were Corpus Christi, Jesus, Gonville and Caius, Clare and King's. Merton College, Oxford, which had owned land in Cambridge since the 13th century was among the substantial owners, with almost 70 acres.

Although the colleges' share of the land was no bigger than it had been before Enclosure, they successfully manoeuvred to get all the best bits, i.e. those closest to the river and to their lands on the town side of the river, mainly in order to prevent any construction there and preserve the land as a kind of green belt. One college, Gonville and Caius, broke ranks and leased land for the building of four private houses on the west side of what became Queen's Road (between what are now Sidgwick Avenue and West Road, but the rest retained their allocations as pasture and playing fields until 1870, when the long agricultural depression obliged the colleges to seek other sources of income. This led to the building of what has been called the "bicycle suburb".

West view of Cambridge dated circa 1750.

SHELLY ROW

9 September 1982

Shelly Row at Castle End is perched on an archaeologist's paradise. Belgic rubbish pits and a Saxon burial ground are under the spot, formerly the Phoenix Gardens, where new flats are being built by the Granta Housing Society at the junction with Mount Pleasant. Behind No. 13 Shelly Row, one of those small higgledy-piggledy houses on the east side of the street, there is known to be another Saxon burial ground, and underneath the house a Roman cemetery.

The slanting pavement, on which the few remaining houses in Shelly Row stand, covers an ancient bank or balk which is known to be of Roman origin, for Shelly Row and Storey's Paddock to the west lay just within the Roman town which stood on the western slopes of Castle Hill, hard against the town's defences. Centuries later, a royal castle, a Civil War fort, a prison and finally the Law Courts were superimposed upon that Roman town. This is historic Cambridge.

Phoenix Gardens – between Castle Street, Mount Pleasant and Shelly Row – lay, according to archaeologist Dr John Alexander who has investigated the site, just inside the north gate of the Roman town fronting the main road. Somewhere nearby there was, in early medieval times, a market cross and a church – All-Saints-by-the-Castle – which may have stood there in the 17th century. Since then the site has been orchards and gardens.

Shelly Row was known as Shallow Row in 1830, and its present name is said to refer to the tons of oyster shells unearthed in residents' gardens within the Roman town. Oysters used to be transported to Cambridge by river from Kings Lynn, where they grew in brackish water. Once in Cambridge they were loaded onto punts and then distributed round the city. There used to be an oyster bar in Shelly Row.

Houses are known to have existed in Shelly Row in the 16th and 17th centuries because cesspits of that period were found under No. 4 when the mid-19th century house was demolished in 1957.

Prior to 1836, the St Peter's Parish "Poor House" was in Shelly Row. H. P. Stokes in an article on Cambridge Parish Workhouses writes: "The St Peter's Parish Vestry Books are not forthcoming, but the Workhouse seems to have stood in Shelly Row opposite Albion Row. The old buildings, which were held on lease from the Corporation, have been pulled down and replaced by houses erected by the Cambridge Improved Industrial Dwellings Company."

After the Poor Law changes in 1836, says Stokes, the inmates of the workhouse were moved to the other classified workhouses until the new building was ready in Mill Road. For a bit of fascinating oral history, Stokes came across "a patriarchal old inhabitant of the neighbourhood still living who well remembers the paupers of St Peter's Workhouse in Shelly Row going away in a cart, and among them 'blind old Dick' and a curious old married couple."

In the *Cambridge Chronicle* and *University Journal* for 5 September 1928, there is in their "picture of the past" series a photograph of what was the workhouse. The caption reads: "An old cottage which stood in Shelly Row and was demolished between 30 and 40 years ago. The last occupant of the cottage was Mrs Smith, a college laundress, whose mother Mrs Burgess for many years held the lease of the property from the Cambridge Corporation. It was at one time the 'poor house' for St Peter's parish." When the building, or rather the lease, was sold in 1838 by order of the Poor Law Commissioners, the advertisement which appeared read as follows: "extensive leasehold estate in Castle Street. Lot 1. House on the Pound Hill, with large yard at the back and gardens bounded at the east by a passage leading to Castle Street and on the west by Pound Hill, etc. Lot 2. Two gardens with an entrance from Castle End, Held by lease from the Corporation for 40 years from Michaelmas 1823 at 22s. and land tax 8s."

Shelly Row in the 1930s showing the Roman balk.

A view of the houses on the east side of Shelly Row in the 1930s.

The charitable associations of Shelly Row however, go far beyond the St Peter's Workhouse: it lies in the heart of the territory of Edward Storey, the 17th-century founder of Storey's Charity, one of the most significant bequests in the history of the city of Cambridge. A farmhouse and eight acres of land in St Giles' parish, known as Storey's Farm on Mount Pleasant, were among the properties and land which he possessed at his death in 1692. It is this extensive site that has become, since the building of Storey's House in 1974, one of the focal points of the Charity's operations. Long before Storey's House, however, there were the almshouses at Nos. 1–9 Shelly Row, rebuilt in 1843–4 for clergy widows.

It is thought that Edward Storey himself lived at one time in Shelly Row. Miss H. M. Larke and Mrs S. Shield in their short history *The Foundation of Edward Storey 1693–1980*, suggest that Storey "perhaps moved to the beautiful old 16th-century house which stood on the Castle Hill side of Shelly Row – later called Cromwell House – because Oliver Cromwell lived there while his troops occupied the Castle in the Civil War. This house was shown to be the property of the Storey's Trust in 1874 when it was demolished by them to provide land for building new small houses." The 16th-century house was built about 1556, with "carved barge boards and pendants outside, a fine staircase, some rooms oak-panelled all over, rush ceilings, wide oak floorboards, a fine carved chimney piece resembling those at Sawston Hall, grotesque door hinges and a fluted cornice of panelling."

Another feature of "vanished" Shelly Row, and much of it has vanished, is recorded for us by Gwen Raverat in *Period Piece*, in which she describes and illustrates the pump and horse trough which used to stand at the corner of Shelly Row and Mount Pleasant. Castle End was a rough slum area when she was a child in the 1890s. Raverat was always frightened of passing through it apparently, and writes:

"The rough gangs of boys who used to rove about Castle End were quite enough to terrify me. To reach our grandmother's or uncles' houses in the Huntingdon Road, we had to pass through a corner of Castle End, called Mount Pleasant."

The sight she remembered with most horror was "a little group of dreadful boys near the pump and horse trough at the corner of Shelly Row. They were wringing the neck of a white hen; and a smaller boy stood apart, sobbing pitifully. I suppose it was his hen. Nana hurried us by."

Mrs Connie Lyne, who was born at No. 8 Shelly Terrace "80 years ago this Christmas," and who has lived at 10 Shelly Row since 1929, has clear memories of the horse trough described by Gwen Raverat. "Yes, it was where the cabbies used to stop to give their horses a drink." Mrs Lyne was Connie Wright before she was married. Her father, Herbert Wright, was a sugar boiler who worked for Whibley & Son, whose shop on Peas Hill sold sweets and groceries. "Father always brought us home 2lbs of boiled sweets every week. They cost 4d a pound."

Mrs Lyne remembers the First World War when men of the Norfolk regiment were billeted in the area: "There were guns across the road in what is now the little park, and horses and mules were stabled at Storey's Farm. My mother had two soldiers billeted in her house."

There were several shops and businesses in Shelly Row in the early days. Mrs Lyne remembers going as a child to Mrs Hall's general store at No. 8 Shelly Row to buy a trundle hoop. It was one of those shops that sold everything. On the opposite side of the road at the junction of Shelly Row and Albion Row was Mrs Harris's sweet shop. Her shop was opposite the Cow and Calf. Mrs Annie Kavanagh of Storey's House, who has lived in the Castle Hill area all her life, remembers that there used to be a baker at the corner of Albion Row and Shelly Row: "Everyone used to go there for their bread. There were so many shops in the area, particularly on Castle Street that there was no need to go down the town," she said.

The Cow and Calf pub at No. 14 Pound Hill, popular for its real ale.

Mrs Connie Lyne has lived in Shelly Row all her life.

William White, the blacksmith, had a smithy at No. 25 Shelly Row (now the children's playground). Mrs Lyne remembers going to see Mr White at work in his smithy: "He was there before I was born." The Street Directory for 1891 lists a William White blacksmith, at No. 24 Shelly Row and next door at No. 25 a Walter White, whitesmith, blacksmith and shoeing smith, together with Thomas Chapman, wheelwright.

Mrs Lyne, who worked as a bedmaker for St John's College for 32 years, has particularly clear memories of one or two of the old characters who used to live in Shelly Row. "There was Arthur Dean, who worked at Trinity kitchens. He lived at No. 17, next door to Albert Shaw." A check in the 1874 Street Directory lists Albert Shaw as a baker.

When Harold Bird of Christchurch Street, Cambridge, read about Connie Lyne in the *Weekly News*, he wrote in to say that he "noted with very great interest 'Down Your Street' for I lived in Shelly Row. "I know Connie Tyne – I knew her as Connie Wright and I lived directly opposite to where she lives at present. I can name her six brothers and two sisters. She says she remembers the First World War – well, so do I. I joined the Cambridgeshire Regiment in September 1914, aged 16 years and eight months, and was in the trenches for three years. Now, I give you some information and ask her how well she remembers me at the outbreak of the war. She and I were rather sweet on one another. She and her sisters and her young brothers were always playing together. Her brother Bill was the first Cambridge man to be killed in the war. I was born in Albion Road. We later moved to Shelly Row and I lived there at No. 26 until 1927, right opposite her house so you can tell her please, that Harold Bird is very pleased to know that she is still alive and well and give her my best wishes."

Of course, there were many more houses in little courts and passages off Shelly Row in the early 1900s, and there was Shelly Terrace itself, a row of five bay-windowed houses, which were pulled down after the last war. Hall's Passage and Miller's Passage led off the east side of the road. On the opposite side, below the clergy widows' almshouses (now council flats), was Porcher's Yard just near Collin's Timber Yard. The terrace at the top of Shelly Row on the east side consisted of one-up-one-down houses with an outside lavatory and a communal tap for the whole block.

Cambridge councillors heard that in 1912 a piece of land in Shelly Row, together with the house adjoining was given anonymously to the Corporation as a perpetual playground to the children of Castle End. It was assumed that the rent of the house would be available for the upkeep and improvement of the playground. £80 would be required to make a really satisfactory playground; it was resolved to spend £20 on putting the ground in order.

In recent times, Shelly Row has been somewhat rejuvenated. Houses have been repainted by the Council and decline has been arrested.

SHELLY ROW

Revisited

Shelly Row may be sitting on an archaeologist's treasure trove, but at ground level, above those historic Belgic, Roman and Saxon burial grounds and cemeteries, it is now a shadow of what it was, say, 100 years ago. Then, it was home to many artisans, packed in to small terraced houses and yards, plying their trade as blacksmiths or running shops such as bakeries and hardware stores and frequenting, before it was demolished, the Cow and Calf pub – one of at least 20 pubs in the area. Incidentally, Cambridge City Council's Conservation area appraisal for Castle and Victoria Road, refers to the Cow and Calf as "a pub of some repute".

Paul Ainsworth writing in *ALE 2000* said when he first knew the Cow and Calf in the early eighties it was very much an Irish pub, with rebel songs on the jukebox and a map of a united Ireland on the wall. "It also had a reputation as a haunt of members of the oldest profession. Local lovers of 'real' pubs were deeply saddened by its demolition in 1999."

A busy route for traffic, cutting through remorselessly all day long from Huntingdon Road and Castle Hill down to Madingley Road, the street is more likely to be home now to less affluent, single young people and students living in privately rented and mortgaged accommodation. The Granta Housing Association's flats at the top of Shelly Row on the east side, and the former almshouses founded by Edward Storey for widows and spinsters from the parishes of St Giles and Holy Trinity, which relocated to Shelly Row in 1843 on the north west side, are now owned by the City Council. These almshouses should not be confused with Storey's House, which also relocated and was built in the same year in Mount Pleasant for widows of Anglican clergymen.

There are however still some local residents who have lived in the area for years and who have seen many of the changes that have taken place, for example Mrs Doris Fuller who has lived at No. 8 Shelly Row since 1967. No. 8 used to be Mrs Hall's general and hardware store, which Mrs Connie Lyne used to visit as a child and which she told me about when I met her more than 30 years ago. Doris Fuller knew Connie Wright who lived next door at No. 10. Mrs Fuller and her late husband Charles, who was an accountant, moved into the former shop, when it was still divided into two rooms on the ground floor. Their landlord sold the property to the Council, who have since modernised it and it is now one room with a kitchen.

Doris Fuller says: "I have seen a hell of a lot of changes round here. There were no houses across the road when we came, and it wasn't so busy with traffic. Also, people years ago were much more friendly. Now there are a few more young people. But then people didn't move so much, did they?" As she points out, her father never moved out of his village. "He was born in Shepreth, died and was buried in Shepreth."

Doris worked as a caterer at St John's College for 25 years, and before that as a waitress at the Dorothy Café in the town centre. "The college was wonderful to me." On one occasion she was presented to the Chancellor, Prince Philip. When she retired in 1996, the St John's Fellows presented her with a grandmother clock, which has pride of place in her living room along with a collection of personal memorabilia. The plaque reads: "Presented to Doris Fuller on the occasion of her retirement by the fellows of St John's. March 1996. Tempus Fugit."

Sharing her home is a spirit which hasn't flown like time! I ask her if it's a friendly spirit, "Yes, of course it is", she says. "He is buried in the wall under the foundations. He is medieval." Perhaps the spirit enjoys the garden too, where Doris has created a pond full of Koi fish. Wires overhead, installed by friendly neighbours, prevent a predatory heron swooping in and scooping up those prized fish.

I was told to call on Doris Fuller by another long-standing resident of the area, Mr Andrew Hawes, who lives across the way at No. 6 Albion Yard. His father,

Some of the original houses still standing above the Roman balk on the east side of Shelly Row.

Ronald Lester Hawes, used to work for Cambridge Police. A retired welder, Andrew Hawes, was taking his dog Elisabeth Longstocking to sit in St Giles Churchyard the day I stopped to speak to him outside Castle End Mission. "I help to clear the churchyard of litter and bottles that are thrown over, and the church gives me a cake in return! My dog sits on clover there in the churchyard."

On a clear day, passers-by may notice an eccentric figure sitting in the doorway of his home up the road from Doris Fuller. When the stars are visible he will be scanning the night sky with his telescopes. He is retired scientist Fred Allen, whose home is swamped with his collection of scientific instruments, including several microscopes. Originally studying biochemistry at St Andrews University, he then worked in the Cambridge University Radiology and Radio Therapeutic departments, as well as in Pathology. A colleague of his was the scientist Dr Donald Cator, who was interned with his family in Shanghai during the Second World War.

With the time of publication coinciding with the 100th anniversary of the outbreak of the First World War, Fred's anecdote about his father's wartime cricketing experience is rather timely: "My father was the second or third fastest bowler in the Army. When he bowled out the Navy team for just 18 runs, the top brass said 'we don't want him to be killed, he is such a good bowler', so they made him a cook on the General Staff of the British Army". So Fred's father, also called Fred, survived the war cooking for huge numbers of troops, and, I am guessing here, serving haute cuisine to Earl Haig and the other "donkeys" who led the "lions". Pure Monty Python!

Edward Storey, with his great bequest in the 17th century, was not the only philanthropist to have left his mark on the area. Castle End Mission, at the bottom of the street on Pound Hill, is the legacy of a doughty Victorian lady, Mrs Mark Ives Whibley. Today, Castle End Mission is a small, independent congregation, linked since 1910 to Emmanuel United Reformed Church in Trumpington Street. It shares Sunday services with Castle Street Methodist Church and has links to Westminster Theological College. The Mission began as a centre for the education of working men, many of whom could not read or write. The first meeting took place in 1879 and the driving force in its early development was Mrs Whibley. It was initially called the Castle End Men's Morning School.

Dr John Kendall, a member of the management committee, who for many years has helped take care of the building, tells me about the work of the Mission. The present building with its impressive main hall was opened in 1884 as the Castle End Mission and Working Men's Institute. It has always been a centre of community activity in this area of Cambridge and continues to provide facilities for a large number of community groups, including drama groups, the opera group CAOS, the Korean Church and yoga groups. The nearby Folk Museum holds meetings there and it is a polling station at election time.

We sit upstairs on rather well-used, old armchairs in the Band Room, where a big drum and a kettle drum are stuffed away in a cupboard and date from the time when the Girls Brigade used to parade through the streets. Frances Whibley looks down at us from a handsome portrait depicting her in Victorian

**Castle End
Mission, the
legacy of
Mrs Mark Ives
Whibley.**

dress, complete with bonnet and cape. The painting captures her determined character and spirit and has pride of place on the wall. Dr Kendall explains that Mrs Whibley and her husband Mark Ives Whibley were prominent in business, local Liberal politics and Church affairs in Cambridge. Mr Whibley was in the grocery trade and when they moved to Cambridge in 1852 he worked for the firm, Brimley & Bond, the grocers on Market Hill, before becoming a partner in the firm, later Whibley & Son. They lived in St Edward's Passage nearby and then later moved to a house on Milton Road.

After raising nine children, several of whom died in childhood, and supporting her husband in his grocery business, Mrs Whibley then committed herself to helping the poor, illiterate and destitute who lived in the Castle area of the city.

On Sunday, 11 February 1879, Castle End Morning School began with two men attending at a small rented room in a cottage in Kettle's Yard. Numbers soon increased and a weekday Night School meeting was added. The undenominational support offered, together with the teaching of the three R's and religion, was welcomed by the community. By 1884 membership had increased to sixty, drawn by the variety of activities that had grown from its modest start. Clubs for women, girls and boys were added to the educational meetings and a Sick Benefit scheme provided a lifeline in the days before any State benefits.

Mrs Whibley, who died in 1915, was the driving force behind the building of the Castle End Mission by raising funds for the work through public appeal. A memorial plaque placed in the Hall on 20 September 1920 commemorates this formidable woman and her work.

STOREY'S WAY

10–24 March 1983

The origins of Storey's Way go back to the Middle Ages when it was called Grithow Field. In the eighteenth century, Grithow – or Grythowe – became Great Howe. The Grythowe was the mound or tumulus at the south end of a gravel ridge which gave its name to the Field.

When John Maxwell Edmonds was building his house in Storey's Way in 1914, to the designs of the distinguished architect Baillie Scott, he decided to call it Gryt-Howe Cottage, thus perpetuating the early origins of the area. Edmonds had been a student of archaeology, which suggests that those antiquarian potterings must have led him to come up with one of the more recherche names in Storey's Way. More about his house later.

The land on which Storey's Way is built became incorporated in the eighteenth century into the estate which Edward Storey, the Cambridge bookseller, left in the endowment of Storey's Charity. It was part of Mount Pleasant Farm. The Charity was founded in the eighteenth century to provide almshouses for four widows of ministers of the Church of England and for widows and maidens of the Cambridge parishes of St Giles and Holy Trinity.

According to H. M. Larke and S. Shield in their book, *The Foundation of Edward Storey 1693–1980*, the trustees of the Storey's Charity decided to develop part of Mount Pleasant Farm – an L-shaped piece of land, which had been allocated to the charity in 1805 by the Commissioners of Enclosure. "It was agreed in 1909 to develop 35 acres of Mount Pleasant Farm as building land, to build a road from Huntingdon Road to Madingley Road and to ask the Commissioners to allow the value of the land to be written up as £20,000 in lieu of the existing £7,000." The upper part of their peculiar L-shaped allocation joined Huntingdon Road when the first part of Storey's Way was built. It was the first of the two right-angles that make up the shape of the road as we know it today.

It was a tricky start to a commercial enterprise for the Trustees, who were "engaged in a perpetual struggle as landlords to make money, curbed by the Commissioners who were bound to take the long view, by the Corporation who were bound to take the broad view, by intending purchasers of plots who beat down prices and demanded rights, and then by the onset of the Great War." At the beginning of 1911, there were no bids for building plots, but by the end of the year they were said to be selling well. This progress was halted at the start of the First World War in 1914, only one plot being sold in the following three years, but building then resumed after the end of the war. Not all of it was built on however, Trinity Hall buying some for its playing field.

In 1917 there was said to be "an unfavourable outlook for Cambridge Trade." The Commissioners desired a new valuation of the land, and strove to push sales by public announcement and to increase income by stricter requirements of buyers. The house plots furthest from Huntingdon Road were not proving attractive to buyers because the road was a dead end at that point, so the Charity asked St John's to sell them a right of way joining the eastern end of their land to Madingley Road. St John's agreed, hence the second right angle in Storey's Way. Until well after the Second World War, that final leg of the road had no houses on it. The land on both sides was owned by St John's, the college kitchen garden and orchard on the east side of it, and that part of Grange Farm which later became Churchill College on the west.

The building plots said to be "selling well" by the end of 1911 were among the first to be built on. By 1912 Edward Cunningham, a Fellow, Praelector and mathematical lecturer of St John's College had built the first house on the north side. For many years, Lord McNair, author of the classic *Law of Treaties*, published in 1961, lived at No. 25. On the south side, Mr Wehrle was having a house built, as was the artist H. M. Brock, who chose the architect T. D. Atkinson, the secretary of the Cambridge Antiquarian Society, to design his stylish home, later numbered 63 Storey's Way. The architect Hugh Hughes, who designed Nos. 25 and 31 Storey's Way, was an apprentice of Atkinson.

H. M. Brock, the well-known illustrator of children's books, had a room on the first floor of Woodstock, later No. 63 Storey's Way, designed as an artist's studio. He must then have become friendly with the neighbours or the near-neighbours, in particular the Chivers family of Huntingdon Road, for he designed the original Olde English Gentleman that went onto the Chivers Olde English Marmalade labels!

Flashback to 23 May 1913 … The *Cambridge Chronicle* illustrates a report of suspected fire-raising in Storey's Way.

1913 saw a bit of a setback to house-building in Storey's Way. Miss Miriam Pratt, a 23-year-old teacher and suffragette from Norwich set fire on the night of 17 May to two houses being built there. The *Cambridge Chronicle* of 23 May 1913 reported that "shortly after one o'clock on Saturday morning, residents in St Andrew's Street and on the route to Huntingdon Road were awakened by the monotonous ringing of the alarm bell on the motor escape, and a few minutes afterwards the steamer followed. Then came large numbers of firemen – some cycling, some running and some riding in a covered van."

The fires had been started at a house that was being built for a Mrs Spencer, of No. 100 Castle Street, and for Professor Punnett, the Balfour Professor of Genetics. His house was next door but one, at No. 44 Storey's Way. Mrs Spencer's house, which was being built by Frederick Henry Jeffs of Letchworth, bore the brunt of the damage. The *Cambridge Chronicle* reported that "all the doors of the premises had been fastened overnight and the glazed windows were closed. The firemen forced an entrance by the front door, but it is thought that the incendiaries gained access to the premises by breaking the study window. There was a strong smell of paraffin in this part of the house, and the soaked flooring, packing cases and shavings in the room were very favourable to a rapid development of the blaze. The ceiling became ignited, and the fire rapidly spread to the other rooms in the house. Then the roof was demolished – the falling ruins doing a considerable amount of damage. The building would have been completed in a few weeks, and would have been worth about £1,150."

The house next door, however, was relatively unscathed. A lady's watch was left on the premises which was to be one of the clues that led to Miriam Pratt, who was later gaoled for arson. She went on hunger strike and was subsequently released from Holloway Prison prematurely. Between the two houses, fired by the young arsonist who was attempting to draw attention to the Votes for Women cause, was a house built for Herbert Ainslie Roberts, of Gonville and Caius College, the Secretary to the University Appointments Board. Miss Pratt made no attempt to fire this house. Had she done so it would have amounted to sacrilege in the eyes of architectural historians, for No. 48 Storey's Way is a jewel among Cambridge houses.

A Sussex-style farmhouse of mock-Tudor design with low eaves and a cat's slide roof, No. 48 Storey's Way (formerly known as No. 33) is the first house in Storey's Way to have been designed by Baillie Scott. It was completed in 1912, and the architect considered by Pevsner to be "one of the best British architects of the Voysey generation" went on to design four other houses in the road that was to become one of the most sought after residential areas of Cambridge. Baillie Scott's houses in Storey's Way are listed buildings and represent a range of different styles, from the Tudor farmhouse to the Georgian "Tortoise" look. How Baillie Scott came to acquire such a clutch of commissions all in one road no one actually knows, but it is probably something to do with imitation being the highest form of flattery.

My guess is that Mr and Mrs Roberts would have been familiar with examples of Baillie Scott's work from articles and photographs in, say, *Country Life* or architectural journals and said to themselves: "that's the man for us – or for our house". Impressed neighbours would have followed suit and hired the golden boy of the period to fashion them a lovely home "a la nature", full of oak floors, oak panelling, hand-tooled hinges, plaster ceilings and period fireplaces, where the emphasis was on handiwork, quality and simple design.

Baillie Scott was a real stickler for the natural look. Graham Pollard, the deputy director of the Fitzwilliam told me that Baillie Scott employed "peasant craftsmen" to work on No. 48. "He insisted that the apprentices were deliberately incompetent so as to achieve coarse plaster work." There is no wallpaper in the house, just the plasterwork which is prickly to the touch, with the exception of the plaster ceiling in the dining room which is particularly fine. The present owners, Mr and Mrs Geoffrey Ridsdill-Smith, said that the dining room was supposed to have been modelled on a room in St John's College. The Tudor Rose is picked out on the ceiling, modelled by J. C. Pocock, and oak leaves form the decoration of the frieze round this low, snug room. Even the curtains have an oak leaf design!

Baillie Scott clearly enjoyed working on No. 48. He wrote in 1933 that: "Nothing but pleasant recollections remain of this early adventure in house building, and the owner continued the good work with appropriate furnishing and a garden scheme of his own devising which makes an excellent setting for the house." The south garden of this house was planned like a church with nave, side aisles, chancels and transepts, and with plants blooming every month of the year. Baillie Scott said: "This will often be found a very satisfactory scheme for the layout of a garden, and its development might lead to the reproduction of the plan of one of our great cathedrals with hedges for walls and pergolas for aisles." There is topiary work and a bird bath built of brick and tile. The cobblestones were laid by Mrs Roberts who taught herself the skill.

The Ridsdill-Smiths said that Baillie Scott wanted the house to look as if it had grown out of the ground; lots of doors open out into the garden. The stone slabs leading up the path to the house are continued in the hall, then the oak takes over on stairs, walls, doors and fittings. There is a cosy rustic feel about this house, enhanced by log fires and mellow light. Baillie Scott was satisfied by the "excellent" builder they had for the house: "His enthusiasm for rustic character led him to choose for the joists over a passageway some unusually contorted branches of oak, the appearance of which the owner described as that of a troglodyte cave, but these were eventually pruned to more chastened lines."

Why doesn't the house have a name though? Baillie Scott himself can supply the answer. He wrote: "The fact that this house is distinguished only by a number may be understood to represent a mild protest by the owner against the fancy names of suburban residences, although he has been known to refer humorously to his house as 'Asphalte Court', presumably because it has no court, and if it had it would not be an asphalte one."

H. A. Roberts died in 1933. The second owner of 48 Storey's Way was Ashley Tabrum, the clerk of Cambridgeshire County Council. Then the Ridsdill-Smiths bought the house in 1958, the same year as Capt. and Mrs John Jago moved into

No. 30 Storey's Way, another of the Baillie Scott masterpieces in which he achieved the familiar cottage look. This was the house built in 1914 for John Maxwell Edmonds, whose lifestyle was clearly influenced by William Morris. For when the Jagos came, they found the house was equipped with a loom and was decorated in the period colours of peacock blue and mustard yellow. It was bitterly cold as a spartan ethic prevailed in those days before central heating. No. 30 Storey's Way – Gryt-howe Cottage – is now a cosy house; what was the lamp room has become a store room, and with low ceilings everywhere you feel you are in a snug burrow.

No. 29 Storey's Way was called by Baillie Scott "Tortoise". The low Mansard roof of brown pantiles seems to suggest the low reticulated carapace of the tortoise, he said. The house is Georgian type but instead of a bedroom floor plus attic floor over Mansard roof, the bedroom floor has been omitted and the roof storey placed immediately over the ground floor.

Cambridge's "Highgate Cemetery"

Between the gardens on the north-west side of Storey's Way and the open land of the University Farm lies the "Highgate Cemetery of Cambridge". St Giles's and St Peter's Cemetery, the city's country churchyard, where in summer the bullfinches and goldfinches feed on the thistledown, is the resting place of some of the intellectual giants of the last 100 years. Born in 1889, the Austrian philosopher Ludwig Wittgenstein, author of the *Tractatus Logico Philosophicus*, who reminded Magdalene English don I. A. Richards of Lucifer, both in appearance and in his capacity for engendering discord, is buried there – he died in 1951.

Charles and Evelyn Dilley who look after St Giles's Cemetery.

People come from all over the world to find Wittgenstein's simple tomb. To do so, these questing scholars in search of a grave need the help of the sexton, Charles Dilley, and his wife, Evelyn. "If I had a halfpenny for the number of times I have shown people to that grave, then I would be a wealthy woman," she said. The Dilleys have looked after the cemetery since 1947, and have opened up the chapel every Sunday at 8 a.m. for a communion service.

The grave of Horace Darwin, 1851–1928, the son of Charles Darwin, and the co-founder of the Cambridge Scientific Instrument Company, lies beneath brambles. Remembered on the headstone is his son Erasmus, born 1881, who fell at Ypres. The epitaph to Francis Darwin, Horace's older brother 1848–1925, reads: "O ye holy and humble men of heart bless ye the Lord." Arthur Stanley Eddington, the mathematician and astrophysicist, Alfred Marshall the economist and John Couch Adams, who predicted the existence and position of Neptune, are buried nearby.

Frank Ramsey, brother of the former Archbishop, and A. C. Benson, the author and at one time Master of Magdalene College, are buried near the perimeter wall of the cemetery, where there is a view of open country and in the distance, Madingley Hill. The temptation to quote from Thomas Gray's *Elegy Written in a Country Churchyard* is irresistible:

Perhaps in this neglected spot is laid
Some heart once pregnant with celestial fire;
Hands that the rod of empire might have sway'd,
Or waked to ecstasy the living lyre.

(from Thomas Gray *Elegy Written in a Country Churchyard*, 1750)

Among the many other people buried in this pre-Raphaelite haunt, are the first residents of Storey's Way, Ada and Ebenezer Cunningham, who in 1912 built the first house on the north side of Storey's Way, now No. 141 Huntingdon Road. The Cunninghams are buried a stone's throw from home. Ebenezer Cunningham was 95 when he died, the oldest Fellow of St John's College.

At the age of 100, Dame Harriette Chick, the distinguished nutritionist who lived with her married sister, Mrs Elsie Blackman, at No. 34 Storey's Way, continued to use the cemetery as a shortcut to her friends', and the bus stop in Huntingdon Road. Brakes squealed as she plunged across the road, stick held out in front. She shinned over the cemetery wall with the help of a neat little ladder strategically placed at the end of the garden. That she could negotiate that ladder (it's still there!) at the age of 100 was a tribute to her agility and determination. The expression "cemetery walls" is synonymous with keeping young and fit for the Abbott family who live at No. 29 Storey's Way.

Dame Harriette Chick, who came to Cambridge from London in 1940, spent her life working on nutrition. She discovered that rickets was due to deficiency, and not disease as was thought. In 1920, she worked on Vitamins A, C and D. When she was 100 years old, she gave a seminal lecture on nutrition in London.

Relatives remember that in spite of her brilliance she did not mind menial tasks. She would help her housekeeper with the washing-up and fruit bottling well into her late 90s. For her 100th birthday Dame Harriette was due a telegram from the Queen. A member of the Royal Household telephoned to check whether she was still alive. Only the home help was in the house, and so she took the call. She said: "Dame Harriette is very much alive – she is now out shopping with her companion." At 100 she was still beautiful and prettily dressed, although despite her work on nutrition, she took very little interest in what she ate herself. She more or less ate anything, and was in no way a crank.

The house she lived in with her married sister, Elsie Blackman, after whom the Blackman wing in Langdon House is named, was built for the Blackman family. The house was designed by the late Professor F. F. Blackman in 1925, in a modern style for the times, for a family with servants. At the time of building, it was still in the countryside – a quiet rural spot. It was completed before No. 32, which was built to a similar style. Professor Peter Blackman now lives in the family house with its spacious grounds, which still has an unimpeded view of the very gently undulating countryside of west Cambridge. Maids used to serve tea al fresco, in the pretty summerhouse on the lawn.

The oldest resident in Storey's Way, at 90, is Enid Lenox-Conyngham. Her house was built in the same year as the Blackmans – 1925 – and being on the north-west side of the road looks across to the cemetery. The house belonged to the Church Missionary Society when the family bought it in 1960.

The houses on the south-east side of Storey's Way have a rural outlook on to Trinity Hall's sports ground. The seven-acre site was acquired by the college prior to 1674. A further three acres between the college's land and Huntingdon Road was bought by Trinity Hall from John Chivers, who lived at Wychfield on Huntingdon Road. He had used the three acres as a kitchen garden and paddock. John Chivers, people may remember, was one of the first people in Cambridge to own a motor car. "Wychfield" was built by Francis Darwin, son of Charles.

The college playing field between Huntingdon Road and Storey's Way was laid out in 1922–4. In spite of tempting prospects for building development, the governing body apparently decided to convert about six acres of allotments into a playing field. Charles Crawley, who knew the college intimately for more than 50 years as a Fellow, senior tutor, Vice-Master and Honorary Fellow, wrote in his history of Trinity Hall that the playing field was the "enduring monument" to the Bursar at the time, the Hon. I. M. Campbell, DSO, Scottish laird from Eton and Trinity, who also did some teaching in estate management.

The work of creating the playing field was achieved under the daily supervision of the Bursar and the groundsman, Ernest Coote. A pavilion was built, followed a little later by a groundsman's house, and after that by two squash courts.

Ernest Coote retired in 1951 after 46 years of hard work. He died in 1953, and was succeeded by his son Leslie, who had been groundsman for Peterhouse. Another son, Cyril, had in 1875 been the groundsman at Fenner's, the Cambridge

University Cricket Ground in Mortimer Road for nearly 40 years, and a third son, Claud, was long groundsman for Trinity.

One of the houses with a particularly fine view of the Trinity Hall playing field is No. 7 Storey's Way, the home of Peter and Anne Chivers. A house with some Baillie Scott-type flourishes, it was built in 1924–5 by Arthur Negus, the builder, for himself. When Mr Negus and his wife died, their daughter let the house to James Macgregor, who was head of the School of Architecture.

Mrs Romola Oddie bought No. 3 Storey's Way in 1958, after a fire destroyed her thatched cottage in Bourn. She regrets that Professor Baker, the mathematician, who built the house on a double plot, decided to build an adjacent house on his plot of land. No. 5 Storey's Way deprives No. 3 of any sunlight. You have to get right out into the garden before you feel any warm rays! A Belgian nun, Sister Agnes-Marie of the Order of Sisters of St Mary of Namur, who lives with Mrs Oddie at No. 3, is a familiar figure to people who live on the King's Hedges estate. Sister Agnes was instrumental in helping to establish the King's Hedges Ecumenical Centre and this church-cum-social centre, which looks like a big bungalow, celebrated its first anniversary last November.

Opposite No. 34 Storey's Way is a den of ecological activity. It is the Culture Centre of Algae and Protozoa, part of the Institute of Terrestrial Ecology. This Culture Centre of Algae and Protozoa derived from the collection started by Ernst Pringsheim in Prague in 1928. Pringsheim's collection was expanded and eventually taken over by E. A. George for Cambridge University in 1947. In November 1975, the Centre became part of the Institute of Terrestrial Ecology.

One of the 2,000 strains of algae, seaweeds, etc. in the Centre was in fact identified by none other than Dame Harriette Chick! A marine biologist at the Centre, Nigel Pennick, told me that she described the organism "chlorella pyrenoidosa", a small green freshwater algae, which probably came out of her garden opposite! What a small world!

At the back of the Culture Centre is the Department of Zoology's Field Station. From time to time locusts are released from here, but hovering sparrows are quick to pounce and devour them. They deal with country matters in Storey's Way!

Treasures in the Archives Centre

When Sir Winston Churchill was a little boy, he was packed off to board at prep school. He hated it, and wrote sad little letters home, craving affection, visits and treats. The letters were frequently signed with rows of loving, giant-sized wobbly kisses, which demonstrated the unfulfilled needs of a lonely affectionate child.

His mother, Lady Randolph Churchill kept all his childhood letters. They are now stored in the Churchill College Archives Centre which was embarked upon principally in order to house Sir Winston's own papers. But the scope of the collections now extends to the Spencer-Churchill family as a whole, and to the history of the Churchill era 1880–1970.

Other treasures I spotted during my visit to the Archives Centre last week was Nelson's prayer book, given to his daughter Horatia by Emma Hamilton, who has inscribed a warm-hearted message on the fly-leaf in a strong, spidery hand: "This book belonged to the Reverand [sic] Mr Nelson the father of the virtuous great & glorious Nelson & it belonged afterward to that victorious lamented

"Damn the Dardanelles!"

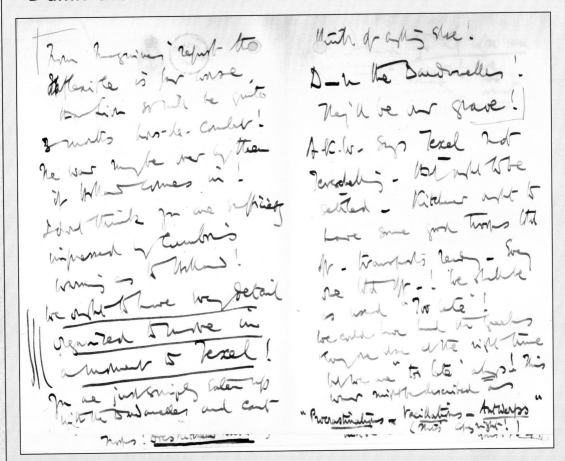

Churchill Papers, CHAR 13/57/2b.

In 1915 the relationship between Winston Churchill, the first Lord of the Admiralty, and Admiral Lord Fisher, the First Sea Lord, broke down over the failure of an operation to use ships to force the Dardanelles Straits. On 5 April 1915, Fisher wrote to Churchill complaining about the amount of time that was being used up on the Dardanelles Campaign, exclaiming: "D-m the Dardanelles! They'll be our grave!" and ending, "We could have had the Greeks & everyone else at the right time but we are "too late" ALWAYS! This war might be described as <u>"Procrastinations – vacilliations (sic) – Antwerps"</u> (That's copyright!)"

cheif [sic] it was left to me & as I consider it as belonging to the only child of this great man I theirfore [sic] give it to my much loved Horatia Nelson. May God bless her amen prays Emma Hamilton."

There is also an inscription on the facing page reading: The Book of Horatia Nelson who was born October the 29th 1800.

Among the boxes and boxes of papers – nearly 300 collections – acquired by the Centre and stored in the Strong Room, which with its hydraulically operated bays and advanced anti-theft systems gives the place the air of a *Star Wars* set, are vast collections of naval papers. From these papers, the Keeper of the Archives, the defence historian and journalist Correlli Barnett, chose to show me the log book of Admiral Sir John de Robeck, compiled at sea when he was a young midshipman.

Among the illustrations in the log are detailed watercolour sketches of the ship and its rigging, sometimes in mountainous seas, sometimes in calm tropical waters. These accomplished watercolours are reminiscent of the soft hues and textures of Edward Lear in his much prized scenes of Greece and North Africa. Correlli Barnett and his full-time professional archivist at the Centre, Miss Marion Stewart, share an exuberant enthusiasm for, and dedication to the job. Mr Barnett pads about the place with a chatelaine of keys dangling from his waist.

"My wife complained about the holes made in my trouser pocket by the number of keys I used to carry there", he said, effecting an entrance to the Conservation Workshop where the conservationist Victor Brown works on both modern and 17th and 18th century documents.

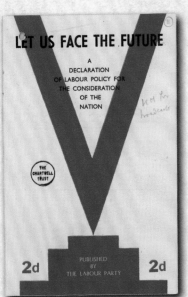

The published version of the Labour Party's 1945 General Election manifesto, Churchill Papers, CHAR2/554/11.

Among the papers of General Thomas Erle (one of the Duke of Marlborough's subordinates) and now part of the Ernle-Erle-Drax Papers held by the Centre, some of the letters were so badly affected by damp and rot that after chemically treating them, the conservationist suspended the fragments between sheets of fine silk gauze, and married them into matching spaces cut out of sheets of handmade paper.

Churchill College's fine Archives Centre, built and endowed by, or in memory of, former American ambassadors to this country and other eminent Americans, is one of the outstanding features of the college; interesting though to have a building dedicated to modern history in a college which is predominantly science-orientated.

Sir Winston himself wanted the college to be a centre where the emphasis was on science and technology. "Our statutes require us to have 70 per cent of all our students reading natural sciences, engineering or mathematics," said the Bursar, Mr Hywl George.

The proposal to found a college in Cambridge bearing the name of Sir Winston Churchill was approved by the University in February 1958. A trust was established by deed shortly after, with Sir Winston as chairman of the trustees. The college was financed largely by British industry.

In 1958, a 42-acre site in the north-west part of Cambridge was bought from St John's College, The land had been farmed by a tenant and had no buildings on it. A competition to choose an architect was held in 1959 under the auspices of the Royal Institute of British Architects. The winners were Messrs Richard Sheppard, Robson and Partners of London.

Building started in January 1960 with a block of 20 flats in the north-west corner of the site. These were used for about four years as temporary college offices and Common Rooms, and are now occupied by visiting Fellows.

The main college buildings have been sited on the eastern part of the college land, where in October 1959 Sir Winston planted a black mulberry tree and an oak tree. The college consists of ten small courts round a main central court. The Duke of Edinburgh formally opened the college on 5 June 1964.

But things didn't go smoothly when it came to building a chapel at the college. One of the original Fellows was the biologist and Nobel Laureate, Francis Crick. When he heard that the college was planning to build a chapel on the site, he said: "I will not be a Fellow of this college if it has a chapel." That was a bit of a gauntlet! So what happened? The college formed a Churchill College Chapel Society which built a chapel on land at the end of the playing fields – a rather clever fix, as Churchill College does not have a chapel, but Churchill College Chapel Society does and members of that society can attend. (The original plan was to build a chapel on what are now bike sheds and a squash court by the Storey's Way entrance.) Francis Crick was a powerful man! My thanks to the astronomer and Churchill Fellow, Professor Douglas Gough, for this story.

Kilsyth, No. 66 Storey's Way, the home of James and Katherine Cameron has an interesting history. It was commissioned in 1912 by the two sisters Mrs Lewis and Mrs Gibson of Castlebrae and Westminster College fame. The Rev. Islay F. Burns, the librarian and tutor of Westminster College lived there during the First World War.

Westminster College was endowed by Mrs Lewis and Mrs Gibson and in *The Ladies of Castlebrae*, his biography of the twins. A. Wigham Price recounts that Islay Burns was a guest of the sisters at one of their gatherings "but was rather nervous of them". The house was acquired by Mrs Cameron's father, Brigadier General Turner in 1919 ("Mrs Lewis and Mrs Gibson were relations of my mother's and told her the house was for sale"). Mrs Turner was the niece of Grace Blyth, a young teacher at the sisters' Westminster finishing school, who was persuaded to come with them on their first trip to the Middle East as they needed a chaperone and thought she was respectable enough to serve the purpose without stifling their newfound freedom, according to A. Wigham Price. Grace Blyth later followed the sisters to Cambridge and they set her up with an endowment that was worth £10,000 at the time of her death in 1917. She was living at the time in Douglas House, Trumpington Street. The twins recovered the £10,000 and used it to

The Austrian philosopher Ludwig Wittgenstein, born in 1889, died in Cambridge in 1951. He is buried in St Giles Cemetery.

endow the Chair at Westminster College. Mrs Cameron has lived in the house for most of her life. Her mother died in 1967.

Nearby, No. 76 is another of the noteworthy houses in Storey's Way. Called "Storey's End", it was built in 1913 to the designs of the architect A. H. Moberley for Sir John Clapham. the Vice-Provost of King's College. It was built on a grand scale – a family house with servants' quarters.

Since 1947, Storey's End has been the home of Dr Edward Bevan and his wife, Joan, a professional artist who has sold her work to the conductor Sir Leonard Bernstein ("He bought one of lobsters and a mermaid"). Storey's End has been dubbed "The Bevanry" – an affectionate reference to a house where a social scene has been provided by the young students who have lived there over the years as guests of Dr and Mrs Bevan.

From August 1950 until his death in April 1951, it was none other than our friend Wittgenstein who lived there. The Danish Royal Princess, now Queen Margaretha of Denmark also stayed there when she was 18 and dodged the Press with her lady-in-waiting, the Countess Armfeldt. Now it is the turn of "Sloane Rangers" to enjoy life at the Bevanry, while sorting out boyfriends on the payphone in the hall.

It is clear that while Wittgenstein was living – and dying – at the Bevans' home, he was shown great kindness by his hosts. As an antidote to all the mental effort he undertook, Wittgenstein used to enjoy reading detective stories, doing puzzles, listening to music with Dr Bevan, and going to films with Joan Bevan. The latter told a *Radio Times* reporter, Robert Shelton in April 1973, that she often accompanied Wittgenstein to the Rex Cinema in Magrath Avenue to see cowboy films. "We sat so close to the screen, we were almost trampled by the horses," she said. One of his idiosyncrasies was to rush out of the back exit of the cinema before the National Anthem began.

Joan Bevan told the *Radio Times* that she made many discreet sketches of Wittgenstein while he lived with them. And for the next 20 years after his death, she did "hundreds of sketches of him and several oil paintings," a posthumous tribute to a man of whom it was said: "He put his whole soul into everything he did. His life was a constant journey, and doubt was the moving force within him …"

News travels! It appears that Storey's Way is not only renowned for Churchill College and Baillie Scott, but also for Wittgenstein. Japanese visitors are constantly rolling up on the doorstep at Storey's End to pay homage by association, to the man who was one of the world's outstanding philosophers.

It's an illustrious road but did you know that the planners, about 20 years ago, wanted to put a by-pass through Churchill College grounds and the northerly part of the road? What a relief that the speedily formed Storey's Way and District Residents' Association contributed to the ultimately successful fobbing-off process by appointing Mr Sam Silkin QC to represent them at the planning inquiry.

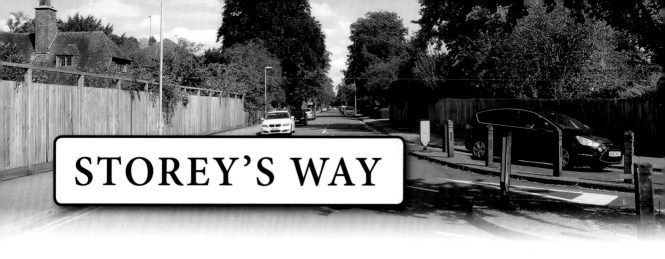

STOREY'S WAY

Revisited

So what has changed in Storey's Way in the last 30 years?

Apart from St John's new development The Crescent, built in 1993 on what was formerly the college's kitchen garden and orchard, together with Churchill College's Møller Centre opened in 1992, to name two new projects, a visitor returning from a long absence, would not detect major changes on a cursory drive through.

That drive through though would be slower than in the past because of the traffic calming measures which have been installed, including pinch points to deter lorries, coaches and farm vehicles. Churchill, Fitzwilliam and St John's were required to pay a sum for traffic calming measures in order to obtain planning permission for their various building projects, which paid for the width restriction and the bumps in the road.

Nothing has been demolished; no Baillie Scott house has bitten the dust, heaven forbid. In fact, the area was designated the Storey's Way Conservation Area in 1984, followed by an appraisal in 2008. You can still walk through from Storey's Way down to the University Observatory on Madingley Road, and many of the trees in the area have grown into giants over the years and the mistletoe is flourishing!

The changes have been social rather than architectural. One reason is that with current house prices in Storey's Way now averaging in excess of £1.5m, they are way out of reach of most families with young children, who 40 years ago could have moved there. Nowadays many of the houses in the road are home to older retired professional people, many of them academics who have lived there for many years, and whose children grew up in Storey's Way, roaming the big gardens and getting together for the annual fireworks party.

As in other west Cambridge streets, such as Newnham Road, Cranmer Road and Adams Road, these social changes have been reinforced by the practice of colleges buying up large family houses in their vicinity when they come on the market, to house mainly graduate students. This practice has been repeated in Storey's Way. Take Churchill College, the building of which began in 1961 on

No. 48 Storey's Way – one of the first houses to be designed in Cambridge by the famous Edwardian architect Baillie Scott.

the edge of the Conservation Area. It used to own just two houses in the road, now it owns seven properties: Nos. 36, 42, 44, 64, 70, 72 and 76 (formerly "The Bevanry"), and 40a, 40b and 40c. For a while No. 48, the five-star Baillie Scott house was the home of Churchill's bursar, although it is now back in private ownership.

No. 44, known as Whittingham Lodge, formerly the home of Professor Reginald Crundall Punnett, who used to breed mice there for his genetic work, now houses post graduate students. No. 46 Storey's Way is a spare plot of land next to No. 48. It was kept vacant as there was a plan once to put a road directly through to Madingley Road.

No. 74 – Atholl Lodge – the brick, pebbledash and stone house with the turret, built in 1931, is the Master's Lodge of Fitzwilliam College. The college itself has been turned back to front, so to speak, its main front entrance now being on Storey's Way rather than Huntingdon Road. Murray Edwards College (formerly New Hall) has its back entrance on Storey's Way. No. 69, built in 1931, has been incorporated into the college.

But these changes of ownership, together with proposed building schemes, have had subtle repercussions. There are fewer families with children living in the road, but the residents who remain are loyal supporters of the Storey's Way Residents Association which has managed to preserve much of the special sense of community in the area. Their current chairman is John Chaplin, who moved with his wife Jenny into No. 50 Storey's Way 30 years ago. The Chaplins bought their house from a family trust of the Countess Rietberg, the morganatic wife of the Prince of Liechtenstein. She lived there from 1953–1983 and tended the garden with its walnut and mulberry tree and climbing roses.

Mr Chaplin recalls that "the original owner of our house was Hugh Francis Russell Smith, who bought it in 1913 to the design of the architect Charles James Tait. Sadly, he was killed in the First World War on 5 July 1916 and the house was sold to Mrs Ludlam in May 1917."

The holding of a garden party has become a regular social function of the Residents' Association in this desirable area with its handsome houses and extensive gardens. Who would sell up and leave unless they had to? It seems not many people do. The first three parties were given by Harriet Gillett and Phil Trathan, Sue and Nick Finer, and Janet and Alan Windle, each in their own gardens. In

The Grove, built in 1813, once the home of Emma Darwin, widow of Charles Darwin, now part of Fitzwilliam College. The house was bought by her three sons, Francis, Horace and George in 1882.

2013, the party was held in the Chaplin's garden which as it happened was the 100th birthday of their house.

A reminder that five of them built by Baillie Scott, an architect of the Arts and Crafts movement, are Grade II listed. And there are three more Grade II listed in the area: Nos. 63 and 76 Storey's Way, and The Grove, the house built in 1813 to the designs of the architect William Custance on Huntingdon Road. The Grove, forms an integral part of Fitzwilliam College.

Complementing the many lovely houses are their extensive gardens, with legions of trees ranging from copper beech, walnut, limes, silver birch, yew, crab apple, willow, fir, cedar and mulberry, to name but a few, as well as planting that would not be out of place in a National Trust or botanical garden! These gardens continue to be the "lungs" of the residential part of the road. Bigger lungs are provided by the Churchill and Trinity Hall playing fields, where colleges, including Fitzwilliam, rub shoulders with the substantial detached houses of Storey's Way.

The Fitzwilliam College gardens with their magnificent trees, including a primeval Gingko biloba and a gigantic plane tree, are tended by a five-strong gardening team. The College grounds were once Emma Darwin's garden. By then Charles Darwin's widow, she wrote in 1883: "I never saw such a display of primroses anywhere, especially under each of the beech trees; they were like a carpet." These two beech trees are still standing and the 100-year-old lime tree avenue still creates a vista from Storey's Way to The Grove.

Safeguarding the special features of Storey's Way, requires constant vigilance on the part of the people who live there. Of course, the same goes for all the major residential streets in this area of west Cambridge, as well as throughout the city.

View down Storey's Way towards Madingley Road. On the right Atholl Lodge with its turret – the Master's Lodge of Fitzwilliam College.

Yes, the City Council plays a crucial role together with councillors, but from the researches I have been doing, and the many conversations I have had with local residents in west Cambridge, it is these people, getting together with fellow, like-minded residents who really man the barricades against those who want to make unwelcome changes to the character of the area, and who are prepared to go to great lengths to do so.

Nowhere is the fighting spirit more evident than in Storey's Way where the Residents Association has fought several battles over the years. Without seeking to push the military metaphor too far, it is fair to say that, as in other roads, the colleges in particular have had their drive to expand somewhat thwarted.

When St John's College wanted to sell No. 34 Storey's Way to developers, a house left to the college by Professor Frederick Frost Blackman, the plant physiologist and a Fellow for whom it was built, local people went into action, particularly when they heard that the developers' plan was to demolish the house and build sixteen units on the site. The house backs onto the burial ground where Professor Blackman and his wife Elsie are buried.

The battle over No. 34 proved to be a protracted one, and the house was left to deteriorate badly. The developers failed to gain planning consent to build three apartment blocks behind the original house, built in 1925, then lost a plan to build four substantial houses.

Eventually the developers appear to have been worn down. The house was to remain and be restored, and eventually planning permission was given for the building of just two new houses in the garden, not the original number that was sought. St John's did not escape censure by fearsome local residents over their behaviour towards their deceased benefactor.

Now, No. 34 has been restored in a magnificent way, and Nos. 32a and 32b have been built in the former garden. These two new houses, completed in 2010, are impressive mansions designed as a pair in the Arts and Crafts style by local architect James Snell.

When the Gould family moved into No. 32b in August 2011, the neighbours were quick to highlight that their new home was called Mulberry House after the mulberry tree that had flourished in the garden alongside a rhubarb patch that locals used to raid while No. 34 was derelict. No 32a is called St Giles House, presumably after the local parish. Andrew Gould points out that the houses are built to a very high standard with the red hand-made tiles, little cobbles and beech hedging. "These are all the themes that pick up what makes Storey's Way so special."

The view from the back garden of No. 32b takes in on one side the rolling wheat fields of the University Farm, which is part of the site of the university's huge £1bn North-West Cambridge development covering 150 hectares. It is hard to imagine the scale of it. The project includes 3,000 homes, of which half will be available as housing for University and College staff. It will also include post-graduate student accommodation, 100,000 square metres of research facilities and a local centre with public amenities such as shops, a school, etc. Heather Topel, the deputy project director expects the first house to be built in 2016.

Archaeologists at work on the North West Cambridge dig.

Before any building work can start on the site however, archaeologists have the run of the open fields, as they have the statutory right to explore the past beneath the land that is to be developed. On an early spring afternoon, members of the University's archaeology unit based in scruffy buildings at No. 34b Storey's Way, took me on site to show me in particular the earliest known example of Roman irrigation – ditches which could have been used to grow grapevines or asparagus.

Chris Evans, head of the unit investigating the site, told the *Cambridge Evening News* that the irrigation had been discovered on a ridgeway where settlement had begun in the late Neolithic period. He said: "Our findings from excavating around the ridgeway have unearthed zebra-like stripes of Roman planting beds that are encircled on their higher northern side by deeper pit-wells. The gully-defined planting beds were closely set and were probably grapevines or possibly asparagus. Extraordinarily, after carefully peeling off the clays, we saw a series of ditches lining the wells and the horticultural beds. Clearly, in dry spells, water could have been poured from the pit-wells into the ditches to reach the beds. This is a tremendously significant find that reflects the area's intense agricultural regime from the Roman period."

At another site on the University Farm, further along Huntingdon Road archaeologists have discovered the lost medieval settlement of Howes Close.

Back at No. 32b Storey's Way, the Goulds are braced for the huge development and obviously took it into account when they bought their new home. However, they are concerned that no faith centre has been designed in the new development. The view to the east of their garden is of the burial ground in All Souls Lane where so many famous Cambridge alumni are buried. There is a glimpse of the chapel roof and many trees, which form the backdrop to what is a very peaceful, almost rural setting. But there is no sign now of the little ladder that Dame Harriette Chick once used when she climbed over the cemetery wall at the bottom of the garden of No. 34 to cut through to Huntingdon Road!

On the other side of the wall is what used to be known as the Cemetery of St Giles with Peter (St Giles' Cemetery), which opened in 1869. It is now called the Ascension Parish Burial Ground and you reach it via All Souls Lane, off Huntingdon Road. On the left-hand side of the approach to the Burial Ground are a row of lime trees with tree preservation orders on them. The Burial Ground was designated a wildlife site by Cambridge City Council in 2008 and butterflies and vegetation were flourishing there in the hot summer of 2013.

In the heart of the cemetery is the former Chapel of All Souls. It is now the workshop of the lettering artist, Eric Marland, who carves letters in stone and wood and also engraves on glass. Most of his work is for gravestones in church-yards and memorial plaques. He uses a hammer and chisel for his work as did the Romans, and invites people, often the bereaved, who are commissioning work from him, to bring their own ideas to the project.

Eric Marland, who was born on Harvard Street in Cambridge, Massachusetts, owns the chapel. He began his business there in 2000 after a tortuous process of negotiating with the Church Commissioners from whom he bought the building, together with the freehold. "It was being used as a mower shed, the roof had started leaking, there was no water or electricity and the Church could not justify repairing the roof of a mower shed. The plan of last resort was to knock it down which would have cost £10,000, so they agreed to sell it to me."

Roman coins found by the team from Cambridge University's archaeology unit working on the site of the University's North-West Cambridge development.

The figure of
Christ crucified
on one of the
many graves in
the Ascension
Burial Ground.

It took him more than two years to buy the freehold, because it involved deconsecrating the ground, and the sale had to be approved on behalf of the Privy Council by the Queen (as Head of the Church of England) – that was a lengthy procedure. Eric quickly realised why it had been designated a Mortuary Chapel in the deeds. In Victorian times there was no refrigeration, so to keep the bodies stored prior to burial at a low temperature, the building had three-foot thick walls and tiny windows. Eric has since installed double glazing to stop himself from freezing!

In addition to working there, he holds seminars and workshops as well as directing a stream of visitors from all over the world to Wittgenstein's grave. These visitors, many from Japan, often follow their customary practice of leaving money, flowers, sweets or model ladders as little offerings. When he took me there one afternoon, there was a tiny statue of a Buddha sitting on the tomb.

Going into Cambridge, just along the road from All Souls Lane, is the site of the mock-Tudor building that used to be the Cambridge Lodge Hotel. Built in the early 1900s, it stands on Huntingdon Road at the junction with Storey's Way. When its former lessees could no longer sustain the business, the owner of the freehold sold it to developers. Alarm bells started to ring in Storey's Way because the developers wanted to knock it down and build 12 flat-roofed apartments there. The tenacious members of the Storey's Way Residents Association went into action to stop the hotel's demolition. Some 80 letters were written to the City Council objecting to the plans.

At No. 20 Storey's Way, Paula Farman, widow of Joe Farman, the British Antarctic Survey research scientist whose discovery in 1982 of a "hole" in the

Pyotr Kapitza and his Cambridge house

Beyond the cemetery, about 300 metres along Huntingdon Road is No. 173, a distinctive looking house called Kapitza House, built with layers of different coloured bricks. It was the family home of Pyotr Leonidovich Kapitza, a Nobel prize-winning Russian physicist who worked in Cambridge for 13 years, originally starting as a research student of Ernest Rutherford. The house was designed and built by him and his friend, the architect H. C. Hughes, in 1930. Kapitza became a Fellow of Trinity College and in 1929 was elected to the Royal Society. He pioneered research in low-temperature physics, and the Royal Society's Mond Laboratory was built for him on the site of the old Cavendish Laboratory in Free School Lane in 1932.

On a visit back to the Soviet Union in 1934, the government there decided not to let him return to Cambridge but subsequently negotiated with the university to buy all his equipment and to relocate it to his newly-built Institute in Moscow. Kapitza was eventually permitted to visit Cambridge again in 1966. The house is still owned by the family and, according to his will, used by visiting Russian students and academics of both arts and science. Is it going to get a blue plaque?

Pyotr Kapitza, the Nobel prize-winning Russian physicist who worked in Cambridge for 13 years, and designed and built No. 173 Huntingdon Road.

ozone layer was considered to be one of the most important scientific finds of the 20th century, said: "The hotel has always been part of Storey's Way and not Huntingdon Road. It is the gateway to our road."

Despite the residents' arguments though, the Council granted planning permission to the developers. But soon after, the site was included in the Conservation area. This meant that permission to knock down the existing house had to be separately obtained. The concerns of the residents about environmental damage to the area now became more central. The Council accordingly refused this second application. The hotel building was saved and was bought by Fitzwilliam College in August 2010. They have now turned it into accommodation for graduate students.

Further along the road at Churchill College, I have an appointment with Dr Allen Packwood, the director of the Churchill Archives Centre. As we head across the grounds, he points to a magnificent oak tree. "Winston Churchill planted this oak tree in 1959." In the same way that the sapling has since grown into a fine, strong tree, so the Archives Centre has flourished too.

The Centre was purpose-built in 1973 to house Sir Winston Churchill's papers contained in some 3,000 boxes of letters and documents. The papers range from those first childhood letters to his war-time speeches, as well as the writings which earned him the Nobel Prize for Literature, all now contained on a huge database of about 7,000 entries.

Then the project grew! In addition to the Churchill papers there is now a substantial archive of the Churchill era and after, covering the areas of public life in which Sir Winston played a role or took a personal interest. Today, it holds the papers of 570 important figures and is still growing. When it ran out of space an extension was built, which was opened in 2002 by Lady Thatcher who subsequently gave her papers to the Churchill Archives Trust. The new wing houses her papers and those of her successors: John Major and Gordon Brown.

In 1983 the Centre was run by a part-time director, the historian Correlli (Bill) Barnett, one secretary, an archivist and a conservator. Now the team is eleven strong, with full-time director Allen Packwood, four archivists, three archives assistants, a secretary, a conservator and a conservation assistant. As the number of staff has grown, so the collection has doubled.

On a tour of the new wing, Dr Packwood showed me a selection of iconic artefacts which are preserved there. Out of a specially constructed cardboard box, he produced Margaret Thatcher's famous handbag. On a little note she had written: "This is the handbag that I was given by friends in 1984 and which I used every day during my time at Downing Street. It always brought back many happy memories." A separate cardboard box contains the contents of her makeup bag!

Another iconic gift given to the Archives Centre is one of Churchill's cigars! It was sent by Mr Paul Keane, who was one of Churchill's many American fans. The story

One of Margaret Thatcher's famous, and heavily-used handbags dating from the 1980s. Stored in the Churchill Archives, the bag is black and imitation crocodile. Thatcher Papers, THCR 9/1/1

explained on the Archives website states: "In 1961, when he was just 16, he waited for more than 24 hours in the rain on a New York pier for a chance to see his hero disembark from Aristotle Onassis's yacht *Christina*. His patience was rewarded at last, not only with a sight of Churchill, but also with the gift of matches from the *Christina*, one of Churchill's handkerchiefs, and last but not least, the famous cigar."

Just as the Archives Centre has grown these past 30 years, so has the college itself, the largest physical addition being the Maersk Mc-Kinney Møller Centre for Continuing Education which was formally opened by Her Majesty, Queen Ingrid of Denmark, on 2 October 1992. The Centre was built with a donation to Churchill College by the A. P. Møller & Chastine Mc-Kinney Møller Foundation, a Foundation which makes contributions to good causes, especially those involving national heritage, shipping, industry and science.

The Centre's website explains that A. P. Møller's son, Maersk Mc-Kinney Møller, was contacted in 1988 by Churchill College, seeking funding for a building project at the College. "Maersk was keen to support a development at Churchill College in memory of Sir Winston Churchill, because of his support to Denmark and the Maersk shipping industry during the Second World War. The Centre is built in the shape of a ship: the lecture theatre represents the bridge of the ship, and the east end the bow. Drive along Madingley Road out of Cambridge and look across the Churchill Playing Fields to the Møller Centre and you get the nautical picture!

The Maersk Mc-Kinney Møller Centre at Churchill College.

GRANGE ROAD

26 July – 4 October 1984

In a testy letter to the *Cambridge News* in 1973 complaining about the surface of Grange Road, a correspondent from Orwell, Mr M. Salim-Khan described it as "the only road which epitomises the academic and cultural dignity of this great city." That was, of course, "until one looks at the road itself and its surface, and feels that surface in a vehicle." The bumps over Grange Road, he said, were reminiscent of the tracks in the wildest part of the tribal territory in his own north-west frontier province. "But a rough ride there is the least of one's concerns in the face of the possibility of rifle bullets from any direction. It is different in Cambridge, or it should be."

His 1971 model car had already aged six years at least, he said and he urged the powers-that-be to spend some money on resurfacing Grange Road. I wonder what Mr Salim-Khan would have thought if he knew that a graded and gravelled road, for what would become Grange Road, was first discussed in 1805.

Grange Road has a complicated history. Begun in 1805 at its southern end on Barton Road, the road was built in stages and did not reach Madingley Road until almost a century later, in 1910. Before the enclosure of Cambridge's West Fields (the parish of St Giles), there was an unploughed strip of land called the Great Balk[1] and when the Commissioners of Enclosure laid out the road network to support the new ownership layout, they specified that a new road, graded and gravelled, be built on what had been the Great Balk.

Starting from Barton Road (in those days called the Arrington Turnpike until the Enclosure Award of 1805), it was to be a carriageway 40 feet wide until a section now defined by the northern edge of the University Rugby ground, at which point it narrowed to a bridle path 12 feet wide. That point became what Philomena Guillebaud has called the "Kink" in her *Cambridge's West Side Story: Changes in the Landscape of West Cambridge 1800–2000*. So it remained until the mid-1880s when St John's College decided to develop the land it owned north

---

[1] Balk derives from an old Norse word 'balkr', meaning a ridge of land between two ploughed strips used as a cart track for taking out the harvest in the open field era.

of the 40 foot-wide carriageway for houses. The first person to take out a lease from St John's in 1884, was Professor Walter William Rouse Ball, a mathematician and Fellow of Trinity. His one-acre plot on which he built "Elmside" lay on the west side of Grange Road, immediately north of the point at which the road narrowed to 12 feet.

Robert Scott, then Senior Bursar and later Master of St John's, negotiated a lease with him, which unfortunately left the eastern boundary ambiguous, and when it was realised that the road at that point would need widening from 12 to 40 feet, Scott tried to persuade Rouse Ball to give up part of the easternmost end of his site to permit this. Rouse Ball was uncooperative, and only after lengthy wrangling was an awkward compromise reached: Rouse Ball yielded a small strip, and the unfortunate owner of the house "St Martin's" on the opposite side of the road, the Rev. Charles Graves, Fellow of St John's and lessee of St Catharine's College, was made to give up a strip of his garden, thereby creating the "Kink".

Even so, the road at this point was (and is) only 30 feet wide, though it widened imperceptibly further north until it ended at the intersection with Bin Brook. The brook was bridged in 1898 when Adams Road was built, and progressively thereafter Grange Road extended northward to Madingley Road.

The road has had some interesting names. Since it was a brand new feature, the Commissioners of Enclosure must have been stumped to find a name for it. Eventually they hit on the peculiar solution of calling it "The House in the Fields Road", because the only feature in the nearby landscape, otherwise composed of flat fields, was a solitary house – which wasn't even in the parish of St Giles, but across the boundary in the parish of Grantchester.

A study of the Enclosure Award of 1805 shows that the House in the Fields Close belonged to Storey's Charity (see Barton Road chapter). How long that name persisted is not known, but on Spalding's map of 1875 the road appears as Parallelogram Road. Parallel to what? Was this an academic joke? Whatever, it was not long before the name changed to Grange Road, reflecting the importance of St John's College's Grange Farm which was served by the road. That was the only function of the road for a surprisingly long time. The first structure of any kind to be built along the road was the first of two real tennis courts in 1865, which are still there, at the corner of Burrell's Walk. Real tennis, riding and shooting were the main sporting activities of students at that time.

The first house to be built in the road was "Pinehurst", now the flats of the same name. The landowners, Corpus Christi College, granted a lease in 1871 to Augustus A. Vansittart, the auditor of Trinity College, who built a large house there in 1875 and named it "Grata Quies". The house was described in an 1883 sale notice as "a moderate-sized house in white brick with stone dressings and tiled, with a lodge, entrance and carriage drive and a coachman's house".

Professor Walter William Rouse Ball, who built "Elmside" on the west side of Grange Road. He was the first person to take out a lease from St John's in 1884.

By 1891, the house had become the home of Charles Finch Foster, JP, of the Cambridge milling and banking family. He renamed it "Pinehurst", and lived there for many years. As well as Pinehurst, Corpus Christi College in 1871 leased land for the building of houses between Cranmer Road and Selwyn Gardens. Housing development in the road took place from the middle outwards, that is from the intersection of Grange Road with West Road once called Green's Road, the latter being the access road and the first road to be developed by Caius College for housing, as it owned all the land on the south side of the road up to Grange Road. It was called Green's Road, according to a map of 1840 in the University Library, probably because there were three nurseries towards the western end of the road, respectively identified as Green's, Stittle's and Green's. The Spaldings map of 1878 shows four houses on it and a nursery, and marks it then as New Road. The Ordnance Survey for 1888 shows Gonville Nursery up at the west end of West Road. The further north or south you go along Grange Road from that point, the later the construction date.

In 1906, St John's decided to build four houses in Grange Road near their playing fields. In 1955, these were sold to Trinity College – an instance of collegiate cooperation. Had St John's not sold, Trinity would probably have had to sacrifice part of their "Backs" to house their undergraduates.

More than 10 years after Mr Salim-Khan's complaining letter, and a brand new college – Robinson College – later, traffic, parking and road surfaces still tediously exercise Grange Road residents and commuters. Just as in the early days of this

Pinehurst, the first house to be built in Grange Road in 1875.

residential road, there were raised eyebrows and complaints about the first bus that went down it. One hundred years ago, Grange Road would have echoed to the sound of horses' hooves (the story goes that George V and Lord Kitchener rode down it), just as today it shudders under the weight of coaches bringing the hordes to our local "Twickenham", the University Rugby Ground, or under the collective tonnage of cars unloading offspring at St John's College and King's College Choir Schools.

"St Martin's", No. 50 Grange Road – that first house to be built on the east side of Grange Road, is a large redbrick Victorian building with massive chimneys. It has for many years been the junior house of King's College School. Built with a conservatory (now a boys' changing room full of muddy football boots), it has a fine galleried staircase, which leads to classrooms 4RF and 4NL.

St Martin's was acquired by the school in 1952. It had a large rambling garden, even though it lost land at the front to the road widening. Good use was made though of this extensive overgrown garden, as R. J. Henderson explains in *A History of King's College Choir School, Cambridge*, published in 1981:

Augustus Vansittart who built Pinehurst.

> "Teams of boys were set to work to cut down the nettles and very long grass and level the area to the south of the house, which became a very playable grass tennis court. By the side of the court the boarders constructed a number of brick huts in which they were allowed to cook the type of meal which only the young can digest. To the east of the house the garden was 'rediscovered' and the boys themselves planted a variety of plants and vegetables."

A man of scholarship, the original owner, Mr Graves, would no doubt have approved of the change of use of his home from spacious residence to educational institution for generations of high-spirited children who have thrived on the intellectually rigorous and slightly laissez-faire standards of King's. Speech day al fresco, whatever the weather, is one of my memories of my daughter's time there. The school took the historic decision to admit girls as day pupils in 1976, but it was not intended that girls should ever become boarders.

King's College School is mainly all about music for the 16 pupils who are choristers at the school. That is all thanks to King Henry VI who, at the age of 19 in 1441, founded King's College, King's College School and Eton College. It was stated in the school's Charter that there were to be 16 choristers who were to be of "honest conversation and able to read". The original statute is still in place. The choristers form the core of the school.

The main school, housed in a large redbrick building overlooking the school playing fields, was built in 1878 by King's College. Before that only the choristers

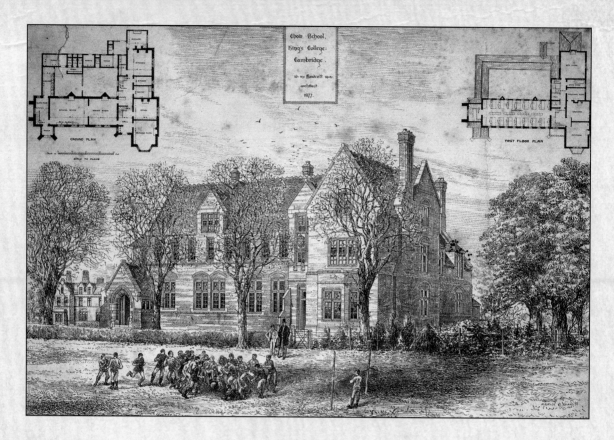

Plan and drawing of King's College School by W. M. Fawcett and Maurice B. Adams, 1877 KCD/65.

were living in the college. Originally, the headmaster lived in the main School House with his family, but since 1979 the headmaster has had his own house, a College property called "The Pavilion", tucked away off West Road down the road leading to the University Library. It was formerly the cricket pavilion shared by King's and Clare College before the First World War.

Famous King's College School pupils include: from that pre-First World War era, Rupert Brooke. Three centuries earlier the composer Orlando Gibbons (1583–1625) was a chorister at the college. Fast forward to the 1960s, the mathematician Andrew Wiles, who in his thirties solved Fermat's Last Theorem, was also a pupil at the school.

His father was Maurice Wiles and the family lived at No. 9 Grange Road. The story goes that Wiles came across Fermat's Last Theorem on his way home from school at King's when he was ten years old. He stopped at his local library where he found a book about the theorem. Fascinated by the existence of a theorem that was so easy to state that he, a ten-year-old, could understand it, but nobody had proven it, he decided to be the first person to prove it. However, he soon realised that his knowledge was too limited, so he abandoned his childhood dream, until the age of 33.

Roman and Saxon remains

In 1911, builders digging the foundations of "Saxmeadham", No. 71 Grange Road, uncovered Roman and Saxon remains. Their finds, which included several skeletons, a quantity of Roman pottery, coins and pieces of Saxon bronze, meant that Sir Frederick Gowland Hopkins, who was Professor of Biochemistry, Fellow and Praelector in Biochemistry of Trinity College and discoverer of enzymes, had a ready name for his new home.

The place where these remains were found is close to where the line of the Roman road from Castle End crossed Grange Road on its way to the south west of England. It was the road commonly known as Akeman Street, according to an account of the finds by the Rev. F. G. Walker, in a Cambridge Antiquarian Society communication of 13 May 1912. Mr Walker's article gives a precise account of the remains, while Dr J. P. Bury, the French historian, and Fellow of Corpus Christi College, who with his wife has lived in Saxmeadham since 1956, adds that the playing fields of St John's College opposite his house, were an important site for Roman remains, too. Six Roman skeletons – or parts of skeletons – were found: four male and two female, all less than two feet below the surface of the Saxmeadham site. Two of the skeletons were of special interest. Mr Walker writes: "A male, about 5ft 7in in height was found in undisturbed ground close to the wall between Saxmeadham and 'Coleby', the adjoining house."

Coleby, No. 69 Grange Road, was then the home of Mrs Clover and her daughter Miss Mary Clover, the secretary to Girton College in the 1920s. Later, the house was bought by Col. Sir Gerald P. Lenox-Conyngham, a Fellow of Trinity who renamed the house "Desertlyn". Colonel Lenox-Conyngham was one of those rare breed of academics who had a professorship without having a degree. He had been trained at Sandhurst and was a senior surveyor in the Army, but because he hadn't been at Oxbridge, it is said that he felt at a disadvantage in the university here.

But back to the Saxmeadham skeleton, which was lying with the head towards the south-east. The lower part of the body and the legs had been partially destroyed some considerable time earlier, when water pipes were being re-laid in the conduit to the fountain in Great Court, Trinity College, from the water source in what is now Conduit Head Road, off Madingley Road. It was the monks of the Franciscan Monastery (that later became Sidney Sussex College) who built the conduit all the way to the college in Sidney Street.

A Roman jug, six and a half inches high, was found touching the left side of the skull. From among the rib bones of the skeleton, Mr Walker picked out the "broken bone pin and also a small plain bronze dress or cloak fastener with one hook broken off". Near the side of the body was a socketed iron spearhead, six and a half inches long, leaf-shaped and flat and also one scale of Roman bronze armour, shield shaped, one inch in length and three quarters of an inch in breadth.

No other scales of armour were found because of the laying down of those water pipes for Trinity College. There is a reference to the pipes in the deeds of

Saxmeadham. As Dr Bury says: "We have to allow people from Trinity to come in if their conduit goes wrong." It runs down the south side of the garden.

Another of the skeletons discovered on the Saxmeadham site aroused a great deal of interest in archaeological circles. It was of a young Saxon girl of about nine to 11 years of age. Resting against the child's skull was "a handsome bone comb three and a half inches wide. The comb was in four pieces which fitted together accurately and were kept in position by two curved pieces of bone, one on each face of the comb, each ornamented with a design of rings and dots". The girl wore round her neck an amber and glass bead necklace fastened by a plain, flat, circular, bronze brooch with, apparently, an iron pin. The necklace, said Mr Walker, was made up of 38 beads, 28 of amber and ten of glass. Five of the amber beads had been broken by the workman's pick, but the others were perfect.

Two Saxon urns, both broken, were also dug up while the drive to the house was being laid, and Roman and English coins were discovered on the site. The haul numbered an English Henry VI farthing, two farthings dated 1626 from the reign of Charles I, an Irish halfpenny and a farthing token dated 1667.

Perhaps Sir Frederick Gowland Hopkins and his family, for whom the Edwardian house was designed by the architect Wright, wondered about those early shades. Sir Frederick's younger daughter, the writer Jacquetta Hawkes, who married J. B. Priestley, described in an autobiographical account how as a child she used to swing on the big ash tree at the bottom of the garden of No. 71.

Wandering in the Bury's peaceful garden where the view at the back, before Girton College built Wolfson Court, was of open cornfields, one wonders whether the garden is not the final resting place of other Roman and Saxon inhabitants of an earlier Cambridge.

Dr Bury and his wife have a pleasant relationship with St John's College Choir School next door at St John's House, No. 73 Grange Road. Cheerful voices and errant tennis balls ("Please sir, can we get our ball?") are all part of being neighbourly.

Education of the choristers

Choristers have been singing in St John's College Chapel since 1637. College records, dated 1660, refer to Peter Gunning, the Bishop of Ely, bequeathing money for the better provision of music in the college chapel. The education of the choristers in those early days was the responsibility of the curate or parish clerk of the Holy Sepulchre (the Round Church). Whether the college had established a school for the education of the choristers at that stage is not known, as there is no known record of the actual foundation of the school, which since 1955 has been in premises in Grange Road.

In the early days, there was probably just a schoolmaster and a college room. It is not until the 19th century that a site in Bridge Street, in the triangle of land formed by All Saints Passage, Bridge Street and St John's Street, can be identified as the school where the choristers of St John's and Trinity Colleges were educated together. That site was also where the church of All Saints in Jewry was located, later demolished for road building, and later rebuilt in Jesus Lane.

It was a pretty poor sort of educational establishment in the 1820s, held in low esteem by an educational inspector called Maria Hackett who said: "I forbear to comment" when asked for her opinion of the place. It soon improved though. Later in the century, the two choirs separated. For a period of time, St John's school occupied a house in Malcolm Street.

In 1955, a strong faction at St John's College determined to defeat any opposition to the rejuvenation of the school as a proper preparatory school. They won the day and the school was re-established at No. 73 Grange Road in a large house built in 1913 for Sir John Sandys, a classical Fellow at St John's who had obtained permission from the college to call it St John's House, which was all very appropriate. To Sir John Sandys' horror, however, the college signwriter made, as schoolboy slang would say "a blog of it", and wrote "Sir John's House" instead.

Two subsequent inhabitants of No. 73 Grange Road were, from 1924–1930 Dr A. H. Lloyd FSA, and from 1938 onwards Dr Rex Salisbury Woods, the Olympic athlete and physician.

St John's College School opened as a fully fledged day preparatory school on 20 September 1955, under the headmastership of the late Rev. Cyril Walters. He had been told that the maximum number of pupils was to be 100. "He thought he had got it right", said Mr Alan Mould, the present headmaster, "But when they called the roll, it came to 103. Within two years the school had opened dormitories.

No. 73 Grange Road looks like any other large house in this part of west Cambridge. A cursory glance at the redbrick house, with its mullioned windows set in stone surrounds, would give the passerby few clues as to the nature of the establishment. The game is given away, though, when you are going past at 8.45 a.m. or after 4 p.m., when the road outside is filled with jostling school commuter traffic. It must have been peaceful in the days when people came by bicycle. (Incidentally, the school's bicycle shed has a very distinguished looking entrance! "It must be the only bicycle shed in Cambridge with a four-pointed perpendicular arch", says Alan Mould.)

The school's forecourt was originally set out as a little proscenium stage and in the early days of the school, plays were staged there. Among the first efforts was the production of *Caribbean Gold*, which involved the creation of a beach with "miles" of golden sand. The local contractor, who delivered the sand, over-enthusiastically covered the whole of the forecourt, thereby giving the headmaster rather a shock when he woke up and looked out from his bedroom window.

Four years ago, a northward extension was added to the back of what is called Senior House. In June 1983, the School's new hall, named Hinsley Hall after Professor Harry Hinsley, the Master of St John's College, was opened by the Duke of Edinburgh, the Chancellor of the University. Designed by the architect Peter Boston, it is a multi-purpose building which acts as theatre, chapel, gymnasium, concert hall (it has its own organ) and badminton court. Senior House at No. 73 Grange Road provides for 200 boys aged seven to 13, of whom 20 are the choristers of the college chapel.

St John's has also been a coeducational school since 1973, the year it acquired Byron House School, No. 63 Grange Road. The acquisition of Byron House brought pre-preparatory classes *and* girls into St John's College School. Byron House School has its origins not in Cambridge, but in London. It was founded in 1897 at 13 North Road, Highgate, and named Byron House, not because of any sentimental associations with the great poet, but because in the 18th century the house in Highgate was occupied by a man called Edmund Byron.

Poets have, however, been connected with Byron House – one in particular, if readers of *Summoned by Bells* have done their homework. Yes, it was Sir John Betjeman, poet laureate who wrote warmly of his days as a pupil at Byron House. But he was in love wasn't he?

Peggy Purey-Cust.
Along the Grove, what happy, happy steps
Under the limes I took to Byron House,
And blob-work, weaving, carpentry and art, Walking with you ...

During the Second World War, Byron House was evacuated to the "Orchard" in Huntingdon Road, once the family home of Horace Darwin and his family. It is now the site of Murray Edwards College. After the war, part of the school returned to Highgate, while another part stayed in Cambridge, moving to premises in No. 56 Grange Road. The school later crossed the road to No. 63 Grange Road, a large stylish house built in 1922 for Sir Richard Glazebrook.

For many years, Byron House was a girls' preparatory school under the headship of Miss Gimingham. Today, as part of St John's College School, Byron House contains a coeducational pre-preparatory department of boys and girls aged four to seven, and four further classes of girls aged seven to 11.

"Maryland", No. 67 Grange Road, is the headmaster's house. It was built in 1923, originally for the scientist and engineer who was responsible for the building of most of the sewage works of Ecuador – Dr Eric Rideal. His wife was an American and perhaps she chose the name of the house. The look of the house, particularly from the garden at the back, recalls the white boarded houses of New England. An extensive boarded loggia, or sun terrace, would perhaps have prevented Mrs Rideal from feeling homesick. Dr Rideal also incorporated a "motorhouse" with a pit beneath it at Maryland. After all, he did list "motoring and old furniture" as his hobbies in *Who's Who*.

The new development of Cockcroft Place, between No. 63 and 67, was built in 1981. It was located on the site of No. 65, which was originally built for Sir Harry Stephen in 1916. Talbot Peel, the Bursar of Magdalene lived in it in the late 1920s and 30s. However, the house developed irreparable cracks and had to be demolished. St John's College left it empty for more than 10 years but the Choir School got permission from the college to use the grounds as an ecology garden. Until Cockcroft Place was built, bees were kept in the garden and a nature trail entertained and educated the pupils.

By the mid 1920s, it was recognised that the former First Eastern General Hospital, built on the King's and Clare Colleges Cricket Ground in 1914, would be the best site for a new library. The University wanted the library to have the same access, and to be aesthetically compatible with Clare College's Memorial Court. Therefore the architect Gilbert Scott was appointed, due to his success with the design of Memorial Court, which is immediately adjacent to the site of the new library.

Changes in character after the war years

It was in 1926 that Herbert Charles Webb and his family moved into "Mon Abri" at No. 2 Grange Road, the large Victorian house at the junction of Grange Road and Barton Road. A retired barrister, Mr Webb had bought the house in 1925 from the sons of Arthur Rutter, the corn merchant and miller who died in 1925. His son, Hubert Webb, who lived at No. 2 Grange Road from 1926 until he and his wife Doris moved to a smaller house in Grantchester Meadows, was well placed to monitor changes in the street from the unshielded position at the corner.

"My father searched for a long time before he bought the house, which was considered expensive in those days", says Hubert. Arthur Lionel Rutter and Roland Richmond Rutter, the two sons of the deceased Arthur Rutter (who founded the firm of Arthur Rutter, Sons & Company, land agents, surveyors and auctioneers in 1875), wanted £2,500 for the house which was built by Rattee and Kett in 1892. "Father beat them down to £2,175", adds Hubert.

In those days the house was leasehold, the lease belonging to the Ecclesiastical Commissioners as the land was part of the living of the parish of the Holy

Doris and Hubert Webb lived at No. 2 Grange Road for more than 50 years. The house was called "Mon Abri", and was formerly the residence of Mr Arthur Rutter.

Sepulchre (the Round Church). Hubert Webb bought the freehold of No. 2 Grange Road in 1950. A retired lecturer from the Cambridgeshire College of Arts and Technology, Mr Webb himself is well known in Cambridge as a tourist guide.

Grange Road in the pre-war days was a very exclusive road, rather snooty perhaps and considered to be one of the prime places in which to live. But a great change in character took place after the Second World War when some of the large houses became uneconomical to run as family homes, and became institutions, such as schools and college hostels instead.

Among the Webbs' neighbours in the 1920s and 30s – at No. 6 Grange Road, called Eadson Lodge – was Harold Pye, son of the founder of the electronic company Pye's. Also a Mr G. G. Goodman and his family who lived at "Lyndhurst", No. 8, later the home of Dr Archie Clark Kennedy and now the Newnham Language Centre. Mr Webb remembers the Goodmans as "very strong Tory supporters. On VE Day all the flags were out, but not on VJ Day because by then there was a Labour Government in power".

Mr Webb recalls the time when "Glebelands" – No. 10 Grange Road – before it was acquired by the Canonesses of St Augustine, had served as the chaplaincy for Catholic women university students from the 1930s to the 1960s and was called Lady Margaret House. It belonged to W. S. Mansfield, a former director of the University Farm. The Mansfield family built Grange Gardens, a block of flats across the road.

No. 16 Grange Road, now a Newnham College hostel called Eva Smith House, was in the 1920s and 30s the home of Mrs R. W. Atkinson, whose son Basil, an under-librarian at the University Library was, says Hubert Webb "noted for his fundamentalist views. He thought the 1920s were the end of the world".

Two horses pulling a snow plough in Grange Road on 1 February 1935.

Relative newcomer among the colleges

In 1982, Selwyn College in Grange Road celebrated its centenary. Like its neighbour, Newnham
College in Sidgwick Avenue, it is a relative newcomer among colleges. The college was founded as
a hostel in 1882, in memory of one of the greatest
Victorian ecclesiastics, George Augustus Selwyn,
the first Bishop of New Zealand. From 1923 it
was known as Selwyn College. The aim enshrined
in the charter was to "provide a university education, combined with strict economy and simple
living, for practising members of the Church of
England".

Portrait of
George Augustus
Selwyn, first
Bishop of New
Zealand painted
by George
Richmond in
1855. Selwyn
College is named
after him.

Funds for the foundation of Selwyn College
were raised by public subscription, while a committee was formed to promote Bishop Selwyn's
memorial. The secretary of that Memorial
Committee was Charles John Abraham, who had
been Selwyn's suffragan bishop, both in New
Zealand and afterwards in Lichfield, where Selwyn was bishop from 1868 until
his death in 1878.

In 1879, the founders elected a Master, the Hon. Arthur Temple Lyttelton, and
invited the Archbishop of Canterbury to be Visitor. They then acquired from
Corpus Christi College six acres of farm land on Grange Road for the sum of
£6,111 9s 7d. The *Short History of the College* by The Master, Fellow and Scholars
(Selwyn College, Cambridge, 1973) suggests that an alternative site was mooted:
that of the Roman Catholic Church in Lensfield Road, but the argument for
space won the day. The architect chosen was Arthur Blomfield, and building
began in 1880, the cornerstone on the north side of the gateway being laid by
the Earl of Powis on 1 June 1881.

Selwyn's first Master, Arthur Lyttelton, who had been a tutor at Keble College,
Oxford, had useful political connections. His mother was sister to the wife of
the Liberal Prime Minister, Mr Gladstone. Lyttelton himself was a Liberal party
supporter. College annals record that he persuaded Gladstone to make a personal
gift to the college of the louder of Selwyn's two chapel bells, "for Gladstone evi-
dently thought that undergraduates needed to be well woken if they were to get
up betimes in the morning".

Selwyn's Royal Charter acquired in 1882, did not, however, incorporate the
college in the University. This matter had to be settled by the Senate.

Architectural historians busy themselves with Selwyn's chapel and Hall. The
permanent chapel was built before the permanent Hall and was an expensive
project for a college without adequate endowment. It was the new Master, John
Selwyn, the son of George Augustus Selwyn, who set out to find the money. An

ambitious original plan by the architect, Sir Arthur Blomfield was modified to reduce the cost to an estimate of £8,000.

"The Hall", says the Selwyn history, "is a very satisfactory piece of architecture. The woodwork of the west end comes from the altar panelling of the old English church at Rotterdam, built between 1699 and 1708 for the English community of merchants and traders.

"Queen Anne gave £500 to the building (in Rotterdam) and the Duke of Marlborough contributed. The plan and ornaments came from the office of Sir Christopher Wren, therefore possibly being a design by Wren himself.

"A. C. Benson, the Master of Magdalene, bought the woodwork and presented it to Selwyn in memory of his father, the archbishop who had dedicated the chapel."

No one could be more closely associated with Selwyn and its Hall than long-serving college butler, Mr Derek Childerley, who took on the job some 36 years ago. Before being made butler after the Second World War, Mr Childerley had been working for the college since the age of 14, helping out in the gardens in those early days. As well as a college butler, Mr Childerley used to run a college hostel for Selwyn with his wife, Betty. The Childerleys have looked after Selwyn hostels: at "Saxon Barns", formerly No. 43 Grange Road, a house that was demolished when Selwyn's Cripps building was built; also at No. 29 Grange Road where the system of late passes between 10 p.m. and 12 midnight applied.

That was in the 1960s, when gowns were compulsory and no loud music was allowed after 10 p.m. Latterly the Childerleys have been living in "The White Cottage", a Selwyn house in Sidgwick Avenue. Derek Childerley is as loyal to Selwyn as he is to the game of rugby. He still goes to every Varsity match and keeps in touch with the teams. He shares a love of the game with the former Master of the College, Professor Sir Owen Chadwick, OM, a University Rugby Blue.

Robinson's mighty mark

Robinson College has changed the face of Grange Road. On this long, predominantly residential street of Victorian family houses, many of which are now educational establishments, it has imposed the towering contours of a fortified brick castle. It is a major landmark in the road.

Inappropriate images of Corfe Castle spring to mind (Robinson has not been dynamited!) when you hear that the one and a quarter million bricks used in the construction of the college were hand-made in a small brick works in Swanage, Dorset, a mile or so from that legendary castle which came to grief in the Civil War.

Like so many of the Cambridge colleges, Robinson has a fortified air, but I cannot think of any other college whose main entrance suggests a portcullis in the way that Robinson does. The large, sloping ramp to the entrance and front court beyond recalls that great medieval castle of Warwick. The towering upper storeys suggest crenellations. Before 1977, not one of these million and a quarter handmade bricks had been laid. The college, which was still on the drawing board, came about because of a million pound gift to the university – the largest single gift ever accepted by the university – from local benefactor, David Robinson of Newmarket. It previously began its administrative life in "Thorney Creek", a large Victorian house in Herschel Road built in 1895 by the founder of Foster's Bank, now the home of graduate students.

The first warden, Professor Sir Jack Lewis, FRS Professor of Chemistry, had been appointed in 1975, but building work did not start until 1977. Several firms of architects had had a go at designing the college, taking part in a competition organised by the Royal Institute of British Architects. But it was Professor Andy McMillan, Professor of Architecture at Glasgow, and Mr lzzi Metstein, then senior partner in Gillespie, Kidd and Coia, and now the Chair of Architecture at Edinburgh, who were appointed. Their brief was to design a college that did not encroach on the extensive wooded grounds between Herschel, Sylvester and Adams Road, to the side and rear of the college, on the land purchased by Robinson College from St John's, the landowner at the end of Grange Road.

Other designs would have destroyed the shady gardens, creating a busy looking campus on the peaceful banks of the Bin Brook, which meanders diagonally through the garden and is crossed by a wooden bridge. The college opted for Gillespie, Kidd and Coia because their design left this well alone and spared the mature trees in the garden. A walnut tree planted in the garden in 1897 in honour of Queen Victoria, is one of the sacrosanct trees in the tranquil gardens, through which the kingfishers flash, and other wildlife is encouraged. An 80-foot cedar tree creates cover on the Herschel Road side.

Three houses were demolished to make way for Robinson, including "Binstead" in Herschel Road, a fine house with beautiful views whose destruction was generally regretted. The part of the college where Binstead once stood is now called Herschel Court. The two other houses to go were "Bin Brook", No. 53 Grange Road, originally the home of Rev. R. H. Orpen who built the house, and "Overbrook", No. 1 Adams Road. As well as Thorney Creek, the college now owns No. 5 Adams Road and No. 1 Sylvester Road which act as marker points on two of the flanks of the large site.

Robinson College's modern chapel contains stained glass windows designed by John Piper and made by Patrick Reyntiens. The inspiration for the smaller window is acknowledged by Piper to be the Romanesque stone carving over the west door of the village church of Neuilly-en-Donjon, Allier in France. The larger "Creation" window, through which the sun pours in the late afternoon introducing explosions of colour into the chapel, reminds the visitor of Piper's work on the Baptistry window in Coventry Cathedral. The chapel, with its fine organ built by the Danish builder Frobenius (organ scholars in the university queue up to use it) is a feature of the college, of which the founder is said to be especially proud.

Among the college's new trophies is a huge bell, which summons members of the college to hall. It came from the HMS *Mauritius* and was given to the college by the Second Sea Lord. I was told this by the Bursar, Commander George Coupe, who has, hanging in his office up on High Court, two "before" and "after" aerial photographs of the site. These show just how much this part of Grange Road has been changed by Robinson College.

Another big change in the area was the establishment of Clare Hall, the graduate college founded by Clare College in 1966 in Herschel Road, off Grange Road. The college was founded because the growth of research in the University and the broadening of graduate teaching during the 1950s had led to an increase in senior posts unmatched by the growth in fellowships in the Cambridge colleges.

St John's College sold to Clare College the freehold of the land in Herschel Road on which Clare Hall now stands. Richard Eden in his book *The Origins and Development of a College for Advanced Study* explains the early history:

At the time there were three large houses on this land. There were long leases nearing their end for the land occupied by "Elmside", No. 49 Grange Road on the corner of Grange Road and Herschel Road, and for "Huntley" at No. 3 Herschel Road. However Herschel House at No. 1 Herschel Road owned by St John's was divided into flats which were let on short leases, which could be terminated with six months notice. The total area amounted to three acres in all.

Herschel House was built in 1890 for the Rev. John Lock, Fellow, Bursar and Steward of Caius College. In 1925 it was briefly occupied by George Mallory, then a lecturer for the University Board of Extra Mural Studies shortly before he left for the expedition to Mount Everest where he lost his life near the summit.

In 1978, the college was able to begin negotiations to purchase the remainder of the lease of No. 3 Herschel Road from our neighbour Professor Richard Keynes, subject to an arrangement under which Keynes was able to build a smaller house on the far garden. In 1980, the house was converted for use by nine of our graduate students and with the approval of Professor and Mrs Keynes it became known as "Keyneside". The name Keyneside was used until 1996 when postal confusion with our neighbours led to its renaming as Leslie Barnett House.

Dr Keynes was a physiologist, a nephew of the economist Maynard Keynes and a great grandson of Charles Darwin. A Fellow of Churchill College, he later became Professor of Physiology in the University.

Mansions built in the Victorian era for dons and their families

Grange Road like so many of the residential streets in this leafy stretch of west Cambridge, is well endowed with large, stately-looking mansions built in the late Victorian era for dons and their growing families. "St Martin's", "St Chad's", "Bin Brooke", "Saxon Barns", "Leckhampton" and "Pinehurst" were among these grand houses. Another, built in 1891, was "Berry Croft" now No. 12 Grange Road.

"Berry Croft" was originally the home of the solicitor Mr H. G. Few, JP, and his family who moved into their home with its substantial servants' quarters on

23 September 1891. It was Mr Few's second stab at a family home. He had first built No. 16 Grange Road called "College House", but, the story goes, it wasn't big enough for Mrs Few! Berry Croft is thought to owe its original name to a well-endowed holly tree which still thrives there, tempting local residents and passers-by at Christmas with its glowing, seasonal berries.

It is nearly 50 years since the Canonesses of St Augustine bought Berry Croft to establish a "house of studies" there. They acquired the house in 1937 and renamed it Lady Margaret House. To find out about the origins of the Canonesses of St Augustine and their early days in Cambridge, I spent an evening with two of the eight sisters who now run a hostel there for students. Sister St Philip, who is the Warden and Mother Superior, and Sister Edith told me that the Canonesses of St Augustine are a teaching order founded in 1597 in Lorraine, France by St Pierre Fourier and a young woman in his parish called Blessed Alix Le Clerc.

Like Mary Ward who had founded the teaching order of the Institute of the Blessed Virgin Mary (IBVM) a few years earlier, St Pierre Fourier who was a Canon of St Augustine, together with Alix Le Clerc felt that nothing was being done for the education of Catholic girls. The Canonesses first came to England in 1904 to escape religious persecution in France and established themselves at both Westgate in Kent and St Leonards on Sea in Sussex.

Their first move away from Westgate came in 1937 when Father Pettit of St Edmund's House, Cambridge asked Mother Mary Joseph Walters to found a house here for the welfare of Catholic undergraduates. To the house came girls between the ages of 17 and 20, some of whom were preparing for university entrance.

Why did the sisters choose the name Lady Margaret for their Centre in Cambridge? "It is named after Lady Margaret Beaufort, the foundress of St John's and Christ's colleges here in Cambridge", said Sister St Philip, who like Sister Edith, is a graduate of Newnham College. The oldest sister at Lady Margaret House, Sister Veronica was the first person ever to take a degree at Newnham as a nun. She read History. Lady Margaret House was, from 1937 until 1966, the headquarters of the Margaret Beaufort Society, a society which acted as a Catholic Chaplaincy Centre for Catholic women undergraduates until the merger of the two chaplaincies at Fisher House in 1966 following the retirement of Monsignor Alfred Gilbey. Monsignor Gilbey had insisted on presiding over an all-male establishment at Fisher House.

In 1945, the Canonesses had acquired No. 10 Grange Road which was used as accommodation. In 1955–6 a chapel was built between Nos. 10 and 12 and, in 1960 a new wing was added providing accommodation for the small community of nuns, who later chose to wear lay dress after 1968. For many years the sisters have been running Lady Margaret House as a hostel, providing bed and board for students. Now things are to change – No. 10 is in the process of being sold while building alterations at No. 12 will mean that the students, both undergraduates and graduates, will be able to cook for themselves.

Over in Selwyn Gardens, at No. 36, is another religious institution of long standing – Tyndale House, an international centre for biblical research, mostly at postgraduate level.

Grange Road has traditionally been associated with teaching institutions, but not all those who have lived in its large mansions have been academics. One notable exception was the wealthy agriculturalist, Sir Fred Hiam, who lived at "Burrell's Corner", No. 56 Grange Road, until his death in 1938. A former High Sheriff of Cambridgeshire and Huntingdonshire, Sir Fred farmed about 10,000 acres in East Anglia, some of the most productive land in the country.

His great agricultural knowledge was placed at the disposal of the authorities during and after the First World War. From 1918–21, he held office as honorary Director of Vegetable Supplies at the Ministry of Food. He toured Austria for the Reparations Commissions with the result that 50,000 tons of seed potatoes were dispatched there from Scotland and England. The resultant yield, according to his obituary in the *Independent Press and Chronicle*, was 50 per cent greater than any previous crop, and all danger of a potato famine in Austria was ended. Sir Fred Hiam was one of the most popular members, and keenest supporters of the Cambridgeshire and Isle of Ely Agricultural Society and twice president in 1928 and 1933. Incidentally, his favourite sporting hobby was skating, and in 1895 he won the 220 yards speed skating world championship in what remained the world record for ten years. Another first for Grange Road!

Pinehurst banishes the worry of gardening

The Pinehurst flats occupy the site of that first house to be built on the west side of Grange Road. As mentioned earlier, Pinehurst was built on eight acres of ground for Mr A. A. Vansittart. It was a private house designed by the London architect, T. F. Steatfield. Between 1924 and 1930, Pinehurst had been a boarding school for girls, the principals being the Misses W. R. and G. H. Frey.

When referring to the Pinehurst flats, it is important to distinguish between "Old" Pinehurst and "New" Pinehurst. "Old" Pinehurst was built in 1932 as residential flats – Grange Court and Manor Court – by the Norwich Union some three years after the girls' school was pulled down. Pinehurst, the school, was replaced by flats in the traditional architectural style of the 1930s.

In 1965, the Norwich Union Life Insurance Society sold part of the Pinehurst grounds to a building firm called Contemporary Homes Limited at a price of £72,000. It was on that piece of land measuring two acres and three roods or "thereabouts" to quote a copy of the deed of sale, that Marlborough, Westbury and Amhurst Courts were built, in a recognisably modern style with 99-year leases. They are "New" Pinehurst.

During the 1930s and the early years of the war, there were families living at "Old" Pinehurst who brought up their young children there, but since then, the overwhelming majority of Pinehurst flat owners are elderly, retired professional men and women, many with academic connections who welcome the proximity to the University Library, plus the relative proximity to the city centre, although the loss of a bus service down Grange Road has made it harder for some residents to manage a trip into town. Among the residents of Manor Court, in "Old" Pinehurst, are one couple who have lived there almost longer than anyone else: Mr and Mrs W. A. Munford. A London graduate, Mr Munford came to Cambridge after the war. He was made City Librarian in 1951. It is the peace and relative quiet of Pinehurst and the mature gardens with their copious trees that is one of the reasons why the Munfords have stayed on, making their home in what is a very congenial, rural spot with squirrels in the gardens.

Another resident of Manor Court is Dr Rex Salisbury Woods, who, until quite recently, was still practising from his doctor's surgery in Green Street, Cambridge. Several academics also live in "New" Pinehurst. The Praelectors of both New Hall, Miss S. K. Newman, and her opposite number at Lucy Cavendish, Mrs C. R. Cheney both live in Westbury Court. The retired Bursar of Trinity Hall, Mr Stuart Abbott and the current Bursar, Brigadier Curtis both live in Marlborough Court.

THE IDEAL FLAT

AT
GRANGE COURT & MANOR COURT
PINEHURST
CAMBRIDGE
INCLUSIVE RENTALS FROM
PER £130 ANN.
FULL PARTICULARS FROM THE RESIDENT AGENT
PINEHURST, GRANGE ROAD, CAMBRIDGE.

Flats for sale at Pinehurst in 1932.

When I called at Amhurst Court, everyone said: "Go and see Henry. He knows everything." Henry Button indeed does know everything. He was Brain of Britain in 1962, and he has written the *Guinness Book of the Business World*, not the *Guinness Book of Records*, as some have thought.

Educated at Manchester Grammar School and Christ's College, Cambridge, where he took a first class degree in modern and medieval languages, he entered the Civil Service in 1937. He served as Under Secretary in the Ministry of Agriculture, Fisheries and Food from 1960 until his retirement in 1973. He has been collecting facts like a schoolboy collects stamps ever since, and is an entertaining man to listen to as he takes you on a guided tour of his bookshelves and collection of artefacts made by centuries-old companies in all parts of the world.

He points, for example, to a tin of boot polish made by the company Day & Martin, the oldest boot polish firm in the world going back to 1770. "Day & Martin was the boot polish used by Sam Weller in Dickens's *Pickwick Papers*, he said. Other relics on Mr Button's shelves include samples from the oldest brewer, soap maker, builder and candlestick maker, J. G. Rathbone (Dublin 1448).

It was his fascination with company history that led him to become secretary of the Tercentenarians Club, a group of family-run businesses with histories going back more than 300 years.

GRANGE ROAD

Revisited

The biggest change in Grange Road and the adjoining roads is that the area has become increasingly institutionalised. No getting away from that when you consider that Cambridge University has doubled in size every 27 years since 1800! Colleges and university departments have continued to buy up houses in the area and, in the case of several colleges, have built more accommodation to house both undergraduate and postgraduate students. "Creeping annexation" was how it was put to me by one academic.

Trinity College has been expanding extensively in Grange Road. In 1995, they added a large complex to the already existing Burrell's Field cluster of buildings, on the site of a 1960s house designed by Patrick Hodgkinson and built for Lord Edgar Adrian when he stepped down as Master of Trinity.

Back again at Robinson College, 30 years later, my tour guide this time is Dr Martin Brett, the Oxford medieval historian and Emeritus Fellow of Robinson who became the college archivist on retirement. Dr Brett's research interests are "The documents of the Latin Church between 1000 and 1250 AD, in particular its narratives, charters and law". Ideal subject for an archivist, but he seems equally passionate about trees, botany and ornithology because on the guided tour of the college, we focus less on the buildings than on the college gardens, and he adds a visit to that hidden spot, the Sanctuary Club in Adams Road, alongside No. 18 accessible only to key holders.

Wandering in the Robinson College gardens with its pond, a brook and a walkway – one of the few college gardens in which students say they may walk on the grass, picnic and play Frisbee throughout the summer – Dr Brett speaks proudly of the college's horticultural achievements. "I think we have done nothing but good to the site, having planted infinitely more trees than we have replaced." These have included the large collection of Sorbus trees at No. 6 Adams Road. "Two consecutive chairmen of the garden committee have been fanatical conservationists." He says that the aim has been to achieve a tamed wilderness. But hidden in the wilderness at the end of the grounds of "Thorney Creek", one of the college's core buildings, there is a massive private bunker which the college can't do anything about. Was Mr Foster, the banker who built the house, anticipating a Doomsday scenario back in the 1890s? "No", says Dr Brett, "it dates from the Second World War."

Further manifestation of the institutionalisation of the Grange Road area is the growth of Clare Hall. By 1990, the numbers at the college had more than doubled, and there were 95 graduate students. In the summer of 1996, the college purchased No. 11 Herschel Road, a substantial property in a rural setting, formerly the family home of the late Lord Victor Rothschild. Rothschild had built the house in 1960 on land owned by St John's College adjoining Grange Farm, the land that was farmed by Dales dairy farmers.

From 1971 to 1997, Bob Hulyer was Lord Rothschild's gardener. "When I became gardener, Lord Rothschild bought a house for me in King's Road, off Barton Road. It was a tied cottage, an ex-council house which his Lordship bought for £4,250. He built a house for his butler in the grounds of his house and a bungalow for his secretary."

ABOVE: The Creation window in Robinson College Chapel.

LEFT: Robinson College – a major landmark in Grange Road with its towering contours that resemble a fortified brick castle. The main entrance is via a drawbridge-like ramp.

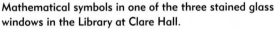

Mathematical symbols in one of the three stained glass windows in the Library at Clare Hall.

Retired Clare Hall gardener Bob Hulyer in the garden at "Elmside".

Bob's gardening duties involved keeping the grey squirrel population under control, but the creatures weren't destined to be buried, because Dr Alice Roughton at No. 9 Adams Road, whose garden adjoined the Rothschild estate, asked him to leave the shot grey squirrels in her garden so that she could add them to her stews! Waste not want not was clearly one of her mottoes!

After Lord Rothschild died in 1989, Bob carried on working for the family until the Rothschild Trustees sold the house to Clare Hall in 1971. "It went for more than £1m and was freehold", he said. In 1998, Bob became gardener at Clare Hall and worked there until his retirement in 2012.

Gardening was clearly in the Hulyer family genes. "My Dad, George Hulyer was an amateur gardener who came originally from Six Mile Bottom. My father's brother, my Uncle Jack was head gardener at King's College who had worked first for Lady Hope, of 'Binstead' in Herschel Road. She bought a house for him in Barton Road, No. 86, and he later bought it from her."

"I was going to work for Uncle Jack, but he died in 1958. Instead I started working for Clare College and became their second head gardener."

During his years working at Clare Hall, tending in particular the lawns and flower beds of Elmside, which now has fine lime trees rather than elms growing there, he became intrigued by strange mathematical symbols in the stained glass window of what is now the Library. He shared his curiosity with a student at the college who promised to investigate. It turns out that the window shows the Coat of Arms of Walter William Rouse Ball (1850–1925), the mathematician and Fellow of Trinity who built the house that triggered the Grange Road "Kink".

Professor Rouse Ball was a keen amateur magician, interested in mathematical creations and puzzles, the problem of magic squares and magic tricks. He was the founding president of the Cambridge Pentacle Club in 1919, one of the world's oldest magic societies. The house includes a billiard room and squash court, which he added for the students.

Building projects are very high on Selwyn College's agenda. The College has seen considerable expansion over the past few years. On the main site, there have been two phases of development in the corner between Grange Road and West Road based on a new court – Ann's Court – named after Ann Dobson, wife of Selwyn alumnus, Dr Chris Dobson. Ann and Chris Dobson provided almost all of the funding for this development, which totalled £7.5 million.

Moving further south down Grange Road, Pembroke College which has owned Eadson Lodge, No. 6 Grange Road, for many years, has recently bought Nos. 2 and 3 Selwyn Gardens to house undergraduate and graduate students. The two houses have since been joined together. One part is for undergraduates, the other for graduates. They have also converted No. 10 Selwyn Gardens into another college hostel.

As for the University departments, some have moved from the city centre and relocated to the West Cambridge site. One department is the Centre for Mathematical Sciences (CMS) in Clarkson and Wilberforce Roads. This is the name given to the physical site and buildings occupied by the Faculty of Mathematics,

The section in Grange Road called the "Kink".

Professor Owen
Chadwick,
former Master of
Selwyn College,
celebrating his
98th birthday.

and its constituent departments the Department of Pure Mathematics & Mathematical Statistics (DPMMS) and the Department of Applied Mathematics & Theoretical Physics (DAMTP), The Isaac Newton Institute and The Betty and Gordon Moore Library. These faculties all decamped from their original site in the Pitt Press Building, off Silver Street.

Meanwhile, what has changed at the two choir schools which both moved to Grange Road in the 1950s, and established themselves in what used to be substantial private houses? At St John's College School there has been no change in the setting. And what a setting it is, looking out across the extensive playing fields of St John's College, which serve a multifunctional purpose – a sports pitch for both the College and the School, a route for the 16 choristers to beetle across to the College chapel every day, and a regular landing pad for the Royal helicopter!

Those playing fields, like the Trinity College ones further down Grange Road, are also one of the key parts of the green, green grass of west Cambridge that keeps the area rather protected, and special.

St John's laid out the first college playing field in 1858. Two years later in 1860, Trinity followed suit and rented (and later bought from St John's) 16 acres of land which had been part of Grange Farm and lay west of Grange Road. It's called Trinity Old Field. In due course, other colleges rented land from St John's for playing fields, or in the case of colleges which had been allocated land in west Cambridge – Gonville and Caius, Corpus, King's and Clare – laid out fields on their own territories.

What with these playing fields and gardens, especially the Fellows' Gardens of Trinity, Clare, King's, Corpus and Gonville and Caius, the colleges had indeed established a special green belt for themselves beyond the river.

For St John's College School, the biggest change in the last 30 years has been the growth in the number of pupils. Prior to 1993, Byron House, as explained in the earlier article, was a pre-prep and single sex school for seven to 11-year-old girls. Boys aged seven to 13 were educated at Senior House, named after the former headmaster, Sam Senior, and only boys were allowed to board. The school became fully co-educational from 1993, with younger pupils aged four to nine educated at Byron House, and nine to 13-year-olds educated at Senior House.

There are now a total of 460 children at the school all enjoying wonderful amenities and inspirational teaching. No wonder SJCS gained the accolade of "exceptional" when the Independent Schools Inspectorate carried out an inspection in May 2013. Why is the school exceptional? What is the special ethos I ask Headmaster, Kevin Jones, an English graduate of Caius College, who has been the Head since 1990. (Incidentally there have only been five headmasters at the school in the twentieth century). From his desk in his comfortable study in

No. 75 Grange Road with a large eye-catching collection of stones on the shelf, Mr Jones explains that "the core of the ethos is about childhood".

"We achieve exceptional results because we start by knowing the children. It is important to protect childhood," he said. "For instance, the percentage of children who have not climbed a tree by the age of nine is very high generally."

"People talk now of the compression of childhood — some say that it is over by the age of ten. When we know that for their best cognitive growth and their well-being, children must have their childhood, why is childhood itself now so threatened?"

He wrote in his Headmaster "Retrospect for 2013" that one third of our children will live to be at least 100. One hundred years ago, the First World War had not begun: "The world has changed unimaginably. We have arrived at what is now called the Anthropocene era, a time when the influence of human behaviour on the earth is so extreme as to constitute a new geological epoch and a terrible threat."

"The Dalai Lama came to St John's last year. In the College Chapel, he said: 'In the last century, we developed the capacity to destroy ourselves. Can we now develop the capacity to save ourselves? Will the 21st century be a century of happiness or of self-destructive greed?'" Mr Jones said that he asked the Dalai Lama what his most important message was for the children of St John's. It was

Choristers at St John's College School crossing the playing fields towards the College for Evensong.

St John's
College School
Headmaster Mr
Kevin Jones with
pupils on Pre
Prep Sports Day.

this: "turn always towards affection and give to others the affection that you have been given."

For Mr Jones, it was a particular joy to have in the school's inspection report such clear evidence that an education rooted in affection, which values childhood and children, which seeks to foster in them the best care for themselves and for others, is one that produces the highest possible achievement.

The report says: "St John's gives its pupils a flying start to their education. What I have tried to say is that it is affection that gives our children their wings." When he writes how a young child from the Kindergarten class whispered in his ear: "I love you" and "Stay weird for the rest of ever" you realise what a much loved head-master he is.

Although there have been many changes since the 1980s at King's College School in terms of refurbishing: adding in 1999 an ICT and Design and Technology Suite, called the "Wiles Building"; in 2004, the "Briggs Building", named after the former headmaster, which houses new classrooms and science laboratories; tightening up security (the place is gated and security coded now), complying with Health and Safety regulations; raising money to build a new sports hall, the ethos of the school has not changed.

I asked Nicholas Robinson, the headmaster, how he would describe that ethos. "I was a gap student here in 1978, helping out with sport in particular. One of the things that drew me back here as headmaster was that King's has a quirky, happy, individual character, where children are allowed to be themselves but the relationship between the children and the staff is one of mutual respect and humorous interaction."

He goes on to add: "Academic standards combined with the musical tradition of the school are second to none. The musical strength stems from having the choristers at the school. It is in the blood. The fact that music is a way of life means that children who start at King's aged four, experience all the music as normal. This is what the school does and they enjoy it."

One tradition at the school has changed though – it used to be ginger beer and ginger biscuits on Founder's Day, but it is now hot cocoa and chocolate biscuits. And there will be many parents and pupils who remember speech days at the school in headmaster Gerald Peacocke's time when a cockerel and hens belonging to his wife crowed and clucked in the background!

Robert Henderson, who will be retiring in July 2014 after 41 years teaching history at the school, and known to all staff and pupils past and present as "Hendy", agrees that the ethos of the school hasn't changed much. By the way, keen chess players at the school and their parents will be relieved to know that after retiring, "Hendy" will be coming back to run an after-school chess club. More than a quarter of the school, 110 children, are members of the chess club.

When King Henry VI founded King's College with its 16 choristers who were to be "of sound mind and able to read", he didn't have chess playing in mind! Nor did he imagine that his choristers would one day travel the world performing in concerts! Recent destinations were China, Hong Kong, Singapore and Istanbul. In the case of China, it was to perform in just one concert under the directorship of Stephen Cleobury, the college's Director of Music.

During term time, however, choir trips abroad are restricted to weekend performances in European cities. Stephen Cleobury and Nicholas Robinson have had to turn down many invitations for the choir to travel and perform. One they didn't turn down though, was an invitation at Easter 2013, to No. 10 Downing Street to sing at a reception to the Prime Minister and his guests. In his headmaster's report in the *Fleur de Lys 2013* magazine, Nicholas Robinson writes: "After they had sung, the boys were given a tour of No. 10 and I will never forget the wonderful sight of all the choristers sitting round the Cabinet table, with one of the boys, Tom Pickard, sitting grandly in the Prime Minister's chair."

While the colleges have extended octopus-like tentacles to many of the large, late nineteenth-century Victorian and early Edwardian houses, there is still a sprinkling of privately owned houses at the southern end of Grange Road and in Selwyn Gardens and there are a number of families with children too. It is an

Choristers at King's College School heading to Chapel for Evensong.

Henry VI
portrayed in a
stained glass
window in the
King's College
dining hall.
CMR/250/5386.

area where neighbours put out windfall apples in baskets on the pavement for others to share, whilst honing bee-keeping skills, and having parties together in their gardens.

They also get together to tackle planning issues. Well, they did when Professor Sir Malcolm Grant, who retired in September 2013 as Provost of University College London, lived in the road at No. 10. He would summon neighbours to drinks and discussions about proposed developments in the area. No one however, goes out now with a shotgun to tackle squatters, as used to happen years ago in the lane alongside No. 15, so I was told!

The Wallises, the Willcocks and the Challises are some of the families who are still there some 30 years after I first wrote *Down Your Street Grange Road*, but somehow missed them out then. I am now making up for that!

Before moving recently to Millington Road, Michael Wallis and his wife Evadne spent 52 years living at "Five Gables", No. 4 Grange Road, the first house to be built in Cambridge in 1898 by the architect Baillie Scott and one of the first in the country to be built by him. It is a lovely, cosy family house with all the Arts and Crafts accoutrements of ironwork, pine floors, wooden doors, window seats, casement windows with leaded lights, with many heart shapes in the leading. Mr Baillie Scott must have been in love at the time, as the place is one big Valentine card with all those hearts!

Michael Wallis having a degree in Natural Sciences from Magdalene College spent a life working on the racecourses all over the country. "I joined the family bookmaking business when my father Laurie Wallis was having trouble."

Good friends of the Wallises were the McBurney family who lived across the road at No. 5 Grange Road. American academic Professor Charles McBurney, who died in 1979, was Reader and later Professor of Quaternary Prehistory at Cambridge. His work included studies of the Upper Palaeolithic in Britain, important excavations in the Channel Islands, extensive excavations in Libya (the Haua Fteah cave) and, in later years, excavations in Iran and Afghanistan. His students included the young Prince Charles and the Queen of Denmark when she was Princess Margarete.

His youngest son, Simon McBurney, the actor and artistic director of Théâtre de Complicité in England, remembers when the family moved into "a huge, rambling house on the outskirts of the town". He remembers it as a draughty, dark, Victorian semi-detached house which was full of strange ghosts and had no central heating.

There was also very little in the way of modern amenities: "It was an age when lots of families were getting televisions and we didn't have one", says his brother.

"We had a radio, which was stored at the top of the house and it was brought out once a year when my father helplessly tried to get it to work in order to listen to the festival of nine lessons and carols from King's but then it was put away again on Boxing Day."

Simon's older brother is the composer Gerard McBurney. He was born in 1954 and studied in Cambridge and at the Moscow Conservatory before teaching at the London College of Music and later for 12 years at the Royal Academy of Music. He is Artistic Programming Advisor to the Chicago Symphony Orchestra.

For the last 30 years No. 5 Grange Road has been the home of William Horbury, also a Fellow of Corpus, and non stipendiary priest in charge of St Botolph's Church. The Horburys bought the house from Anne, widow of Charles McBurney in 1984, and Professor Horbury, his wife, Kathy, and daughters Kate and Mary, moved there from their previous home just down the road, No. 35a, the Coachman's House at Pinehurst which then belonged to Corpus.

Professor Horbury, who is Emeritus Professor of Jewish and Early Christian Studies and a Fellow of the British Academy, explains that there is a special link between St Botolph's and No. 5 and its semi-detached other half, No. 7, since both were built by Edmund Kett of the firm of Rattee and Kett in 1893.

G. F. Bodley, the most influential architect at work in the Church of England at that time, designed the lectern at St Botolph's. He then joined in 1875 with Edmund Kett and his brother in giving it to the church as a memorial to the Ketts' father, the Cambridge builder. In 1898 Edmund Kett designed the cross above the screen in the church and gave that as a gift too.

Rachel Willcocks, wife of Sir David, the director of music at King's College from 1957 to 1975, has spent much of her life in Grange Road. In 1928 as a small child, she came to live in a house in Sidgwick Avenue, close to the junction with Grange Road. The house was called "Selwyn Close". Her father, the Rev. A. C. Blyth was Dean of Chapel at Selwyn College, Vice Master and later, Senior Tutor. She remembers girls coming out of Pinehurst School in the 1920s, and an old man, a retired academic going round in a bath chair giving out chocolate mints to local children.

Another local character was Miss E. L. Heffer, a relative of John Heffer, who lived in one of the 12 flats built in Grange Gardens in the 1930s, and would walk down the road with her parrot on her arm. Neighbours, who were concerned about what would happen to the parrot after Miss Heffer's death, were relieved to learn that she had made arrangements for that eventuality.

Sir David Willcocks, Director of Music at King's College from 1957 to 1975.

What Miss Heffer would make of the news that Newnham College has just bought the Grange Gardens flats to accommodate more postgraduate students is another matter!

During the Second World War, Rachel Willcocks and her siblings were evacuated to Cornwall and her father, who was disabled in the First World War, stayed on at Selwyn to run the college for the small number of under-graduates studying there. Following her father's death, her mother, Mrs A. C. Blyth lived for many years in one of the flats at No. 31 Grange Road, a house that was bequeathed to Selwyn College by one of its members, the zoologist Professor L. A. Borradaile.

Bequeathing your house to your college was frequently the done thing among academics in this part of Cambridge. At this end of Grange Road, No. 7 was left by Enid Welsford, the English scholar, to Newnham. The college subsequently sold it. Similarly, Elizabeth Franklin left her luxury flat at Pinehurst to Selwyn College. The Willcocks, who bought their home from Lady Barcroft, a house built in 1906 by Rattee and Kett have lived in Grange Road since 1957. Kett himself lived at No. 7, a house he called "Redwick". "It was very Town and Gown in Cambridge in those days when we first lived here, but now it is a great place to enjoy retirement."

University of the Third Age (U3A) classes beckon for Lady Willcocks, while Sir David, who conducted his last concert at the age of 90 in the Albert Hall in 2010 attends a bridge club in St Marks every Monday. He was happy to tell me about the secrets of bridge playing – always a closed book to me! He also satisfied my curiosity about why the chorister chosen to sing the first verse of *Once in Royal David's City* at the start of the Service of Nine Lessons and Carols in King's College Chapel on Christmas Eve, was only selected seconds before the start of the service when the broadcasting red light goes on. In brief, it is to stop pressure from the choristers' mothers who would get all worked up in advance and want to bring friends along!

We are in their sitting room on an early spring morning looking out at the long garden which is a carpet of aconites, while hungry birds swarm round the bird feeder. A long-haired dachshund dozes at Sir David's feet, and a signed photograph of a young Prince Charles smiles from a side table.

Good neighbours of Sir David and Lady Willcocks are the architect Tom Challis and his wife Judy, who is an accomplished patchwork quilter. In 1983, they moved with their family into Upton House, Grange Road, one of three families now occupying this large nine-bedroomed villa-style house designed by the Arts and Crafts architect, A. Winter Rose, and built in 1912 for a Mrs Blanche.

Her initials, SMB can be found on the wrought iron gate onto the pavement. The architect's initials are on a cast lead rainwater hopper on the front of the house. Built as one, the house was divided into two in 1980, and then into three separate homes in 1983. One of the homes has an Italianate garden. The Challises had a party in their garden in 2012 to celebrate the house's 100th anniversary!

The Garden House, one of the two surviving structures from the day when the area was a leisure or pleasure garden. Now in the garden of Tyndale Lodge.

Tunku Abdul Rahman, the then future Prime Minister of Malaya, and later of Malaysia after independence, lodged in Upton House whilst studying for his law degree between 1922 and 1925 at St Catharine's College. Apparently overseas students were not permitted to have college accommodation at that time.

During the Second World War, potatoes were grown on the lawn of Upton House, and pigs were kept at the bottom of the garden. Many years later, Tom Challis revived that wartime practice of animal husbandry, by branching into apiculture. He was inspired to take up bee-keeping by another neighbour, the Cambridge artist Pamela Townshend, now in her 90s, who kept three beehives in her garden for many years. Tom Challis thought he would get one, "but I was a total amateur by comparison".

Across the road from Upton House is Champneys Walk, a 1980s housing development – architecturally not quite in the Basil Champneys league. Like St Marks Court, it is built on land belonging to Newnham College that used to be allotments. The college needed money from the sale of the land for its roof repairs.

Running alongside No. 15 Grange Road is a leafy lane, formerly Grange Road Gardens, with six houses built on what used to be one of the celebrated Leisure or Pleasure Gardens of old Cambridge. Of the two surviving structures – what you might call substantial summer houses in this area dating from the days when it was a leisure or pleasure garden (there may be others elsewhere) – one is in the garden of Grange Gardens House, No. 15F at the end of the lane and the other, once rented by Miss Blanche Athena Clough, in the gardens of Tyndale Lodge, the home of Tyndale House's warden. It is called the Garden House. The legend is that Miss Clough used to retreat there from Newnham College for a cigarette.

Miss Clough was the daughter of the poet Arthur Hugh Clough and niece of the first Principal of Newnham College, Anne Jemima Clough. Blanche Athena spent a large part of her life at Newnham, from when she arrived as a student in 1884 until her retirement as Principal in 1923, and for many years was in charge of the College gardens. The brick Garden House, a place for her to escape to, had a small flight of steps leading through French doors into a room with a bay window and fireplace. There was a cellar and an upstairs area. It was after the sale of the land in 1925 that Grange Road Gardens slowly gave way to houses.

Next to Tyndale Lodge is Hawthorne House, No. 15A. It belongs to Wheaton College, a private American Christian liberal arts college in Wheaton, Illinois. The college was founded in 1860 by prominent abolitionist and pastor Jonathan Blanchard. The house is named after Gerald Hawthorne, a popular professor at Wheaton College.

Dr Peter Williams, warden of Tyndale House, round the corner in Selwyn Gardens, tells me that "Hawthorne House is not officially connected to Tyndale House in any way, though we enjoy friendly relations." Dr Williams believes that apart from the house at the very end (west side) of the lane, Hawthorne House is the oldest address in the lane.

Other houses in the lane are called the "Orangery", "Tyndale Court" and "Orchard End", a modern Scandinavian style house, which is the home of Peter and Birgit Carolin. He is Emeritus Professor of Architecture.

The big change at Pinehurst in the last 30 years has been the construction of Pinehurst South in 1990, when two blocks of 30 flats in total, were built at the southern edge of the site in a woodland setting fronting Selwyn Gardens. Two separate mews properties were later added. The two identical blocks of 15 flats, designed by the architect Stefan Zins are called Redwood Lodge, because of the magnificent redwood tree in the grounds, planted in 1871, and The Oast House. This was not because there was ever a brewery on the site, but rather the building gets its name from the design of the roofline which hints at the conical shape of an oast house roof.

The whole Pinehurst South scheme was carried out, developed and managed by the local property company, Midsummer Estates who had to make sure that the design reflected the high standards of the Cambridge Conservation area in this part of the city, when they bought the site from the Norwich Union in 1985. The company's founder and managing director, Nigel Grimshaw, a Resident MA of Queens' College, lives in The Oast House.

Professor Stephen Hawking was the first person to move into Pinehurst South on 1 April 1990. After eight years, he decided to move and asked Nigel Grimshaw to help commission him a striking new chalet-style house designed

The gargoyle from King's College Chapel saved from the skip by Professor Sir Frank Kermode.

Prince Philip, Chancellor of Cambridge University visits The Oast House in 1999. Left to right: The Lord Lieutenant of Cambridgeshire, James Crowden, Prince Philip, Professor Sir David Williams, Dame Gillian Beer, President of Clare Hall and Sir Roger Tomkys, Master of Pembroke College.

by Stefan Zins, nearby in Wordsworth Grove on land which was bought from Newnham College.

An early resident in The Oast House, was Dr Kim Dae-jung, who occupied two flats. He was invited, as a promoter of human rights and democracy in South Korea (for which he had served lengthy prison terms and suffered an assassination attempt which left him with a permanent limp) to come to Cambridge University as a visiting Fellow of Clare Hall. The invitation came from the Vice-Chancellor and former President of Wolfson College, Professor Sir David Williams. Shortly after returning home, KJD (as he was affectionately known) was elected President of South Korea. He touchingly declared that his stay at peaceful Pinehurst in Cambridge had been one of the happiest periods of his life.

KJD was awarded the Nobel Prize for his "sunshine policy" attempt to reunify North and South Korea and a plaque was installed at The Oast House to mark his stay. It was honoured by a visit from Prince Philip in 1999. The event was televised live on South Korean TV with viewers surprised that the Duke of Edinburgh drove directly from Sandringham at the wheel of his own Range Rover. It was presumably assumed that he would arrive by sedan chair carried by the Coldstream Guards! Prince Philip met many residents at Pinehurst.

KJD did not forget his neighbours. Nigel Grimshaw and Stephen Hawking were also invited to meet him in the Blue House, the Presidential Palace in Seoul later that year. In 2001, KJD returned to Cambridge to receive an honorary Doctorate from the University and insisted on visiting Pinehurst before going to the Senate House.

The physicist Dr Alan Walton, a Fellow of Churchill College has lived in The Oast House for 23 years. There is, incidentally, a "splitting the atom" connection with Pinehurst. Dr Walton's father, Professor Ernest Walton of Trinity College was awarded the Nobel Prize in 1951 for this. He was the driving force behind the discovery, sharing the prize with his colleague Sir John Cockcroft of St John's College who later became the first Master of Churchill. His wife, Lady Cockcroft lived for many years in Grange Court, Pinehurst. Walton and Cockcroft's supervisor, Lord Ernest Rutherford, lived nearby in Sidgwick Avenue and also shared the Nobel Prize.

Dr Walton tells the story of how his school, the Methodist College in Belfast, gave the boys a half day holiday in 1951 when his father was awarded the Nobel Prize for splitting the atom. It was Ireland's first Nobel Prize for Science (there had been awards for literature). One boy, when challenged by his mother as to why he had come home early, replied: "We got a half day holiday because somebody broke something!"

Professor Sir Frank Kermode lived in an apartment at The Oast House. Nobly, he saved a King's College Chapel gargoyle which stands in the grounds from the skip but, sadly, had less good fortune in his private affairs. When moving out of his house in Sedley Taylor Road, he assembled many of his rarest Shakespearean and early English literature books in thick black plastic bags which he placed for collection outside his house. Tragically, a City Council refuse team passed at that very moment, spotted the bags and threw them in the refuse cart where they were destroyed in its churning mechanism. He tried to seek redress from the Council but to no avail.

Winter wonderland at 35A Grange Road.

Dr Colin Butler, now 100 years old, lived in Redwood Lodge with his late wife Jean for more than 20 years. Dr Butler was Director of Rothamsted, the Government Agricultural Research Centre at Harpenden, Herts and his field of expertise was bees. He was, of course, fascinated by all insects and discouraged Tony Jobson, the estate maintenance man, somewhat to the latter's bemusement, from removing spiders' webs beside his flat.

Dr and Mrs Butler sold their apartment in Redwood Lodge about four years ago to Professor Antony and Mrs Marjorie Hewish. Professor Hewish won the Nobel Prize in 1974 together with fellow radio-astronomer Martin Ryle for his work on the development of radio aperture synthesis and its role in the discovery of pulsars (pulsar being a contraction of "pulsating star").

Dr Ronald Broom, also living with his wife at The Oast House, is a retired applied physicist. Perhaps because of a long period spent in Switzerland at the University of Bern and the Research Laboratory of IBM in Zurich, his personal hobby has been to make (not mend) complicated clocks. His professional field is the physics of semi-conductors, including laser structures.

Pinehurst South seems to have encouraged longevity. Nigel Grimshaw's neighbour at The Oast House, Stanley Fenwick, moved in with his wife Peggy (aged 97 and still in residence) in August 1990. Stanley died in October 2013, aged 101. The youngest of a family of five brought up in Hackney, he lost a brother Albert (born in 1896) in the First World War. The son of an East End glass bottle warehouseman, he went on to become Head of Beecham Pharmaceuticals in the UK. His hobby was making furniture.

In 2012 The Coach House Mews at Pinehurst was created to resemble an original estate outbuilding from the 1870s Grata Quies estate. It is currently occupied for 18 months by the Whewell Professor of International Law, James Crawford before he heads off to the International Criminal Court in the Hague.

One of the team who helped with the graphic design for the promotion of the Pinehurst South development was Tom Challis, a near neighbour in Upton House.

From the roof terrace and garden on top of one of the penthouse apartments, we look west across Newnham rooftops to open country, and behind to the wooded grounds of the whole 8.8 acre Pinehurst estate where foxes, squirrels and muntjac deer freely roam. Badgers even feature. Owls hoot at night and birdsong is a constant during daylight hours. One lady, moving there from West Chesterton in 1990, said that she found the dawn chorus too loud, for which the management company regretted that there was no immediate remedy!

I don't know if the Waters family now living at No. 35A Grange Road in what was the Pinehurst coachman's cottage are disturbed by the dawn chorus, but they certainly hear and see the greater spotted woodpeckers that make their nests in some of the massive trees that dwarf the house, and give a Hansel and Gretel feel to the garden. It is a real house in the woods with giant redwoods clearly planted when the original Pinehurst was developed. The four Waters children look out of their bedroom windows and watch the woodpeckers making their nests, and are thrilled to watch when the young offspring emerge.

Deterring unwanted callers and scallywags is not a modern phenomenon – sign by a door bell ringer on a house in the Grange Road area.

Sara Waters is the daughter of the late John Lennox Cook who owned the Language School in Barton Road. In 1985, her father sold the business to Anglo World and retired to Grange Road buying No. 35A from Corpus Christi College. He built an extension at the back of the house, which had already been extended in the 1930s judging by the fireplaces.

John Lennox Cook died in 1990 leaving the house to his two daughters. It was let out for several years, before Sara and her husband Mark Waters moved out of London with their young family and settled there.

Sara, a skilled paper conservator, who has kept her maiden name of Lennox Cook works with Penny Heath, the well-established paper conservator at Penny's studio in Wilberforce Road. They work together on the conservation of books, works of art on paper, and archives. Once a week Sara goes to London to work on the conservation of the Law Society's archives.

Mark, a horticulturalist and historian looks after their four young children, two of whom attend Newnham Croft and two King's College School. The family enjoy life in Grange Road. Sara explains: "It is so easy to break into community life here. There are a lot of children in the area, and both schools have a lively mix of people, including the children of a lot of visiting academics."

I was surprised to hear that children on bikes emerge from the Pinehurst flats en route to school in the morning!

Thirty years ago, Selwyn Gardens at the southern end of Grange Road, was not a street I visited for the series. This seems the moment to take a look, particularly as there are some architectural gems in this street of handsome redbrick houses, two of which – Nos. 5 and 6 built in the 1890s, the first houses to be built in Selwyn Gardens are the work of the architect J. J. Stevenson, a talented member of the Queen Anne movement so well represented in the work of Basil Champneys at Newnham College.

Large leafy gardens are a hallmark of the houses and grounds in Newnham, so when Pembroke College bought and joined together Nos. 2 and 3 Selwyn

Gardens and then put in a planning application to build in the garden, the scheme was turned down by the City Council on the grounds that the gardens were an integral part of the large houses in the conservation area.

In 1983, Midsummer Estates purchased No. 5 Selwyn Gardens, a large detached nine-bedroomed house with two staircases, from the Misses Harris. It had been in the family for 60 years having passed from father to mother to oldest son to youngest daughters.

Professor Harris had a large family. The two youngest daughters, well into their 80s, remained unmarried and the house eventually passed to them. They recalled their brother bringing home Army friends during the First World War and the friends sleeping in the garage. They also remembered Pinehurst when it was a girls school. Then, when the new flats (Grange Court and Manor Court) were built in 1931, they recalled local children going up and down in the new elevators which were a novelty in Cambridge at the time.

Professor H. Harris, an anatomist, bought No. 5 around 1922. There is a covenant from 24 June 1918 between Helen Woollgar de Gaugrion Salter (Vendor) and Ernest Howard Griffiths (Purchaser).

Covenants imposed in the 1918 transfer quaintly reveal uses which were considered undesirable in a high quality residential neighbourhood in the Edwardian period:

1) No operative machinery shall be placed on any part of the premises
2) No noisome, noxious, noisy or offensive trade
3) No trade of an innkeeper, licensed victualler, publican, beer house keeper or retailer of wines, spirits or beer
4) No keeper of a lunatic asylum
5) No hut, shed, caravan house on wheels or other chattel intended for use as a dwelling
6) No show booths, swings or roundabouts be placed on the premises.

The first owner, around 1880, was a Trinity Don, Professor Arthur Woollgar Verrall, the eminent classicist and first holder of the King Edward VII Chair of English. Professor Verrall died in 1912 and his sole offspring, Helen Salter, inherited the house.

Henry Harris was elected to the Chair of Anatomy in 1934, which he held until 1951. The current (since 1997) incumbent is a W. A. Harris.

Midsummer Estates bought No. 5 from the 'The Personal Representatives of Mrs Margaret Susan Harris these being Miss Dalbren Harris (the youngest daughter) and Roy Barker Hewitson, the solicitor, Margaret Harris, wife of Professor Henry Harris died on 21 October 1982. Clearly the house had to be sold when the mother died so the estate could be split between her children.

No. 5 was included in a book on haunted houses. This was because the wife and daughter of the first owner, Professor Verrall, became very interested in the supernatural and contributed several articles to the Proceedings of the Society for Psychical Research. Verrall himself was not a regular member of the society,

Professor Arthur Verrall, Fellow of Trinity College and first owner of No. 5 Selwyn Gardens.

which was started in 1882 by a group of Trinity Fellows, but was involved in some of his wife's experiments on automatic writing. The Society held regular séances at No. 5 Selwyn Gardens. Nigel Grimshaw recalls that when his company bought the house it was in a near pristine original condition. "Unmodernised, it didn't appear to have been redecorated for many years but was in a beautiful state. Everything had been cleared out apart from a few old fen skaters with hard leather and a chipped Art Deco teapot. However, on opening a pantry-type cupboard, I and my colleague nearly jumped out of our skins when we were confronted with the skull of a gorilla (so it turned out)."

Midsummer Estates sold No. 5 Selwyn Gardens (retaining the land which is now 5A, a house designed by the architect Stefan Zins) for the princely sum of £120,000 on 9th February 1984.

Ignoring a small garage and outbuildings, there was a distance of 47 metres between No. 5 and No. 4 Selwyn Gardens before 5A was constructed. The planning officer told them that the distance between Nos. 5 and 4 Selwyn Gardens was, until Midsummer Estates infilled, the greatest gap between two detached houses in Cambridge. It provided access for the building of Redwood Lodge and The Oast House flats.

Anne Coombs has lived in No. 6 since 1952, the year she and her late husband, the immunologist Professor Robert "Robin" Coombs got married. At that time he was a prize fellow of King's College.

Anne had come up to Newnham to read natural sciences for two years during the war. She came back after the war to finish her degree and then became a research student. "My supervisor was Robin Coombs."

Robin, as he was widely known, is considered one of the fathers of modern immunology and renowned for the "Coombs Test" – used for detecting antibodies in various clinical scenarios, devised (as legend would have it) while he was travelling on the train in 1945. Professor Coombs, a Fellow of Corpus Christi, was born in 1921 and died in 2006. Robin Coombs qualified as a vet in Edinburgh, did his Ph.D in Cambridge and embarked on a career in immunology. He was the first veterinarian who was a Fellow of the Royal Society.

The Coombs' house, No. 6 Selwyn Gardens, was built in the late nineteenth century for a James Ward, who had been the Minister of the Congregational Church in Cambridge, but had resigned because of doctrinal differences with his congregation.

So how was he able to build No. 6 Selwyn Gardens? Anne Coombs explains that "James Ward had just married a Fellow of Newnham College, who came from Northern Ireland. The Wards were lent money to buy the land by the Misses Kennedy who lived at No. 7 and had a close connection with Newnham College. His neighbour, Professor Verrall, had befriended him and secured him a Fellowship at Trinity. They were close friends and both used J. J. Stevenson as the architect of their houses."

How did the Coombs come to buy No. 6? "Well, when we were engaged and looking to buy a house, we were walking round Cambridge and saw that No. 7 Selwyn Gardens was empty. Robin found out it was a house that belonged to Corpus. Shortly afterwards while scrimmaging round David's bookstall on the market, he found himself standing next to the college Bursar, also searching through the books. He asked him whether the college would give us first refusal on No. 7 if they planned to sell it. The Bursar said that the college also owned No. 6, but they hadn't yet made a decision about which house to sell.

"He promised to give Robin first refusal when they had decided what to do, and in due course he kept his word and Robin, whose annual salary then was £900, was offered first refusal on No. 6, a house which the college used in 1946 as a college hostel for the students who had returned after the war."

There is a gate in the wall connecting No. 6 to No. 7 installed by the Bursar of Corpus Christi so that Professor Coombs, the second Warden of Leckhampton and a Fellow of the College, could enjoy walking with his wife in the grounds of Leckhampton to which No. 7 is connected, there being no boundary. For Anne Coombs the garden is a very important adjunct to the house.

People who have lived in Selwyn Gardens over the years, and who are remembered by Anne Coombs were two senior doctors – two "top dogs". The first two houses in Selwyn Gardens were built for the Surgeon and the Physician at Addenbrooke's Hospital, and a Mrs Hackford at No. 4, a square and functional house built in about 1895 by the Borough Engineer. In war time Mrs Hackford used to run the Thursday concerts. "She was a power in the land." When the Post Office wanted to change the unusual numbering of the houses in the road, she put up such a fight against the scheme that the authorities backed off!

Anthony Hopkinson, the printmaker, and his wife Sylvia lived for many years in Melbourn, ten miles south of Cambridge. "Our house had been in Sylvia's family since the early 19th century but as the years passed we found it too big for us. Seven years ago we moved to Selwyn Gardens."

Their new home, No. 29, was one of a pair built just after the Second World War for Fellows of Queens' College. They stand on land which had been the orchard of a larger house. Originally the houses had three bedrooms, a bathroom, a sitting room and a kitchen. Post-war shortages of materials limited their size. A decade later a dining room was added with a fourth bedroom above it.

Mr Hopkinson is an active member of the Cambridge Drawing Society, and at one time was President: "I was involved each year in the annual exhibition at the Guildhall and became aware of the sad state of the portrait of Thomas Hobson, painted in 1620, which hangs there. It has been damaged over the years and in some places badly restored. I hope to launch a campaign to raise funds for its restoration."

Thomas Hobson (1544–1631) was a carrier, based in Cambridge and bearing mail to and from London. In addition, he hired out horses; his customers had to take the next horse in the row, there was no choice – hence the expression "Hobson's Choice" came into the English language. Hobson was also involved in the construction of a man-made watercourse built in 1614 to provide clean drinking water to the city of Cambridge.

The picture hung at the Black Bull Inn on Bishopsgate, London for about 100 years until it was given to J. Burleigh in 1787. Burleigh was an alderman of Cambridge who, like Hobson before him, ran wagons from Hobson Street to the Black Bull. After his death in 1828, his partner, a Mr Swan, carried on the business and owned the portrait until it was bought by public subscription in 1849. Mr Hopkinson thinks that most portraits of that period that exist today are of persons from royal or noble families: "So this picture of an ordinary citizen going about his business has special appeal."

No. 32 Selwyn Gardens was the home of the senior clinician at Addenbrooke's Hospital. The senior surgeon lived in No. 9 built by the Professor of Anatomy at the University Medical School at Addenbrooke's in 1911. They must have been Anne Coombs' "top dogs".

Another artist, the painter Cecil Collins, lived at No. 35 Selwyn Gardens. He had a full retrospective exhibition at the Tate Gallery after his death in 1989. The Fitzwilliam hold at least one of his paintings. The photographer Bertl Gaye also lived for a time at No. 35 Selwyn Gardens. One of her shots of Benjamin Britten is in the National Portrait Gallery.

Robin Pellew, who now owns No. 32 bought the main front half of the house from Corpus in 2000 when it provided six flats for married postgraduate students: "As part of the sale agreement we were responsible for building the wall splitting off the back half that were the original servants' quarters, which the College sold separately."

No one knows more about the pressures in Cambridge from the University and the high tech businesses sited here, to allow more development on the Green Belt than Sir Robin Pellew, chairman of Cambridge Past, Present and Future, formerly the Cambridge Preservation Society.

His view is that new laxer planning laws favour developers and constrain councils, in our case Cambridge City and South Cambs District Councils, who do their best, he thinks. His message to the colleges and the university in the case of the North West Cambridge development is: don't sell the land, keep control of it and then you will have some leverage over the developers. "Dealing with developers is like tugging a tiger by the tail, which then turns round and snarls, 'I want more!' Or trying to tame an elephant with a pea shooter!"

It's Cambridge PPF's belief that there are under used areas (like the land wasted for surface car parking which could be stacked up into multi-storey buildings) or brownfield sites within the city that should be developed before spreading out at the margins into the Green Belt. All this will be considered at the examination in public of the City's Local Plan in October 2014.

To come up to the present, a house in Selwyn Gardens, No. 33 once owned by the Eaden Lilley family has just sold for £3.5m. That is the house price bubble for you in Cambridge!

Having begun on a traffic note 30 years ago, I will end on one! Around ten years ago, Grange Road was "traffic calmed" with "squeezes", "speed bumps" and a 20 mph speed limit. I wonder what Mr Salim Khan would make of that if he were alive today!

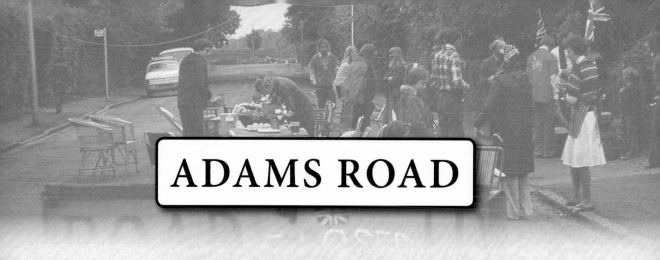

ADAMS ROAD

29 April 1982

Spring is shimmering in Adams Road, one of the choice rural enclaves for academics in west Cambridge. White and blue anemones carpet the spinneys and orchards of the large Victorian and Edwardian houses, commissioned by and built for eminent dons, who by then were allowed to marry, as monuments to family life at the turn of the century.

The road was once called Love Lane, and was romantically leafy and full of ruts. Nightingales sang in the trees in those halcyon days, while in winter local children learned to skate on the pond, now the bird sanctuary tucked away behind Trinity College Cricket Ground, called Trinity Old Field.

Love Lane vanished when St John's College, which owned the land in question as part of its Grange Farm, replaced it with Adams Road in 1898, as part of a long-term plan for residential development which began in 1886, and which also included Herschel Road and Sylvester Road – all three named after eminent astronomers.

This road, where all the houses are leasehold, was named after John Couch Adams, a distinguished alumnus of St John's. Scientist and astronomer, he was director of the Cambridge Observatory from 1891–2, (but declined the office of Astronomer Royal), and made the deductive discovery of the planet Neptune.

"Overbrook", No. 1 Adams Road, which was scooped up and demolished to make way for Robinson College, was one of the first four houses to be built in the road. (The leases for Nos. 1, 2 and 3 were all issued by St John's College in 1898.) It was built for the Selwyn family. Mrs A. C. Selwyn, who lived there for many years, was the widow of John Richardson Selwyn, the youngest son of George Augustus Selwyn, the first Bishop of New Zealand.

It was said to be the least well built house on that side of Adams Road, because while it was being built in 1900, all the great piles of carefully seasoned wood that were to be incorporated into its structure, were seized by jubilant students who lit a massive bonfire with it to celebrate the relief and end of the siege of Mafeking on 16–17 May 1900 during the Boer War. For a time, apparently the word "mafeking" meant to celebrate excessively! As all that seasoned timber had gone up in smoke, the builders had to use new, unseasoned wood, and so it ended up a less solid structure!

The Master of Corpus, Sir Will Spens, lived at No. 1 after the First World War until the late 1920s.

Dr J. H. C. Dalton who built No. 2, called "The Plot" and now the home of the Kaldors, told neighbours that a strata of rock ran right across Adams Road to Madingley Road and that Nos. 2 and 3 were built upon it.

No doubt Professor Kaldor, who was Economic Advisor to the post-war Labour governments and had great influence, would be glad to know that a wise man built his house upon the rock! Family friends remember gathering in the garden there to celebrate the wedding of one of the Kaldors's four daughters. They all sang *The Red Flag* and a good time was had by all. Lady Clarissa Kaldor once mentioned that her cook was busy making cakes for the Labour Party bazaar.

No. 3 Adams Road was also built in 1898 by the Reverend Thomas Orpen, a Cambridge cleric who was curate of Chesterton and later of St Giles, and from 1881–6 vicar of All Saints. He was something of a property developer. He built (and lived in) the house called "Bin Brook" – No. 53 Grange Road, between Herschel and Adams Road. He then went on to build Nos. 6 and 8 Cranmer Road on a site leased from Jesus College. He never lived there, however. A tutor at Selwyn College from 1886–1904, a college to which he was a generous benefactor, he was author of a book called *The Rain Children*. He died at sea in April 1925.

Benjamin Benham, a graduate of Corpus Christi College and headmaster at King's College School from 1887–1905, moved into No. 3 in 1907. From 1905–25 he was deputy University Registrar. He lived at No. 3 with his dog and his aviary until he sold the house to Dr and Mrs Windsor Lewis in 1938.

There is a chapter on Benham in R. J. Henderson's *A History of King's College Choir School*, 1981, which recorded that in appearance "he was stocky with a powerful frame and had a moustache and jutting chin, which gave him a frightening aspect. One of his pupils compared his appearance to that of Rudyard Kipling" ... "the terror he inspired amongst good and bad pupils alike and the uncertainty of his moods made many of the pupils unhappy."

"In 1898, it was arranged that Benham should take a year's sabbatical leave, which he spent touring the Antipodes. It may be that the fellows of the College deliberately arranged it when their sons told them of his paroxsysms."

The Windsor-Lewis house was later the home of Lord Adrian, son of the 1st Lord Adrian, OM, Nobel Laureate and sometime Master of Trinity College. Both father and son were masters of Cambridge colleges, the son becoming Master of Pembroke College in 1981, at which time he sold No. 3 Adams Road.

In 1909, complaints were being made about cyclists and horses being ridden on the footpath from Burrell's Walk to Coton. Part of the footpath known as Love Lane was by then merged into Adams Road where it had been converted into a carriageway. But if cyclists were allowed to use it, why not a carriage and pair? A tricycle would completely impede a pedestrian, magistrates were told at the first prosecution of a cyclist for riding on the footpath.

Before Robinson College, now firmly beached on Grange Road, started excavating and building, they prudently rang up Dr Windsor Lewis to ask about the risks of flooding from Bin Brook. He was able to assure them that they would not be troubled by flooding because they were on high enough ground.

The economist William Reddaway and his wife Barbara live at "Redcourt", No. 4 Adams Road. The house with trim yew hedges was built by Dr Francis Shillington Scales, the first radiologist in Cambridge and designed by the architect Arnold Mitchell.

The lease for No. 5 Adams Road was granted to Mrs Norah Matthews in 1905, but by 1908 it was the home of the Rev. James Pounder Whitney, the ecclesiastical historian, and later Count Ellerburne de Sibour who gave his name "Ellerburne" to the house. It was one of the few houses in the area to have a cellar which was frequently flooded. The next owner was Henry Rottenburg whose grandparents came from Danzig where they were dealers in chemicals. Mr Rottenburg and his wife May bought the house in about 1913.

In 1957, their son Tony Rottenburg and his wife Claudia took over the family home and lived there with their children until 1975 when he sold the house to Robinson College and moved to No. 36 Wilberforce Road, his wife's old family home. Before the family moved, they had a house contents sale on the lawn. The sale was a great draw. Staff from King's College School remember nipping over to have a look during their free periods. Tony Rottenburg also owned Newnham Mill.

During the First World War, two German families faced each other across Adams Road. Dr S. Ruhemann of Gonville and Caius built No. 6 in 1912 opposite what is now No. 19 Adams Road, the home of Dr Eugene Gustav Braunholz and his family. Of No. 19, more later. Allegedly, the Ruhemanns did not have a very happy time because anyone with German connections was ostracised in those days, so it is said.

In 1919, Albert Hopkinson, a family doctor from Manchester moved to Cambridge for the job of anatomy lecturer. He bought No. 6 Adams Road and cultivated a beautiful garden, which included baby cyclamen that had been transplanted from Corfu in 1922. They spread everywhere!

His granddaughter, Patience Thomson (née Bragg) and wife of the famous physicist and Nobel Prize winner J. J. Thomson's grandson David, remembers that Albert Hopkinson's garden was also full of lovely roses, but he would never let anyone pick them. When his wife was dying, he asked the nurse who was caring for her, what he could do to show his love for her. The nurse told him to pick a bunch of red roses and give them to her.

After his death in 1949, No. 6 was sold to Mrs Joan Charnock, the daughter of J. J. Thomson – she has lived there since 1950. Joan Charnock met her late husband when visiting Russia in 1936, at the height of Stalin's purges. "My husband had been a manager of some very big cotton mills 30 miles outside Moscow before the Revolution in 1917. He employed 18,000 people and the mills had their own schools and hospital." Mr Charnock was the third generation

J. J. Thomson, Nobel Prize winning physicist

Joan Charnock's brilliant father, was the Nobel Prize winning physicist whose research led to the discovery of the electron. J.J.Thomson worked in the Cavendish Laboratory after graduation from Trinity College in 1879, under the supervision of Lord Rayleigh, one of the greatest scientists of his era, who at the time was the second Cavendish Professor of Physics at the University of Cambridge (following James Clerk Maxwell) and President of the Royal Society. "J.J", as he was known, was appointed Rayleigh's successor as the Cavendish Professor of Physics at the age of 28.

Both Thomson and his supervisor won the Nobel Prize for physics, Lord Rayleigh in 1904 and "J.J." two years later. We owe so much of all that we take for granted in this modern, press of a button high-tec world to such geniuses.

of Charnocks, a Lancastrian family of Norwegian origin, who had managed the Russian mills.

He was in partnership before 1918 when he returned to England with a Russian called Morosov, who was largely responsible for financing the Moscow Arts Theatre. Morosov had a fine collection of French Impressionists, which are now in the Hermitage in Leningrad.

"Inch-Ma-Home", No. 7 Adams Road, was built for Sir James Frazer of Trinity College of *The Golden Bough* fame, but he didn't live in it for long – apparently because Lady Frazer did not like it. The name reflects Frazer's Scottish connections. He handed the house over to Dr Louis Cobbett, also a Fellow of Trinity and a descendant of the early 19th century writer William Cobbett *Rural Rides*, etc.) Dr Cobbett lived in Adams Road until his death in 1947.

A love of wild flowers led Dr Cobbett to cultivate that little triangular piece of land at the end of Burrells Walk. He planted wild flowers and even introduced oxslips there. The triangle at the corner is known as "Cobbett's Corner". It was maintained privately till the 1970s and then was taken over by the Council.

However, the claim that Louis Cobbett was connected with the Cobbett of *Rural Rides* fame has been challenged. Mrs Kathleen Froment, the daughter of George Wright, for many years the gardener to Louis Cobbett said: "He and the family always denied it and his brother Will wrote a book and had it published privately for distribution to their hordes of relatives. Will had done considerable

Alexis Vlasto — Balkan gardener

Dr Alexis Vlasto, the Slavonic scholar whose expertise is the history of the Russian language (in 1970 he published a history of the Balkans, *The Entry of the Slavs into Christendom*) moved soon after the war to No. 7 Adams Road from Bletchley Park. He has lived there with his family since then. He recalls how Dr Cobbett, an eminent pathologist planned the whole garden with "lovely yew hedges and wildflowers".

Dr Vlasto himself is a wonderful gardener who cultivates whole beds of old roses, Greek poppies and irises not for the sake of their rarity but for their beauty. The garden is full of rare plants and bulbs. His daughter Alexandra recalls that the seed he collected from a very little-known Balkan endemic plant was given to the University Botanic Garden. "It was then distributed to gardens throughout the world, and the subsequent study of it produced information of great value to the development of the science of botany."

He is a lover of music too, who as an undergraduate at King's played the oboe in the orchestra of CUMS and there met his future wife Jill, who was herself in the orchestra and reading music at Girton. She had won an organ scholarship to the college in 1934 and in 1948 was appointed Director of Studies in Music at Girton. Shortly afterwards she was appointed librarian to the Rowe Music Library in King's College. In her care it became one of the best libraries of its kind.

The Vlastos' home in Adams Road is a centre for music and musicians. Alexandra says: "It was a happy home in a sunny house full of laughter, hospitality, friendliness and wise counsel. And all the time there was music-making in the big music room overlooking the lovely garden to which they devoted so much love and care." Her mother died in 1968.

Alexis Vlasto, the Slavonic scholar who lives at No. 7 Adams Road and is as keen a gardener as the previous owner Dr Cobbett who planned the original garden, as shown in March 1928.

research into their antecedents, in his book he even made fun of the fact that all cutlery etc. was marked with an heraldic crow, a pun on the alternative of Corby for said bird.

"What is certain is their considerable fortune came from the China tea trade. Louis's father had retired and lived as a country gent as a young man, though great Uncle Matthew spent years in China handling the business from that end. He sent or brought home cartloads of Chinese gear. Importing tea must have been a very profitable line, to maintain the lifestyle they enjoyed."

Dr John Cuthbert Lawson, Senior Tutor of Pembroke College and Senior Proctor, built "Starcroft", No. 8 Adams Road. When he died, Mrs Lawson sold it to a cousin of the politician Austin Chamberlain, the Rev. Appleford. His widow lived there during the Second World War when the road was home to many evacuees, until her death in the 1950s.

A portrait of Alice Roughton painted by the German artist Ziegler

When No. 8 came on the market, it was bought by Cecilia Scurfield, the youngest of seven daughters of Bertram Hopkinson. Cecilia and her husband George bought the house for only £1,000. George Scurfield ran the kitchen shop in Jesus Lane. He and his wife published two cookery classics: *Home Baked, A Little Book of Bread Recipes* (Faber & Faber, 1956) and its follow-up, *Home-made Cakes and Biscuits* (1963). No. 8 is now the home of the Goodys. Sir Jack Goody and his wife were very well-known social anthropologists who did an enormous amount of work on the tribes of Africa.

Next door at No. 9 Adams Road is a rural smallholding with a couple of rambling acres. Just a little reminiscent of *Cold Comfort Farm* is how I would describe a house that has become rather a legend in Cambridge. It is the home of Dr Alice Roughton and is enough of a rabbit-warren to be home to several students, family and friends. Dr Roughton (née Hopkinson and sister of Cecilia Scurfield at No. 8), entertains round a huge refectory table in her kitchen bought at an auction for £12. The "family" eats well. "We were once 28 to lunch on the lawn," recalls her daughter Dr Rosemary Summers. "Twelve others who were staying had gone into town, and we had people camping in tents all over the garden."

Dr Roughton keeps chickens and pigs, and "at the moment we are eating lots of nettles, which are as good as spinach". I am told that she ate squirrels and had a goose that tried to incubate croquet balls.

No. 9 called "Ellerslie" was built by Mrs and Miss Jebb, the mother and sister of Eglantyne Jebb, founder of the Save the Children Fund, but like Lady Frazer, they didn't like the house and moved out after six months. While their house was being built in Adams Road, the Jebbs lived at No. 7.

Eglantyne Jebb said of the house that it was "too frivolous". The Jebbs were certainly not a frivolous family. Mrs Jebb founded the Women's Institute, Eglantyne the Save the Children Fund, another sister, the Women's Land Army and a third sister was one of the founders of the Papworth Community.

Mrs Jebb's brother-in-law was Sir Richard Claverhouse Jebb OM, the Professor of Greek and University Orator who was elected Member of Parliament for Cambridge University in 1891[2]. He lived in the house at the corner of Sidgwick Avenue and Queen's Road. Much to his displeasure, he lost a strip of his garden when Sidgwick Avenue was built in 1893. It would be hard to imagine another household in England, let alone the road, like the Jebbs and their extended family.

The house was bought from the Jebbs by Dr Roughton's grandmother, Mrs Evelyn Hopkinson, widow of John Hopkinson, the distinguished engineer and inventor, and Professor of Engineering at King's College, London, who died in a climbing accident in the Alps with three of their children – a son and two daughters. They are commemorated in a plaque in Free School Lane.

Father of six, John Hopkinson, as well as an engineer was a pioneer of alpine leisure sports – mountaineering and skiing. In addition to the three children who died with him in the accident, his son Bertram, father of Alice Roughton and six other daughters, was killed in a flying accident in 1918, while his other son Cecil died at home from injuries sustained in the First World War. Only one daughter, the future Lady Ewing, was left. John Hopkinson was supposed to have gone to Africa to harness the Victoria Falls in 1898 for Cecil Rhodes but the expedition was cancelled because of the Boer War. The development of Africa might have been different had he got there!

It is said that a ballroom was added to No. 9 as there were so many Hopkinson daughters to be married off that the family had to have constant parties.

In the garden amongst the trees, one towers above the rest. It is a Giant Californian Redwood tree planted by Evelyn Hopkinson – reputedly so that the chauffeur couldn't see what she was doing in the garden.

Dr Alice Roughton was born in Harvey Road, Cambridge and brought up at No. 10 Adams Road, a fine family house built by her father Professor Bertram Hopkinson, who was a patent lawyer, before becoming an engineer. He was Professor of Mechanism and Applied Mechanics at Cambridge University. He researched flames and explosions, and became a pioneer designer of the internal combustion engine. In 1910 he was elected a Fellow of the Royal Society.

During the First World War he was commissioned into the Royal Engineers and opened a research establishment at Orford Ness where he and his team researched weapons, military sights and ammunition. He learnt to fly but tragically died on 26 August 1918 when his Bristol Fighter crashed en route from Martlesham Heath to London. He is buried in the Parish of the Ascension Burial Ground in Cambridge with his wife Mariana, née Siemens, directly opposite the grave of his brother Cecil, which is marked by a sundial and memorial.

Bertram Hopkinson built No. 10 in 1904 in the Queen Anne Revival style exactly one mile from Great St Mary's. That was the rule then: academics had to live within one mile of the city centre. Dr Roughton was one of seven

---

[2] Between 1603 and 1950, Cambridge was one of the universities that elected members of Parliament to represent the university constituency rather than a geographical area.

The hot and cold taps (warm and kalt) in the bathroom at No. 10, which Paul Hirsch and his family brought with them when they fled Nazi Germany.

daughters. Bertram Hopkinson's seventh daughter then went on to have seven children.

When Dr Roughton got married, her wedding presents included, among the obligatory towels and china, a house in Millington Road, built for her by her grandmother, Mrs Hopkinson, who was a great one for spoiling her! Dr Roughton says her father would have preferred to have lived on Madingley Hill. Adams Road was the next best place.

Alice Roughton's husband, Professor Francis John Worsley Roughton whom she married in 1925, was a Fellow of Trinity and a physiologist who worked on the basic problems of respiratory physiology. He was one of eight generations of doctors in the Roughton family – five men and three women.

Another of the eminent families to have lived in Adams Road at No. 10 was the famous musicologist Paul Hirsch who fled Frankfurt-am-Main with his wife Olga and their children in the early 1930s, bringing with them on a train "The Paul Hirsch Music Library", his famous music collection of 18,000 items. Instrumental in helping Paul Hirsch bring his priceless collection to Cambridge and securing it for the nation, was Edward Dent, the distinguished musicologist, who had been Professor of Music at Cambridge University from 1921 to 1941.

The Hirschs also brought their safe, their hot and cold taps, their firebacks, and even the rose trees from the garden. All these possessions were re-established in what became their new home. They also brought with them their gardener, who stayed with them until he died.

Paul Hirsch, the son of Ferdinand Hirsch, owner of the firm of Hirsch & Co. iron founders, had a special library built for his collection of music in the Adams Road house. Later the collection was acquired by the British Museum. On 16 July 1946 the Hirschs held a 70th birthday party for Edward Dent in their garden as a special thank you to the man who had helped them bring the priceless music collection out of Nazi Germany. It was this library in which the collection was first housed, which made the house such an attractive prospect to the late Professor Jack Bennett, the Chaucerian scholar, who subsequently bought it. His son Edward now lives there with his wife and family.

Mr Edward
Bennett, with
children from
the morning
playgroup at
10 Adams Road,
in April 1982.

Take a walk down the track at the top of Adams Road that used to lead to Grange Farm, a fine homestead built in 1827 but demolished some years ago, and you are in the country, almost on the edge of what used to be the ancient West Fields of Cambridge.

The majority of the houses on the north side of Adams Road – where the Hopkinson family used to graze horses – were built in the 1950s. Dr Roughton calls the north side of the road "suburbia", but these are well cared for with lovingly tended gardens.

No. 11, "West Point", built by Alderman Raynes, a Cambridge Borough Councillor in the early 1900s, replaced a house that had been built earlier. Alderman Raynes decided to demolish the first house, but when his new house was built it only reached first floor level before suffering such severe subsidence it also had to be demolished and rebuilt. It was Alderman Raynes who dug in his toes when the Post Office wanted to renumber Adams Road with odd and even numbers on different sides rather than in sequence and the plan was dropped.

Sir Moses Finley built No. 12 Adams Road in 1957. An American professor who was prosecuted by the McCarran Security Committee, he subsequently became a British citizen and Professor of Ancient History at Cambridge University. Later he was elected Master of Darwin College in 1976 and held the post until 1982. No. 12 is the smallest house in the road and was designed with North American features, its front wall overhung with a distinctive copper beech hedge.

For several years, No. 13 Adams Road was the home of Lucjan Lewitter, Professor of Slavonic Studies at the University of Cambridge between 1968 and 1984 and Fellow of Christ's College. Born in Krakow, he is remembered primarily as an historian of Russia in the reign of Peter the Great. He contributed two chapters on Poland to the *New Cambridge Modern History* and had a profound understanding of Russian modern history.

Tony Durham, the managing director of Cambridge Newspapers recently moved with his family into No. 14, a house built by Dr Alexander Munro, a medical anatomist. The Durhams have joined the ranks of the keen gardeners on the north side.

Built in 1957, No. 15 was the home of Kenneth Budden, FRS, theoretical physicist and mathematician and his wife Nicolette for many years.

No. 16 was the first private house to be built in 1956 by the architect David Roberts. It was the home of Professor Robin Matthews who held the two most senior Chairs of Economics in Britain – the Drummond Chair at Oxford and the Chair of Political Economy at Cambridge, where he was also a popular Master of Clare College for many years as well as a great chess player. He sold the house to another economist, Frank Hahn who was Professor of Economics at Cambridge. Professor Hahn's wife Dorothy, also an economist, was Bursar of Newnham College.

Mr Peter Watson, the eye surgeon, and his wife Ann moved to Adams Road from Highgate in North London in 1965. They bought No. 17, a large family house with a big garden from Mrs Goudy, who had lived in the house ever since it was built in 1935. Peter Watson used to see his private patients in a house on Parkside, originally owned by Dr Graham, a general practitioner who visited his patients in a carriage and pair with two footmen who wore peacock feathers in their hats. When the Parkside property was acquired by Emmanuel College, space was made in No. 17 Adams Road for the private practice. The only real problem that patients had, apart from their eyesight, was that the resident cockerel lived in the tree by the gate and would fly down at those to whom he took a dislike.

There is some very special, ancient history attached to No. 17, or at least to its garden. Peter Watson reminds me that the old Roman Road from Roman Hill in Barton to Castle Hill in Cambridge went diagonally across the garden of No. 17. "We had a conservatory that came detached from the wall because of subsidence (which affects most houses in Adams Road), the soil being clay. We had to dig down deeply to lay foundations for the new conservatory, and one day the young man carrying out the work found bones. They looked like human wrist bones. A rapid trip to Tony Palmer the veterinary pathologist at No. 12 excluded animal bones. This meant we had to tell the Coroner. I told him we had found a body 'How old is it?' A skeleton. 'Ring the City Archaeologist,' who said, 'Oh dear, I can't come now, but I will be there in an hour!'

"By the time the archaeologist arrived, the whole pelvis was exposed and, because of the east–west orientation of the body, the absence of artefacts buried with it, together with the presence of a post hole visible in the ground nearby, he was able to conclude that this was a Roman graveyard covered by a thatched roof dating from 300 AD. We gave our skeleton a wake and called him Gordon, after the person who found his remains. Then we filled his middle (which had gone to the museum), with concrete."

There is said to be a Saxon graveyard on the same Roman Road now in the middle of the Trinity College playing field and, nearby on the New Cavendish site, preliminary excavations there uncovered a big Roman villa and the bones of animals.

Both Peter and Ann Watson have Cambridge connections going back many years. He was an undergraduate at Queens' College in the early 1950s. He lodged with a family in Newnham, but didn't share their bathroom. When it came to serious washing he put on his dressing gown, and, along with other Queens' undergraduates living locally, caught the bus into college to take a shower!

Ann Watson (née Macintosh) is the great-granddaughter of Alexander Macintosh, the founder of Macintosh's, the ironmongers who had their whole-sale and retail business at No. 23 Market Street. Mrs Watson is a volunteer at the Cambridge Folk Museum, sorting out all the old photographs, listing records on card indexes and helping to raise money for the Museum at fund raising events.

From 1904 for many years, Dr Eugene Braunholz, a Fellow of King's College mentioned earlier, lived at No. 19. He was a university reader in Romance lan-guages, who clearly gave the house the name of "Goslar" to remind him of a favourite haunt in the Harz Mountains, or perhaps because of the poet Heinrich Heine who wrote his famous poem *Die Harzreise* whilst staying at Goslar. The house is now the home of Mr Terence English and his family.

Mr Terence English, the cardiac surgeon and heart transplant pioneer, who performed the first successful heart transplant in the UK in 1979, bought the house in 1974 from another medic, Dr Douglas Montague Gairdner, consult-ant paediatrician at Addenbrooke's Hospital. Research scientist, academic, author, and for fifteen years editor of *Archives of Disease in Childhood*, Dr Gairdner spent much of his childhood in Egypt where his father was a missionary. Neighbours remember how Dr Gairdner and his wife Nancy held madrigal parties at their home and Douglas played the tuba in the Cambridge Philharmonic Society.

No. 18 stands in substantial grounds. It is a large house, built in 1938, by pro-fessor Basil Willey and is hidden away at the end of a track alongside the approach to a "secret garden" of a spot called the Adams Road Sanctuary – a pond behind the ivy and couch grass and hidden away behind trees. It is looked after by the Sanctuary Club.

Local families are among the members of this Club, which was founded soon after the place became a sanctuary, at a time when vandalism was proving a problem. It is a tranquil oasis to which woodpeckers, grebes, spotted flycatchers, kingfishers and lesser whitethroats are all drawn.

Inquiries were first made about renting the old skating rink as a bird sanctu-ary by the Cambridge Ornithological Club in 1928. In 1935, St John's let the

The street party held in Adams Road on Tuesday 7 June 1977 to celebrate the Queen's Silver Jubilee.

ground to Mr Ogilvie, whose son, while an ailing undergraduate, had enjoyed sitting watching the birds in the wild spot. There was provision for subletting to the Sanctuary Club, or local bird society as it then was. The club which now has 100 members has put seats there and one member, the orthopaedic surgeon Bill Butler, built a hide.

The pond was first established as a skating rink in 1894, when a lease was granted to the Rev. Austen Leigh and others. The site was developed by the University Skating Club into a wooded area surrounding an ornamental pond. It had once been a plot of land crossed by a rivulet. Dr Nedderman of the Sanctuary Club tells me that there was once a racing-cycle track through this area and the track extended into the garden of No. 1 Clarkson Close.

Writing to the *Cambridge Evening News* in 1959, Mr A. P. Rottenberg wrote: "Adams Road has changed little in the last 40 years apart for three major upheavals: the decline of domestic staff, which is part of a national pattern, the introduction of a bus route which was bitterly resented by residents who have been prominent bicyclists, and the new houses erected since the war. They have made the biggest impact. All the older houses were of a substantial character, whereas some of the new ones are out of place in the neighbourhood. It has always been a family road with many childish pleasures including ice skating."

But walk up to the end of the road heading towards the Coton footpath and all you can hear are Dr Roughton's chickens and the wind in the tall Wellingtonia trees which mark the boundary at the end of No. 10. And remember – you are only one mile from the city centre!

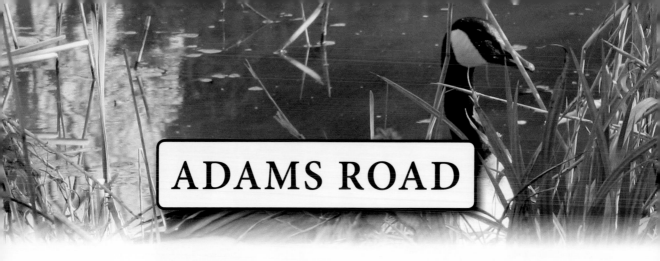

ADAMS ROAD

Revisited

Up to a point, it is still "a choice rural enclave", but no longer home exclusively to the academics who once filled those rambling subsidence-prone houses on the south side with their libraries, servants and children. Nowadays, the road is shared between private residents, particularly on the north side where there are several families with young children, and Robinson College, which dominates the lower part of the road on the south side. The College has bought up all the older houses on that side – Nos. 2, 4, 5 and 6 Adams Road leading up to the junction with Sylvester Road. That is with the exception of one house No. 3, the home since 1982 of Sean Jackson and his family. Mr Jackson bought the house from the late Lord Adrian.

Street parties for special events are still held in the road. The Queen's Golden Jubilee was celebrated on Monday 3 June 2002 with a party for the residents of Adams Road and Wilberforce Road and the road was closed from 10 a.m. to 4 p.m.

Spring as ever is particularly magical when, for a brief period of about three weeks, the trees are in blossom. A walk or cycle ride to Coton along the Coton Footpath which leads west from Adams Road at the junction with Wilberforce Road adds to the rural feel of the area, as do all the college playing fields in this special part of west Cambridge. However, despite in the past feeling as if it was a road on the edge of the countryside, some residents think it more like a commuter car park nowadays!

Adams Road is the main route from the city centre colleges to the West Cambridge site, and prospectively to the North West Cambridge site which is currently being developed and on which some 2,000 accommodation units will be built in the coming years. The volume of traffic has increased massively.

Driving down Adams Road you wouldn't, however, detect the social change in character that has taken place over the last 30 years or so, not least because the original houses on the south side are all still standing as monuments to the Victorian and Edwardian era, when large meant large! They haven't been knocked down and had blocks of flats built on the land, although a new large mansion has been built on the site of the demolished No. 15 Adams Road.

Robinson College has also built student accommodation in the grounds of "Sellinger", the 1930s house with a mansard roof at No. 3 Sylvester Road, which was the home of Charles Darwin's granddaughter, Lady Barlow. The college's original plans for two new linked blocks of housing for research students in the garden, strongly contested by the West Cambridge Preservation Society, were thrown out by the City Council planning department in 2005, but a modified version, dubbed the "Travel Lodge" by a college porter, got approval and was built.

Morcom Lunt and his wife Sandra moved into No. 7A Adams Road in 1986. He recalls: "I still vividly remember the view of Cambridge surrounded by countryside, as we came over the A603 hill east of Wimpole. Visibility was excellent with the radio telescope dishes in the middle distance and the University Library standing proud, and the Addenbrooke's chimney marking the southern boundary of the city."

Their new home, No. 7A, is a substantial bungalow built in 1983 when the owner of No. 7, Professor Alexis Vlasto, sold the land (including that on which No. 9 Sylvester Road was built) in order to buy the freehold of the remaining property from St John's College. No. 7A sits on what was the Vlasto's rose garden.

Morcom Lunt came to Cambridge to join Cambridge Electronic Industries (a spin-off of some thirty small companies from Phillips) as Director of Manufacturing. "For the first 23 years of our time in No. 7A we had at least one dog, two for almost fifteen years. Consequently we walked around the neighbourhood twice a day. A banal but striking example of the changes over the last quarter century, is the extent to which the hedges have been allowed to grow over the pavements", illustrative of the creeping pressures on the area.

Sellinger, No. 3 Sylvester Road, once the home of Charles Darwin's granddaughter, Lady Barlow.

A cricket match in progress on Trinity Old Field.

"The traffic levels, the on-street parking, the gradual degradation of the very qualities that the Conservation Area was supposed to preserve and the expansion of the University and its peripheral activities in the area are the key changes.

"In 1986, apart from a few vehicles travelling from Madingley Road onto Grange Road, the only traffic was residential, plus a small number of cyclists and pedestrians going between the Cavendish Laboratory and the city centre. Since then, the University West Cambridge site, between the Coton footpath, Madingley Road, and the M11, has been massively developed with faculty buildings, business units, the University Sports Centre and large blocks of flats for post graduate and post-doctoral people, many with families."

He explains that the North West Cambridge University developments along with Darwin Green and the completion of the West Cambridge site will inevitably further increase university-related traffic along Adams Road. This need not have too serious an impact on the amenities of those living in the area if the commuter and shopper parking can be reduced considerably.

"Past experience suggests that this will not happen unless there are some serious accidents, which are quite likely given the congestion and aggressive driving by some young and 'Chelsea Tractor' drivers.

"Visually, the planning guidance from successive governments and the pressures on the city's Planning Officers means that almost inevitably, more and more of the full frontage of properties in the area will be filled with buildings, regardless of the Conservation Area's defined characteristics.

"My concerns relate to the nature of what we are bequeathing to our grand-children's generation. One minor change here, and another one there, and then another one, when done often enough, results in a different place altogether. Cambridge is well down that road!"

Morcom is chairman of the Federation of Cambridge Residents' Associations, but he says it takes a huge effort to get local people involved in planning issues and the implications of growth and development in the city. "Too many residents in Cambridge will only get excited and involved if someone starts digging a hole at the entrance to their house!"

At No. 9, I am back round that £12 kitchen table thirty years later, this time talking to Dr Alice Roughton's daughter, Dr Rosemary Summers. Dr Roughton died in 1995. Dr Summers is keeping up her mother's tradition of welcoming paying guests into her home. "My mother believed in quantity, I believe in qual-ity. Most of the people living here are sort of tenants and they nearly all do a certain amount of quid pro quo. We have all sorts living here including one chap, a postgraduate student who has a job, and three Ph.D students, and my cousin who also has a job while she does a part-time fashion design degree." She calls them "BYTs" (Bright Young Things).

The lodgers all have their own rooms, unlike in the past. "My mother never allowed people to have their own rooms. You didn't know where you were going to sleep! She was very keen on control."

Some of the lodgers occasionally sleep out in the yurt in the huge, rather wild garden where Dr Roughton used to keep three cows, four goats, two pigs, ducks, about 100 hens, as well as her bees. During the Second World War, as well as Frances Ward, the Land Girl, who helped her, she employed conscientious objec-tors to work with the animals. Dr Roughton found anyone who had no money and then would employ them to use their skills on whatever needed doing.

Beyond the garden is what used to be the estate of the Rothschild family in Herschel Road. It is now part of Clare Hall. Dr Summers recalls how her family used to say: "We don't have fairies at the bottom of the garden, we have Rothschilds." I suggest that life at No. 9 sounds like a community. "My mother used to get very angry if anyone said that," replies Dr Summers. "She would say it is *not* a community – it is my house."

One of the traditions of life at No. 9 which continues to this day is the ritual of eating together round the refectory table in the kitchen (there is an identical table in the house's Oak Room also bought for £12. "I like companionship, I like people eating together; after all, the word 'companionship' means sharing bread together."

"My philosophy of life is that I have done whatever I have been told to do by my mother and by others". Her mother clearly told other people what to do too, and was never deterred by what today might be called political correctness; she was a pioneer and she always brushed party politics aside. She is remembered as a very loving person.

Dr Summers recalls the day the Second World War ended when her mother invited to tea all the German prisoners of war incarcerated just beyond what was the Plant Breeding Institute in Trumpington. This became a regular Sunday afternoon event. Dr Summers recalls that, "Every Sunday about 20 came to tea, and we sat in the Oak Room".

Some years later, Dr Roughton headed off to lecture to British troops in Occupied Germany, and told them that the German people were lovely. Students from Hamburg, a city devastated by Allied bombing in the Second World War, were invited to come and stay in Cambridge, and were probably told where to sleep at No. 9.

After the Hungarian uprising in 1956 when huge numbers of refugees – mostly young men – fled the country, academics in Cambridge convened a meeting at King's College to see what they could do to help them. Dr Summers tells the story of how, as no one at this meeting could speak Hungarian, or had a Hungarian dictionary, the secretary was instructed to acquire a dictionary from one of the bookshops. "She reported back that she had rung round every bookshop in Cambridge, only to find that Dr Roughton had bought up every Hungarian dictionary in the city."

Teresa Deutsch in her obituary of Dr Roughton focused on the people who filled the Adams Road house. "It was almost possible to map the world's oppression through the refugees at her door. No one was turned away; Arabs lived alongside Jews, anti-Communists from the former Soviet Union beside Latin American revolutionary militants. It was Roughton's earnest intention to see, even to prove, that of course peace is possible within humanity; that there were no political issues that couldn't be thrashed out around the fireside during 'open house' every Sunday evening."

Another of Dr Roughton's war time protégés was the German dancer Kurt Jooss, who before the war had been installed with his famous school and company, the Ballet Jooss, at Dartington Hall in Devon.

With the coming of war, Jooss's company was stranded while touring South America. Jooss, who had stayed in England, was interned on the Isle of Man. After his release he found Roughton, and with her help engineered the return of his stranded dancers by merchant ships and men-of-war. By 1943, with Dr Roughton's influence, he was able to reform his newly assembled company in Cambridge, augmented by one or two English dancers. A remarkable feat.

Dr Roughton's driving power established Jooss as a cultural entity in wartime Britain. Jooss and his family lived in her house. He shared closely her humanitarian beliefs.

One of the "BYTs" who lived at No. 9 in those days, was the Hungarian Gabor Cossa. He was part of the Jooss Company, but when it dispersed, he remained in Cambridge and started up his landmark antique shop in Trumpington Street.

I ask Dr Summers how she would describe the way of life at No. 9. What is it doing – is it serving a purpose? She gives a philosophical answer: "Sometimes in life you get to a crossroads, and don't know whether to go straight on, or turn right or left. You pause before deciding. This house is where you have a little time out before making your decision. We help people who are, or have been victimised, either by themselves or by others, and who are at a crossroads in their lives."

Rosemary Summers' cousin is Margaret Heath, elder daughter of the Nobel laureate Sir Lawrence Bragg the Australian-born British physicist and X-ray crystallographer who discovered in 1912 Bragg's law of X-ray diffraction, which is key for the determination of crystal structure. He was joint winner with his father Sir William Bragg of the Nobel Prize for Physics in 1915. He was knighted in 1941. His daughter explains that he had his "eureka" moment about crystal structure while walking along the Backs!

Rosemary Summers and Margaret Heath are second cousins once removed on their mothers' side. Margaret Heath explains that: "John, killed in the Alps, was the very much older brother of my mother's father, Albert Hopkinson, so Alice, later Roughton, was a generation down from my mother and a first cousin once removed."

Both mothers were born Alice Hopkinson – perhaps it was a family tradition, in that many of the first-born girls were given this name! They were descendants of a line of brilliant engineers and doctors. Their families are part of that academic aristocracy of Cambridge, which flourished long before, and after both world wars. West Cambridge was home to so many of them. Think of the Darwin and the Keynes families too.

Margaret Heath, widow of the diplomat Sir Mark Heath now lives in Bath, but she was visiting her son Nicholas Heath and daughter-in-law Penny who is Chair of the North Newnham Residents Association, at their home in Wilberforce Road looking out across the driveway over the Emmanuel College playing fields. Some of their neighbours, however, have chosen to block out the view at ground level with gates fitted with intercoms and in some cases cameras.

The Heaths's home is a striking looking house designed in 1938 by Dora Cozens in the Bauhaus style of the architect Walter Gropius who was in Cambridge at the time. I was invited to meet Margaret Heath there on one of those warm spring mornings with the blossom out and the fritillaries growing in the long grass at the end of the garden. A tributary of the Bin Brook flows through it.

Her memories of her grandfather Albert Hopkinson at No. 6 Adams Road are rather vivid. "He had bran tubs full of human bones. He used to get his students to dig in to the tubs and pull out a handful!"

"We used to have grandfather to family lunch. Being an anatomist, he did the carving but only ate very small portions. After lunch, we played a game called 'Who Knows?' which involved reading out literary quotations, from the likes of Pope and Shakespeare. Other players had to identify the quotes." Sounds rather a high brow Cambridge parlour game!

Nick Heath chips in: "Mum grew up in No. 3 West Road, Cambridge, a period house which was pulled down to build Caius College's Harvey Court". His mother describes a house built in 1820 that had stabling for four, together with a coach house, a harness room, a hayloft, a dung pit and a cobbled yard and two acres of garden with wonderfully fertile soil (it had once been a nursery garden). The maids lived in the attic rooms, a long way from the bathrooms. The Braggs who lived there from 1938 until 1952 when Caius wanted it back, had a cook called Nellie, two maids, a faithful nanny Hilda and a gardener. The houses in West Road at that time were all private, although during the Second World War, Nos. 5 and 7 were used by the Army. Now West Road consists of University departments, college houses and King's College Choir School.

Margaret Heath continues: "When I was growing up in Cambridge there were very few cars. It was bliss and there were no tourists. I used to canter my pony along the green verges of the Backs and used the mounting block outside King's, whilst stopping to buy an ice cream cornet for one penny from the Walls ice cream van."

Whereas academics of that era settled in the large houses with servants' quarters in the enclaves in and around Grange Road, Margaret Heath comments on the social changes in Cambridge: "Nowadays you get retired bishops and heads of colleges living in what used to be 'bedders' houses in the area round the Kite." And I would add that some of those Victorian and Edwardian mansions in west Cambridge are now home to professionals and entrepreneurs as well as college postgraduates.

During the Second World War, several academics sent their children as evacuees to the United States or Canada for safekeeping, but Margaret's parents decided to keep the children with them in Cambridge, their thinking being: "We'll all be bombed together!" They followed the example of Will Spens, Master of Corpus, nicknamed "The Will of God", who thought it right to show solidarity with other parents in Cambridge for whom the trans-Atlantic evacuation route for their children was not an option.

Margaret's parents had plans for her to follow in her mother's footsteps and become an undergraduate at Newnham College. She had other ideas, and told her parents she was going to Oxford instead. "I did not want to go to Newnham and be subjected to my mother's spy network. Would you go to a college where your mother had had 13 proposals in her first term? No, I went to Oxford, married a diplomat and lived happily ever after". Her husband's last posting was to Rome, where it is said in diplomatic circles "if you live in Rome, your beds are always warm".

Her sister Patience was "Daddy's girl". She got an exhibition to Newnham and later married J. J. Thomson's grandson, David – "Daddy's best friend's son". Margaret's son Nicholas, an estate agent, became the black sheep of the family, when he too chose to go to Oxford!

Margaret's older brother Stephen Bragg is another brilliant engineer who was chief scientist at Rolls Royce, and who now lives in retirement in Brookside, Cambridge with his wife Maureen, a former City magistrate. "Proceedings of the Royal Society" fill the shelves in the downstairs cloakroom. This is a comfortable academic home.

Stephen remembers going to stay with his grandparents before the war at No. 6 Adams Road. "It was virtually the edge of Cambridge, and Wilberforce Road was called the Drift." When he visited great aunt Evelyn Hopkinson at No. 9, he was given a Beatrix Potter book "to keep me quiet".

Lawrence Bragg, youngest Nobel laureate

William Lawrence Bragg, was born in North Adelaide in 1890. The family returned to England in 1909, when his father W.H.Bragg realised that that is where the action was. He became Cavendish Professor of Physics at Leeds University. In 1909, his son Lawrence entered Trinity College, Cambridge to study physics.

Margaret Heath tells of her father's wartime service: "In 1915, he was out in France working on sound ranging methods for locating enemy guns when the padre came up on his bike to tell him that his only brother had died on the hospital ship from terrible injuries sustained at Gallipoli. Some time later when the padre again appeared on his bike, my father thought: 'I have only got one brother, what can this be about?' The padre had come to tell him that he had won the Nobel prize for his work on X-ray crystallography. He was only 25, the youngest Nobel laureate ever, and the first Australian one".

She remembers her father as not being at ease with people. "Rather than going in to dine in Trinity where he was a Fellow, to help with the wartime rations, he would prefer to stay at home and have macaroni cheese. But he and my mother used to have students to tea at No. 3 West Road and if they stayed too long, my father would show them the garden, then say: 'let me see – did you have a coat indoors?'" When Caius College claimed No. 3 West Road back,

the Braggs moved out to No. 10 Madingley Road.

Sir Lawrence Bragg was the director of the Cavendish Laboratory in Cambridge, when the discovery of the structure of DNA was reported by James D. Watson and Francis Crick in February 1953. He later went to the Royal Institution as director and lived in a flat in Albemarle Street.

He recalls that his father, Lawrence, was Professor of Physics at Manchester University from 1920 until 1937 when he moved to the National Physical Laboratory at Teddington for a year. "When Lord Rutherford, the Cavendish Professor of Physics died, my father was his obvious successor and in 1938 the family moved to Cambridge and he took up the post."

Stephen remembers a very happy relationship with his father. "I was lucky in a sense that professors had lots of free time in the days before the war and he joined me in my hobbies and also created hobbies for me. He made me a model railway and together we made boats and collected butterflies. When war broke out he was very busy and on lots of committees, and so didn't have that spare time any more.

"Before the war though, life here gave people an enormous amount of freedom. Academics who were appointed to teaching posts had a fixed post, a job for life, and it was assumed that it would not be full time. It was a comfortable base from which to follow your own research. Nowadays research is more expensive, whereas before the war experimental work done at the Cavendish was very cheap.

"In those early days everything went at a slower pace. Take trains for a start. The first train to London in 1938 was at 6.30 in the morning and took two hours. Now everything, including the trains, has speeded up, the ethos of the city has changed and Cambridge is in danger of being swamped."

Stephen Bragg followed his father to Trinity College, where he read engineering between 1942–4. He was directed by C. P. Snow who was in charge of scientific manpower. "The careers counselling was very rudimentary then. C. P. Snow just said to me, 'I think you had better go and work for Rolls Royce.'"

Another member of the Bragg family who has vivid memories of growing up in west Cambridge and visits to the bird sanctuary in Adams Road is Stephen and Margaret's younger sister, Patience. Patience Thomson, who now lives in Wallingford with her husband David, remembers visits to Grandfather Hopkinson in Adams Road and all those intellectual parlour games accompanied by pink and white iced buns and croquet matches.

Patience recalls the social life of the time. "There was a huge circle of friendship and intermarriage among the academic intellectual families in west Cambridge living in the large family houses in the area. They were all so well read! For example, my father re-read the *Odyssey* in Greek every 10 years, while my father-in-law read the *Iliad* in Latin. A near neighbour was G. M. Trevelyan, the Regius Professor of Modern History and later Master of Trinity College, who lived at No. 23 West Road. Now the property of Selwyn College, there is a plaque on the wall commemorating G.M.'s time there.

Two anecdotes about "G.M." are recalled by Patience. "He used to take Nicholas Barker, son of the art historian Sir Ernest Barker who lived in Cranmer Road, for walks. 'Do you think about death a lot?' he asked the 12-year-old boy. 'No, I don't, sir', the boy replied. 'Well I think about it all the time,' replied G.M. G.M.'s passion for the poetry of Tennyson was legendary. He used to declaim in a squawking voice, 'Maud, Maud, Maud'".

Patience's husband was "the boy next door"! When G.M. went to be Master of Trinity, succeeding J. J. Thomson, Thomson's widow moved into Trevelyan's old house. David Thomson, J. J.'s grandson, aged 11, then lived there with his grandmother. "He used to come to tea with us Braggs and have chocolate cake."

Of her cousin Rosemary Roughton, Patience recalls: "How we envied Rosemary who had a beautiful horse, a half Arab pony, which she rode across Cambridge to the County High School. She was allowed to keep it on an adjacent farm. That was really cool in those days."

With a father like Lawrence Bragg, Patience had a pretty cool childhood by the sound of it. Writing a tribute to her father in the Bragg Centenary issue of "Foundations of Crystallography", she wrote:

"My father told us many tales of his childhood and teenage years in Australia. He had obviously loved the wide open spaces, riding on the beach, picnicking in the hills, the family excursions. Dad enjoyed cooking on an open fire, building a log cabin or carving a boomerang that really worked. He had inherited a measure of the pioneering spirit from his grandfather, Sir Charles Todd, with whom he spent a lot of time. Dad was endlessly creative with a very visual imagination."

Christopher and Friederike Jeans have lived at No. 10 Adams Road for about 30 years. This is the house that has had a long line of distinguished owners, as listed in the original article. The Jeans are the latest.

When they bought the house from Edward Bennett in 1982, they found all sorts of relics or features dating back from the time when the Hirsch family arrived from Germany in the early 1930s bringing with them all their possessions and artefacts, including their taps. The taps with "warm" and "kalt" on them are still in use in what was the butler's pantry, and in the bathrooms upstairs. And there is still the gadget on the floor in the dining room which Mrs Hirsch used to press to summon the butler. A bell box in the kitchen, dating back to those days of servants, lists the music room, four bedrooms, three bathrooms and the sewing room.

On the door of what was the tradesman's entrance there is still the original notice: "Please wipe boots and shoes". Mrs Hirsch was obviously a German housewife par excellence. Neighbours feared that Friederike Jeans, who is also German was going to be the same, but, she says with a smile, they were quickly relieved to find that she was not in the same mould! Friederike was a professional mezzo soprano who now sings in choirs.

As I wrote in the original article, the Hirschs brought the rose bushes from their garden in Germany and planted them in their Adams Road garden. Mrs Jeans has kept one of them "in memory of Mr and Mrs Hirsch".

Although the character of the road has changed, Friederike Jeans still feels it is a very good neighbourhood. "If I need an egg or a lemon, I feel I can call on most people for them. That's easy, but people don't come to me!" Her neighbour Dr Rosemary Summers challenges this. "I have gone to her for herbs", she said. "And neighbours have lent her a mosquito net too."

Dr Christopher Jeans, who founded the West Cambridge Preservation Society together with Sean Jackson, is a research earth scientist specialising in the geology, petrology and geochemistry of sedimentary rocks and soils with extensive experience in their application to the needs of industry and society. He is a veteran campaigner against intrusive developments, having done battle in particular with the university over lighting at the University Sports Centre West Cambridge site up at the top of Wilberforce Road behind Adams Road, to name one campaign! "The bigger the university gets, the less flexible it becomes," is how Dr Jeans sees it.

Claudia Rottenburg, who now lives at No. 36 Wilberforce Road, a house built by her father, the economist C. W. Guillebaud of St John's College in 1934, for less than £2,000, lived in the house as a child until she married Tony Rottenburg. She had met him at the Roughtons, and moved with him to Surrey in 1950. As mentioned in the earlier article, she and her husband Tony Rottenburg, a chemical engineer and a manufacturer of sports equipment, moved into his parents' home, No. 5 Adams Road, in 1957.

"It was a house with large baronial rooms on three floors, a cellar which flooded after the extension to the University Library was built – 'our wine bottle labels floated away' – and it had 52 doors which didn't shut properly because the house was built on clay soil and suffered from subsidence.

"My mother-in-law, Mrs Henry (Harry) Rottenburg had five servants: a cook, nanny, parlour maid, nursemaid, gardener and a cleaner for the rough work." Claudia Rottenburg brought her own three children up there. Her children played with all the other children in the area, the focal point being Dr Roughton's house and garden. "It was a lovely road in those days. You never locked the back door! A fairy ring of children played out in the road and they would scatter whenever the bus came down Wilberforce Road and then turned into Adams Road. The driver would hoot as he turned the corner."

In 1975, she persuaded her husband to sell the house, hence the sale of household goods on the lawn, and they moved, in her case, back to No. 36 Wilberforce Road bringing with them among the artefacts not sold, her mother-in-law's New World gas cooker, made in 1931. Now converted to natural gas and still going strong, it took six strong men to carry it to the factory for the conversion work. Mrs Rottenburg remembers how she once cooked a 30lb turkey in it, a gift from Dr Roughton, although she did have to go and help with the plucking in the kitchen at No. 9, which was deep in feathers! No. 36 adjoins the Emmanuel College playing fields and has wonderful views across to the cricket pavilion.

Tony Palmer, the veterinary neurologist and his wife Shirley live at No. 12 Adams Road. They bought the house from the Fellows of Darwin College to whom it had been bequeathed by Sir Moses Finley. "Apart from buying No. 12 in 1987, my interest in the road started in 1949 when as a student I lived with the Willeys at No. 18 for three years. These were happy days. Later, working at the Veterinary School I cycled up and down the road most of my working life!" He finds Adams Road very busy. "Now that there is a barrier in Wilberforce Road, Adams Road is no longer a shortcut to Madingley Road, thus reducing the rush of homeward traffic in the evening. However, it has also become a parking lot for people working in the city. Cars parked on both sides of the road result in a narrow highway for passing traffic. This in turn slows the pace of the cars, but is also dangerous for cyclists, many of whom are students and graduates taking this route to the science laboratories on the University's West Cambridge site."

Although now retired, Peter Watson, who developed the operation commonly used to treat open angle glaucoma and whose specialism is diseases of the sclera (the white of the eye), is as busy as ever working at the causes of this potentially blinding disease together with several global projects and, as a hobby, trying to find out why such famous people as Galileo Galilei and Milton went blind.

How does he feel about the changes in west Cambridge in recent years? "I don't mind West Cambridge becoming a University campus but what they must not be tempted to do is to lose the open space which gives the area its character, or over-develop it with tasteless, poorly designed structures."

Jonathan and Nicole Scott, bought their home, No. 19 from Terence English ten years ago. For the previous ten years, while Sir Terence was Master of St Catharine's College, it had been let out. "We are extraordinarily privileged to be living in this middle class ghetto", says Mr Scott, a solicitor working in London, as we sit round a table on a warm summer evening in their secluded garden drinking tea, while one of their sons heats the coals for a barbecue.

Mr Scott is a graduate of St Catharine's College, but unlike his neighbour, Peter Watson, as he had rooms in college for his three years there, he didn't have to don a dressing gown and catch a bus to get into college for ablutions! His wife, Nicole, is a graduate of Homerton College.

You can hear the chickens next door, and actors rehearsing in the Trinity College Old Field Sports Ground for the Shakespeare Festival held in college gardens nearby. When Robinson College have their May Ball, fireworks light up the sky. Foxes roam round the garden with its backdrop of magnificent trees.

Inside the house, Mr and Mrs Scott show me the architect's watercolour drawings for the house built in 1904. There is the original servant summoning bell system in place, and it still works (minus the servants!) and an original sturdy wooden cistern fitted to an original downstairs lavatory. In those days things were made to last, much like Claudia Rottenburg's gas cooker.

The Adams Road Sanctuary – a hidden nature reserve.

Mr Scott is not minded to man the barricades when it comes to change and development in west Cambridge. "Cambridge is international. What makes it so special is the university. If you want it to continue to be a world class university, not a National Trust relic, you have to accept there will be changes and evolution." He is sympathetic to the view that the colleges need money. "The supervision system comes at a price." He reminds me that the wealthy colleges such as Trinity and St John's subsidise the poorer ones.

As for the Sanctuary Club in Adams Road, it is still going strong. Records go back 90 years. Membership is now around 150 and the annual membership fee has risen to £10, which still seems excellent value. Among the club's members is an employee at the Patent Office in Munich who enjoys his visits to Cambridge and the Sanctuary. For the club's members, all nature lovers who have access to the lake hidden among prolific vegetation, the mass of trees and the hide for bird watching, this is a jewel of a place. Surprising vagrants have included recently a goosander and little egret. And the cuckoo is back this year! At the moment still a rural retreat then in Adams Road!

But what of the future for Adams Road and the surrounding area? St John's College has plans to develop what is left of the old, derelict Grange Farm site and orchard, a popular fruit tree scrumping spot at the end of Wilberforce Road, down the track alongside the University Sports Centre. The college has plans to build 25 houses there, and then behind the Sports Centre itself there is another plan to build 400 houses – all at an early planning stage at the time of writing.

The University and colleges have repeatedly sought to have land to the south and west of the Athletics Centre and Playing fields on Wilberforce Road (Emmanuel College and the Cambridge Tennis Club site) reclassified as being available for housing. The 2014 Local Plan Review Inspector will decide on their most recent application in autumn 2014.

Congestion! A breakdown van and commuter parking in Adams Road.

CRANMER ROAD

7–21 July 1983

Cranmer Road, off Grange Road, deep in the heart of university territory, used to be called the professorial road or less reverentially, "Dons' Alley". The amount of learning concentrated in it was astonishing.

"When I came to the road in 1938, Cranmer Road was a very distinguished road – every house housed a professor." This is the observation of one of the road's distinguished residents, Lady Lauterpacht, widow of Professor Hersch Lauterpacht, who became Whewell Professor of International Law at the age of 40 – the youngest professor in Cambridge at that time.

The Lauterpachts bought their house, No. 6 from Professor Arnold (later Lord McNair). Lord McNair, whose daughter Mrs Sheila Barwell lives at No. 13 Cranmer Road, also passed on his Chair to Hersch Lauterpacht. He too was a distinguished Professor of International Law and Hersch Lauterpacht was his pupil.

No. 11 Cranmer Road has connections with Sherborne School. The Rev. Percival Gardner-Smith, the Emeritus Dean of Jesus College who, at the time of writing is 95, bought the house in 1960 from the Rev. John Boys-Smith, a Fellow of St John's College. The previous owner, Mrs Shirley Blanch, had links with Sherborne too. Her husband was a housemaster there.

The academics of Cranmer Road appear in several cases to have played "pass the parcel" with either their chairs or their houses. Professor F. Debenham OBE handed over No. 23 and the Chair of Geography to Professor Alfred Steers.

The significance of the name Cranmer Road is that the land on both sides belongs to Jesus College, of which Archbishop Cranmer was once a fellow. The road was developed by Jesus College from 1891 onwards.

In 1896, the Reverend Thomas Orpen (see Adams Road chapter) leased a site in Cranmer Road from Jesus College on which he built Nos. 6 and 8, two semi-detached houses.

The historian, Sir Ernest Barker, who moved into No. 17 Cranmer Road with his family in 1927 wrote about the road in *Age and Youth* – his autobiography. When the Barkers moved in, the road was marked "No Thoroughfare," and it

Gathering by the letterbox … Mrs Elizabeth Gardner-Smith, Glynn and Hugh Barwell, four-month-old Charles Hamilton with Mr John Fairbanks, Mrs Jinny Fairbanks, Mrs Philippa Hamilton, and in the front, the Rev. Percival Gardner-Smith and Leigh Barwell.

came to an end, after 400 yards, in fields that stretched away to the west for mile upon mile upon mile."

Most of the houses, he believed, were designed and built – or at any rate most of them were – at the end of the nineteenth century by a mathematician who was also the bursar of a college. "They still show traces of his genius and the mathematical bent of his mind. They are, as a Greek poet says: 'foursquare and wrought without blame': in other words, they are quadrangular, and well and solidly built." Sir Ernest found that the houses had one notable merit: "The merit is that almost every room has windows, or some form of light, on two sides."

"The defect was that the mathematical designer, possibly being a man who needed only a small stock of books, was content with a small space for a study and conceived other men in his likeness. This is a little hard on a diffuse and scattered humanist, who accumulates books by the thousand, and is compelled to clutter up rooms and passages, even to the very top landing, with wandering shelves and cases." (Sounds like our house!)

Mrs Elisabeth Gardner-Smith remembers being told by the late Miss Reid who lived in Grange Road in a house built by her father at the top of West Road, that she had watched the houses being built in Cranmer Road. "Miss Reid's father was a fellow of Caius who lost his fellowship because he married in the days before fellows were allowed to marry. When this permission was given in 1882 he was given his fellowship back. Dr James Smith Reid used to go to Hitchin to coach the girls who were the first students at Girton College in the days before the college was welcomed into the city. It used to be said that fast 'mails' didn't stop at Hitchin," said Mrs Gardner-Smith.

Miss Reid, the source of this very early account of Cranmer Road died in her 99th year in 1976. Her father built a house at 23 West Road, later the home of the late Professor G. M. Trevelyan, Professor of Modern History and former Master of Trinity College.

When the Barkers came into Cranmer Road, they found a little society which was very different from the society of 25 years later. Sir Ernest writes: "I think it was an older society – certainly there were far fewer children. I do not remember the average age: I should say that it was over 60, and perhaps even verged on 70.

"At one end of the road were two maiden ladies, the daughters (by his second marriage) of the great German scholar Pertz, the editor of the *Monumenta Germaniae Historica*. It carried you back in time to reflect that the father of these two ladies had been the friend of the Ritter von Stein (a contemporary and antagonist of Napoleon), and that under his auspices and with his encouragement he had published the first volume of the *Monumenta* as long ago as 1826."

The Misses Pertz had, he wrote: "a fine instinctive culture: they combined it with grace and courtesy; they remembered that their father, born in Hanover in the allegiance of George III, had acknowledged the sovereignty of the same man whose sovereignty my own forbears had also acknowledged."

Among the scholars who lived in Cranmer Road in the early days were Professor Arthur Bernard Cook, one-time Professor of Classical Archaeology, who moved into No. 19 Cranmer Road in 1899. He was the author of *Zeus*.

Dr A. C. Haddon, the famous anthropologist and fellow of Christ's College, lived at No. 3 Cranmer Road. Dr Norman McLean, at No. 12, the former Master of Christ's College worked with the Rev. Dr A. E. Brooke, of No. 8, an Honorary Canon of Ely and a former Provost of King's College, on the preparation of the larger Cambridge edition of the Septuagint.

Also in Cranmer Road was Professor Bethune Baker, a fellow of Pembroke College, and for many years Lady Margaret's Professor of Divinity at Cambridge. Sir Ernest Barker describes Professor Bethune Baker as "a driving power and force in the movement of modern churchmanship". The road was strong in theology in those days, but "that was perhaps a relic of an earlier Cambridge age, when theology played a larger part in university thought and studies, and the clergy were still a considerable part of academic life and society", wrote Dr Barker.

But even in the early days of Cranmer Road there were many who were not clergy. There was a retired Senior Tutor of Trinity College, who used to pedal his tricycle up and down the road as form of exercise. Nowadays he would probably have been a jogger. The paleographer, historian and vice-provost of King's College, Montague Rhodes James – best known for his ghost stories – used to live at No. 1 Cranmer Road, a house that has always been a King's House.

Sir Ernest Barker describes Miss Jane Campbell Allen who lived at No. 15: "Our next-door-neighbour on the east was a lady from Northern Ireland who had some connection, through her menfolk, with one of the Cambridge colleges. Her Irish voice is a delight in the memory: she mixed austerity and generosity in a unique blend which had a rare and refreshing tang: she kept her garden a lovely wilderness; in front of her house grew a spreading white double cherry, which made me somehow think, when it was glorious with blossom in May, of a passage in Meredith's *The Egoist*, and by its side grew a Judas tree, its purple contrasting with the white of the cherry as the colours are contrasted and blended, in the pictures on the walls of Byzantine churches, and its vivid hue making me think each year of the Judas trees I once saw in the spring on the summit of the Aventine." Sir Ernest was writing about Cranmer Road in the 1920/30s.

Behind the houses and gardens on the south side of Cranmer Road, in Corpus Christi College territory, lies hidden what was once one of the finest private mansions in Cambridge. It is "Leckhampton", a Victorian country house with Cotswold features which stands in grounds of stately home proportions behind Cranmer Road, and up a long drive leading off Grange Road.

Leckhampton, No. 37 Grange Road, was built in 1880 to the design of the architect, William C. Marshall just before the houses in Cranmer Road, on land belonging to Corpus Christi College. Since 1960, it has been the graduate wing of Corpus, part of the residential community of the College, and its garden is the haunt of Corpus Fellows. Corpus leased the land on which Leckhampton is built on a 99-year building lease to F. W. H. Myers, a renowned psychical researcher, who was an inspector of schools, and a one time Fellow of Trinity College.

Myers was a man of considerable private means, and in Leckhampton he created one of the great private houses of Victorian Cambridge. He was very hospitable and entertained many famous people there. At one lunch party in July 1884, the guests included the novelist Henry James and A. C. Benson, English essayist, poet, and author and later the 28th Master of Magdalene College.

Why the name Leckhampton? Is there a Cotswold connection? Dr Peter Lewis, the physiologist, knew the story. "Yes, Myers' father was a housemaster at Cheltenham College, and the house where he lived looked across to Leckhampton Hill. If you look at the house you can see certain Cotswold features, such as the gables." The house is not built in mellow Cotswold stone, however. That would be asking too much for Cotswold exiles like myself who miss the sunlit uplands, and the remote valleys of *Cider with Rosie* country, the chalky escarpment of Minchinhampton Common and the Beacons, such as Haresfield and Uley above the River Severn. But the gardens at Leckhampton, a blend of the formal and the wild, where mature beeches and cedars cast long shadows over the croquet lawn, remind one of the best country gardens in the south Cotswolds, around Leckhampton Hill, in fact.

Leckhampton gardens were laid out by a landscape gardener called William Robinson, who shared the views of the Victorian gardener Gertrude Jekyll. "Both deplored the 'pastry cook' type of garden – a garden that was entirely formal where plants were rotated in the beds depending on the season", said Dr David Dewhurst, a senior observer at the Royal Institute of Astronomy and a Leckhampton Fellow of Corpus. "Robinson's idea of the gentleman's country garden was of a small formal garden leading into a wild garden and orchard beyond." This was the formula devised for Leckhampton.

Myers instructed his landscape gardener to plant cedar trees, a copper beech and cherry trees. In the wild garden, which contrasts with the formal croquet lawn, flowers such as bluebells and cowslips grow in abundance in the spring, and lupins in the early summer.

Visitors to the gardens, which are open to the public once a year in aid of charity, can explore the far end of the garden where there is a swimming pool and a little folly of a temple at the end of the garden. The swimming pool was originally a lily pond. The temple was built on the spoil heap which came from making the garden and was built so it is said, so that Myers could commune with his late wife. The rose garden at Leckhampton, was once a tennis court, but when Corpus took it over in 1960 they had their own courts on the playing fields at the end of Cranmer Road, and a tennis court at Leckhampton was unnecessary.

F. W. H. Myers was one of Britain's foremost mediums and psychical researchers at a time when it was very fashionable to be interested in the occult and seances. He was a founder member of the Society for Psychical Research, and classical experiments including seances attended by mediums who were celebrity figures, were carried out in the drawing room at Leckhampton. When he died, his son Leonard Myers, a novelist, took over Leckhampton.

Corpus Christi College later rented Leckhampton to Professor Louis C. G. Clarke, who bequeathed his collection of Old Master drawings and ceramics to the Fitzwilliam Museum, of which he was a director. His bequest is considered to be one of the Museum's greatest benefactions, Professor Clark's treasures adorned Leckhampton before they were bequeathed to the Fitzwilliam.

The only part of the garden used by Professor Clark was the terrace, then surrounded by a yew hedge. The rest of the garden at that time was an impenetrable, overgrown wilderness.

Because Professor Clarke's descendants declined to live in Leckhampton he arranged that on his death the house and grounds should revert to Corpus Christi. He died on Boxing Day 1960.

Just after Professor Clarke died, a report was published recommending that one or more graduate colleges be established in Cambridge. The committee which made this recommendation was a sub-committee of the Bridges Committee which had been set up to examine the University. There were two members of that sub-committee – Michael McCrum, then Senior Tutor of Corpus, now the Master, and Professor of Biochemistry Frank Young, the first Master of Darwin College. The late Eric Ceadel, who was the secretary of the Bridges Committee became one of the first Leckhampton Fellows of Corpus.

Portrait of Michael McCrum by Michael Noakes, 1977.

The inspired initiative for turning Leckhampton into the graduate wing of Corpus came principally from Michael McCrum who had long been enamoured of the house and its "secret garden" grounds, ever since 1946 when he came up to Cambridge after four years war service and used to roam round the gardens as a bit of a trespasser! Of the older colleges, Corpus has the highest ratio of research students to undergraduates – 100 graduate students to about 220 undergraduates.

Mrs Pat Stokes, assistant domestic bursar on the lawn at Leckhampton.

In 1964, the college built the George Thomson building to house more graduates at Leckhampton. It was named after the then Master of Corpus who had been very supportive of the scheme to develop the graduate wing of the college in 1960/61. Sir George Thomson was the son of the physicist J. J. Thomson, who was awarded the Nobel prize in physics in 1906. His son George was awarded the Nobel prize for physics in 1937.

Corpus' graduate wing has expanded into Cranmer Road where the college owns Nos. 15 to 23, houses, which it has been acquiring since 1965 to provide accommodation for senior research scholars on sabbatical leave and for married graduate students.

The gardens of these Corpus properties in Cranmer Road lead across the lawns to Leckhampton which has become a residential community with a social life of its own. Leckhampton has its own assistant domestic bursar, Mrs Pat Stokes, who took over the job from Mrs Megison, of Selwyn Gardens. No. 25 Cranmer Road is the home of the Corpus groundsman, Mr Dan Hayward, who looks after the college's extensive playing fields.

No. 21 Cranmer Road, now a Corpus house, was formerly the home of the criminologist Professor Sir Leon Radzinowicz, who used to go pounding up and down the road with Professor Alfred Steers whose home was at No. 23.

The Bell School of Languages bought No. 9 Cranmer Road during the war and started their school there. They added an extension to the house and sold it in the early 1960s before moving to Red Cross Lane.

Miss Phyllis Cook, daughter of Professor A. B. Cook of No. 19 Cranmer Road ran a nursery school there. Among the pupils who started on the first day were Ann Keynes and Michael Swann. Miss Cook's successor moved the school to Malting House Lane. No. 3 Cranmer Road will be opening shortly as the Cambridge Day Nursery and Nursery School. The tradition of learning persists!

It was the war-time upheaval that brought about the visit to Cranmer Road of Emperor Haile Selassie of Ethiopia. He came in 1936 with his retinue that included his Prime Minister, to consult Professor McNair, the international lawyer about his legal position following the Italian invasion of Abyssinia that forced the Emperor and his family to flee the country.

Lord McNair's daughter, Sheila Barwell who lives at No. 13 Cranmer Road on the opposite side of the road from No. 6 where she grew up, remembers the visit. "Four Ethiopians arrived at our house, but only the Emperor wore traditional clothes – a long dark cloak with a little stand-up collar and under the cloak the lion of Judah embroidered on the undergarment.

"He was a small handsome man and he didn't speak any English at that time, so he conversed with my father in French, but his Prime Minister spoke English." The McNairs' staff were quite overawed by the Royal visit, and one maid enquired whether she should "come in backwards with the tea tray".

The great philosopher Professor Whitehead, who migrated to Harvard to become Professor of Philosophy, used to live at No. 11 Cranmer Road. He was visited there by Bertrand Russell, who collaborated with him on *Principia Mathematica*.

When war broke out, the "contours of life" in Cranmer Road were altered, to quote Sir Ernest Barker's *Age and Youth*. It became a new road, "not in its aspect or in its buildings," he wrote, "but in the general tenor of its ways and the main contours of its daily life".

Sir Ernest Barker, whose daughter Juliet, now Juliet Beament, used to hang her violin in the tree, was far from complaining of the change. "I think the new road is more interesting, more varied, and a good deal more hopeful", he wrote. "The average age is much younger, and there are far more children about: indeed I can count them in tens where once I could only count them in ones."

Professor Alfred Steers, who used to live at No. 23, told me that when *Age and Youth* was published near Christmas-time in 1953, he bought a copy and on his way home decided to tell Ernest Barker. "He was sitting in his room and I told him I had a job for him. He looked rather fiercely at me, and then I said 'I have just bought a copy of your autobiography and I want you to sign it'. Then all smiles! He then said George Trevelyan always referred to him as the 'prose poet' so my copy of his book is inscribed: 'Ernest Barker, prose poet' of Cranmer Road in honour of its geographer J. A. Steers."

No. 10 was constructed at the end of the nineteenth century on land belonging to Jesus College. No record of the house is to hand other than that the Fairbank family came to the road in the late 1940s. Dr John Fairbank was a consultant surgeon at Addenbrooke's hospital. He died in 1998, and his widow moved away from the road several years later, so No. 10 was the residence of the Fairbank family for more than 50 years.

Permission to build on the land now constituting 12 and 14 Cranmer Road was granted by Jesus College to Rev. John Lock, a fellow of Gonville and Caius College, in 1891. By an agreement between Lock and Jesus College in 1904, two dwellings (12 and 14) were to be constructed.

No. 12 was completed in 1905 and became the residence of Dr Norman McLean and his wife. Norman McLean subsequently became Master of Christ's College in 1927, remaining so until 1936. It is believed that the mulberry tree in the grounds of Christ's College was grown from a cutting taken from the tree still growing in the garden of No. 12. Norman McLean stayed at No. 12 until his death in 1947. Thereafter No. 12 was inhabited successively by two college bursars: the Scotsman William Hutton at Pembroke College, who had been in the army at Dunkirk in 1940, and then Brigadier Michael Crosthwaite at Darwin College.

Literary matters were very much in the minds of Professor John Margeson and his wife Sarah when they moved into 14 Cranmer Road in 1959. "When we bought No. 14, there was a partly burnt bonfire smouldering in our new garden", said Mrs Sarah Margeson. What was smoking on the fire were hundreds of letters

Professor Jack Hamson, tutor to POWs

In the cool recesses of Newton's old rooms by the Great Gate of Trinity last week, an elderly law don summoned up the shades of post-war Cranmer Road, and explained why after the war he had had a passion to live in a large room.

Emeritus Professor Jack Hamson, who moved into a big house, No. 7 Cranmer Road in January 1946, had spent four years at a prisoner of war camp at Dossel, 150 miles from the German–Dutch border. "When I came back from the war I longed to live in a large room," he said. Life as a PoW was restricting and monotonous, but Professor Hamson met the challenge of boredom for himself and his fellow prisoners by establishing a law school in the camp. He taught law to many of his fellow prisoners, some of whom went on to take solicitors' and Bar exams while still in prison.

Did he ever try and escape from the camp? "No, not personally, but I helped to organise several escape attempts." One successful escape involved a short circuiting of the perimeter lights. "We managed to short circuit the lights while another lot made a fuss in one part of the camp, then the remainder got out over the wire. Of the four who got out, three actually got home by walking across country to the Dutch border." One of the successful escapees, who is a member of Trinity College and a good friend of Professor Hamson's is Henry Coombe Tennant, who joined the War Office after the war, and then at the age of 50 became a monk.

Professor Hamson and his wife bought No. 7 Cranmer Road from a Mrs Matthew. "She

was a Miss Lilley by birth, who had married Mr Matthew, the solicitor. There went with the house a Miss Dickens who had joined the Matthew family as governess in 1913." Professor Hamson remembers the road as being much more reserved. "People kept themselves to themselves. All the houses would have had two or three live-in maids. Our kitchen still had 15 hanging bells, each with a different tinkle."

The Hamsons had a laundry woman called Mrs Woodyate, who used to send her nephew to collect the laundry. She was obviously the local Mrs Tiggy-Winkle.

from the Rev. James Bethune Baker, the former Lady Margaret Professor of Divinity. "We still have them and they date from the 1870s or 80s", said Sarah Margeson.

Mrs Robin Orr lives at No. 16 with her second husband, Professor Robin Orr, who was Professor of Music between 1965 and 1976. He was also a composer of operas. They married in 1979. "I moved into No. 16 in 1950 having arrived in Cambridge in 1946 as one of the first exchange students from Switzerland after the war. Instead of finishing my studies in Zurich, the following year, I got married and never returned. With two small girls we were desperately looking for a house." As Junior Fellow at Jesus College, her then husband heard about an ultra modern house becoming available at the end of Cranmer Road.

"Carless, with our babies in the cycle baskets we cycled across the town in search of the not quite finished construction in light London brick with large double windows built by Ivor Smith, then a student (later of King Street Housing fame and Professor of Architecture at Bristol) to the specifications of Professor von Wright who was at Trinity editing the Wittgenstein papers. Rumour has it that his Scandinavian wife did not take to Cambridge academic life, so he returned to Helsinki.

"It turned out to be the house of our dreams, but the snag was that according to the hierarchy of the college system, every fellow above our station was entitled to first option in strict pecking order. A. P. Rossiter took one look from the outside and decided against the flat roof, others objected to the open staircase, some could not do with the open plan living/dining room, others missed a scullery and separate dining room for large scale entertaining.

"Nobody seemed to want it and there was our chance. Soon after the move and while still decorating our unfinished new house, the formidable Miss Stanley, who lived at No. 5, the grand house with the topiary, called to formally welcome us to the road." Miss Winnie Wentworth Stanley was one of a large group of unmarried brothers and sisters who had moved in from Longstowe to Cranmer Road. "They reminded the company that moving to Cranmer Road was slumming it," said Professor Hamson.

The tradition of the topiary work hedge has been maintained by the Neild family who are shortly moving to Brooklands Avenue. One day, when she was trimming the lion and the unicorn, Liz Neild was accosted by a German tourist who said of the patriotic figures at which she was clipping away, "you are very nationalist".

From the end of Cranmer Road beyond the dog rose shrouded field where engine driver Terry Knox has the grazing rights from Jesus College and keeps horses, the view stretches away into mile upon mile of fields. Residents feel the fields may soon be a thing of the past if Jesus College go ahead and develop a housing estate on part of the Rifle Range and allow access from Cranmer Road, It would be sad for the once "No Thoroughfare" street of learning. Happily, this has not come about.

CRANMER ROAD

Revisited

You couldn't call it "Dons' Alley" any more, the road where once professors occupied nearly every house! Nowadays, wealthy businessmen and their families outnumber the academics as house prices have topped the £1.5 million mark. In addition, more of the private properties have fallen out of private hands and into the hands of colleges and an academic institution, the Lauterpacht Centre for International Law. No property has ever been released from institutions to private buyers.

Academics, even on professorial salaries, cannot afford now to buy houses in this part of west Cambridge. Money – not learning and scholarship – is the god nowadays.

Since 1983, almost all the houses in Cranmer Road have been either extended or significantly modernised – whether as individual residences or multiple College accommodation. Nos 2 and 4 were demolished in the 1960s to make way for Selwyn College's Cripps Court (further expansion of Cripps Court is still continuing) and five family houses: Nos. 15, 17, 19, 21 and 23 were bought up by Corpus Christi College, also in the sixties to form part of the Leckhampton estate, the college's graduate accommodation.

King's College already owned No. 1 Cranmer Road, also called No. 41 Grange Road, together with "Grasshopper Lodge" at No. 39 Grange Road. In 1993, No. 3 Cranmer Road came on the market and King's stepped in and bought it from the Coppersmith Family, who had run the Copperfields Nursery School there on the ground floor for several years. With their latest purchase, King's have three adjacent properties, now one big site for postgraduate students.

No. 5 Cranmer Road, built in 1892, was bought by the entrepreneur and businessman, Peter Hoskins from the economist Robert Neild in 1983. Two years later, Mr Hoskins sold it to the Lauterpacht Centre for International Law, one of the specialist centres of the Faculty of Law. The Centre was founded by Sir Elihu Lauterpacht QC in 1983 in memory of his father Sir Hersch Lauterpacht, who was a member of the United Nations' International Law Commission from 1952 to 1954, and a Judge of the International Court of Justice from 1955 to 1960.

Sir Eli first ran the Centre from his home at No. 7 Herschel Road while looking for premises to establish the Centre in a place that would be more like a home than an institution. "We gradually grew, and acquired No. 5 Cranmer Road in 1986 for £300,000, then the most expensive house in Cambridge. Various people and institutions gave us money, in particular Edward St George, a successful businessman in the Bahamas, who gave us £100,000."

After the late Professor Jack Hamson moved into rooms in Trinity College from his home at No. 7 Cranmer Road, shortly after the death of his wife in 1978, the College turned it into a college lodging house for Trinity College research students. It was run by an Irishman, Paddy Stronge, and his wife Irene.

In 2002, the Lauterpacht Centre made the college an offer for it and the Stronges retired. The Centre now owns the two adjoining houses, three feet apart and plans to link the two buildings when funds are available. No. 7 is now called Bahrain House. It has offices, a library and upstairs, eight apartments with en suite bathrooms and kitchenettes for postgraduate students at the Centre. A palm tree flourishes in the large garden and foxes and muntjac deer roam freely.

Elisabeth Gardner-Smith, widow of Rev. Percival Gardner-Smith, Dean of Jesus College between 1922 and 1956 stayed on in their home, No. 11 Cranmer Road, after "Perks" death in 1985. Her friend and neighbour in Pinehurst, Dame Rosemary Murray, founder of New Hall (now Murray Edwards College), and

Still some of the West Fields left! View at the end of Cranmer Road from the footpath that leads from Gough Way.

Vice Chancellor, insisted on doing the garden at No. 11. Mrs Gardner-Smith died in 2001, and is remembered with affection by many people in Cambridge.

Her neighbour, Dr John Wilkes at No. 13 recalls that Mrs Gardner-Smith had intended the house to be a retirement home for clergy when she left the house to the Diocese of Ely, but the endowment was not enough to sustain the plan.

The Diocese sold the house in 2004 to a businessman, Nigel Street and his wife Sarah, an architect. They chose the location because of schools for their four children. Modernising the house was a challenge. "We walked into a Victorian house with gas and no central heating." They then employed Sindalls the builders who had built the house originally for Harry Marshall Ward, to make major changes and refurbishments. These included adding a new kitchen/dining wing. An engineering graduate of Sheffield University, who used to work for Rothschilds, Nigel now runs a company building solar parks. Sarah works for the charity SOS Children.

Dr Wilkes, a retired lecturer in computer science from Anglia Ruskin University, has lived with his wife Rita and their family at No. 13 since 1987. It is a semi- detached house joined to No. 11, and was built in 1895. It has the comfortable feel of a family home with a secluded garden and huge trees that characterise this part of west Cambridge. The house previously belonged to Professor Sir Percy Winfield, a distinguished academic lawyer.

Dr Wilkes, one of the last two academics living in his own home on the south side of the road, is working on a full history of Cranmer Road, and would welcome reminiscences from those who lived in the road, or know those who did.

The groundsman's house on the Corpus playing fields, a house built in 1935 and lived in by two generations of the Hayward family, Reg and his son Michael, was knocked down in 2012 and a small hostel for Corpus students was built there. There were no objections.

On the north side of the road, walk up past Cripps Court and you get to No. 6, where Lady Lauterpacht lived until her death in 1989. The Lauterpachts then sold the house to Rob Hammond who was the chief executive and town clerk of Cambridge City Council until 2012. He was awarded an honorary doctorate in business administration from Anglia Ruskin University in 2009.

No. 8 has changed hands several times. It was the home of Professor Harold Davenport, who was appointed to the Rouse Ball Chair of Mathematics in Cambridge in 1958. He remained in the post until his death in 1961. His widow, Annie lived there after his death. The house was sold in 1989 to Michael Walton, an architect. When he moved out of Cambridge, he sold the house to Christopher and Veronica McDouall, who lived there from 1991–4.

Christopher McDouall is a company director and business consultant, his wife Veronica a psychotherapist. Mr McDouall's memories of Cranmer Road go back a long way. "I remember well Percy Gardner-Smith as I was an undergraduate at Jesus College shortly after he stepped down from being Dean of Chapel, though he continued teaching for a while longer. In those days, he had a house in Fen Ditton, where he, and later with Elisabeth, would entertain undergraduates to tea and croquet of a summer Sunday afternoon.

"He was famous for his sardonic aphorisms: for example, Junior Fellow to the Dean: 'Good morning Dean, what a beautiful spring morning!'. Percy G-S in response in a gravely voice, dropping his aitches. 'Yes, I'ave just passed a dead 'edge 'og in the road.'

"It was later they moved to Cranmer Road, and while we were living there Elizabeth used from time to time to invite a selection of fellow residents to Sunday lunch, which seemed invariably to consist of tomato soup served from a vacuum flask with bread or rolls and fillings to go with it." The McDoualls found Cranmer Road was a good place to live. "It was quiet and there was no trouble."

John Fairbanks, the orthopaedic surgeon, who lived with his wife at No. 10 until his death in 1998, was the second of three generations of orthopaedic surgeons. Mrs Fairbanks lived in the house from 1949 until 2005, more than 50 years, which must be almost a record!

No. 12 was acquired from the Crosthwaits by Eva McLean, who has since taught for many of the colleges of the University. Her husband, Professor David McLean, when a Fellow of Pembroke College, was a colleague of William Hutton (mentioned earlier). Professor McLean points out that the house has been owned by only four families since it was built.

Referring to the account of the Ethiopian visit to No. 5 Cranmer Road in the 1930s, recalled in my 1983 article, Professor McLean recalls that No. 12 has also experienced overseas visits in so far as academic staff from Japan were annual visitors in the 1980s.

"These visits developed after I was initially contacted at Pembroke College from Nihon University in Tokyo in the late 1970s, and subsequently went to Tokyo as a visiting scholar in 1985. Building upon that connection and the visits to No. 12, Nihon University formalised a regular scheme for visiting scholar exchanges by staff with Cambridge University and, a few years later, entered into an institutional arrangement with Pembroke College, whereby Nihon students came to Pembroke annually for a Summer School."

And what of the changes at Leckhampton? I put the question to the Leckhampton Warden, the Rev. James Buxton, who is also Dean of Chapel at Corpus. He is west Cambridge born and bred, having grown up in Barton Road at No. 24. His mother, Mrs Mary Buxton now lives in Grantchester, a village where the church, St Michael and St Mary has been a Corpus Christi College living since 1352. There is a Corpus Fellows Memorial (a classical pillar with the College's emblem, the Pelican in her piety, on top. A mosaic pelican is also found in front of the altar, in the churchyard to the west of the tower where "the clock stands still at ten to three and is there honey still for tea", and Mr Buxton has buried the ashes of Dr David Dewhurst there. Michael McCrum is also buried in the churchyard just beside the Corpus Memorial.

"There are no longer Leckhampton fellows, and the majority of postgraduate students here who are studying for M.Phils or Ph.Ds are single, though there are flats for students with partners. Most of our postgraduate students live here and have meals together, as we promote the community life. No other college focuses

Leckhampton house and gardens – a blend of the formal and the wild.

all its postgraduates in one place." He explains that a lot of the overseas students, who come to Leckhampton expecting it to have similar provision to other colleges, "can't believe their luck". I can understand that!

He tells me that in 2004, to mark his 80th birthday, Michael McCrum and his wife Christine, presented the College with a redesign of the Leckhampton gardens by the award winning landscape designer Tom Stuart-Smith, a graduate of Corpus and regular gold medallist at the RHS Chelsea Flower Show.

On 4 September 2010, his widow Christine, eldest son Robert and granddaughter Isobel were at Leckhampton with many others, who played a part in the earliest days of this graduate wing of the college, to see the first part of that design unveiled in the Prairie Garden which used to be the Rose Garden.

There is a new building too. Leckhampton have just built the Kho building to house more postgraduates. The principal benefactors and generous doners were Mr and Mrs Kwee from Singapore, whose son Philip graduated from Corpus three years ago.

Mrs Doris Orr at No. 16 has lived in Cranmer Road since 1950 and at the time of writing was 90 years old. We last met in her home some 30 years ago. "I am the oldest inhabitant in the road now", she says.

Reclining in her chair, in a sitting room whose focal point is her late husband's rare walnut harpsichord, which she persuaded him not to sell, she is happy to share more memories of her life, roaming from her childhood in Solothurn, the finest Baroque town in Switzerland, where her father had a watch factory, to her mother's time in India under the Raj, and then to the early Cambridge years with her first husband, James Winny, the father of her three children. She met him as one of the first two Swiss exchange students sent to England just after the war, and remembers that "she had a grand wedding and then it all came to nothing". The happiest years of her life were those from 1979 with Professor Orr, her second husband until his death in 2006. "I married him after he retired. I was 12 years younger. That didn't bother me at all. He was so charming, above all loved by everybody, a very nice man and a good composer." She smiles as she remembers how her son gave her away in marriage on the lawns of St John's. "As a student, he gave his mother away to the Professor of Music at Cambridge." She reminds me that "Robin was most famous for building the Concert Hall in West Road. He fought tooth and nail for it. When the Duke of Edinburgh opened it, he said: 'if it weren't for Robin it would never have been built'." But it was Doris Orr who suggested that they appoint Sir Leslie Martin, the architect to design it. "That was my contribution to the Music Faculty!"

Mrs Orr's house is the last on the north side, there is just an open field to the west and then the footpath leading over Bin Brook to Gough Way. Three months after reminiscing to me again, Doris Orr sadly died in November 2013.

The plan to develop housing on part of the Rifle Range was rejected by the planning authorities. Cranmer Road remains a "No Thoroughfare" and fields and open country to the west of the city can still be viewed from the end of the road.

RHS Chelsea Flower Show gold medallist, and Corpus graduate, Tom Stuart-Smith designed the Prairie Garden at Leckhampton.

SILVER STREET

14–28 October 1982

Until 1615, Silver Street was called Small Bridges Street. That is because there was once an ancient branch of the Cam which was spanned some 80 yards to the west of the present bridge, by the lesser of two "Small Bridges", as they were called. The other Small Bridge was the forerunner of Silver Street bridge.

There is a good account of what Silver Street must have looked like some 400 years ago in Clark and Gray's commentary to John Hamond's plan of 1592. The area is shown on the map as crowded with houses, courtyards and gardens. "The Bridge at the western end of Silver Street where we cross the united courses of the river as it comes from the two mills, was a railed bridge of planks without arch or piers. The smaller bridge near the Hermitage was not even railed," they say.

"The southern side of Silver Street where the Anchor Inn and boathouse is now, in Hamond's day was open to the Mill Pool. Above the King's Mill stretches Sheep's Green on which grazing sheep are figured. Beyond the bridge, in Hamond's plan, all appearance of a road ends, and traffic found its way over an open green to the second of the two bridges, which together with the first bridge were known as Small Bridges. This second bridge crossed a considerable branch of the river, which came from Newnham Mill, and survives in an attenuated form as the ditch which bounds Queens' Grove on its western side.

We know that both small bridges were destroyed by Parliamentary troops in 1643, but restored five years later. The small bridge by Queens' College was replaced in 1841 by a cast iron version made by Charles Finch at his Market Hill foundry. The present stone bridge was built to designs by Sir Edwin Lutyens in 1959, when the street was widened."

Silver Street at its eastern end used to be a commercial street lined with fine sixteenth-century timbered houses. Many of these disappeared when Cambridge University Press developed the site on the southern side of the street towards Trumpington Street, and St Catharine's built their Master's Lodge in 1875 on the north side. Among the businesses which went were several public houses – The Cock, the Wheatsheaf, the Three Crowns and the Black Lion, which was No. 22

Silver Street. There was an extensive yard behind the Black Lion, called Black Lion Yard, where a college servant, a fly proprietor and two butcher's men lived shortly before the pub and yard were demolished to make way for the Pitt Press machine rooms.

The one pub left in Silver Street is The Anchor. A cottage once occupied the site, and the pub was not licensed until 1872. George Jarvis, who was the first publican, was also a bricklayer, builder and boat proprietor. The Dolbys took over from him, and ran The Anchor boat houses as well as The Anchor inn for more than 30 years. The Anchor is a popular haunt with foreign students, tourists who debouch there by the bridge in search of historical detail and Cambridge atmosphere, and undergraduates themselves.

Since the earliest days of the University, there have been undergraduates living in lodgings in the town, and it was soon found necessary to appoint somebody to look after their interests and well-being. The Lodging Houses Syndicate, whose offices are in Nos. 17 and 18 Silver Street, began in 1265 when King Henry III issued letters patent appointing a board consisting of Members of the Senate and two Burgesses, whose duty it should be to regulate the rent paid by undergraduates for houses which they hired in the town.

The Syndicate still carries out this duty, beside many others, which in the words of Miss M. C. D. Kennett, former secretary of the Syndicate: "have been thrust upon it in the course of centuries". Undergraduates are not allowed to live out of college except in rooms licensed by the Syndicate, representing the University, and a licence is given only after inquiry about the character, of the applicant and after inspection of the house.

Harraden's view of Queens College (1798) showing one of the old bridges with Beales granary on the extreme left.

Any serious charge against a lodging-house keeper may lead to the licence being revoked. Details of the misdemeanours which could lead to a licence being revoked were recorded by the Secretary in a little black book. When I called at the Lodgings Syndicate last week, Mrs Margot Holbrook, successor to Miss Kennett, unlocked the little black book that had been used more than 100 years ago to note down the weaknesses and "crimes" of landladies and their families.

G. Flack, the plumber's shop in Silver Street in the 1870s.

Peccadilloes ranged from leaving the shutters undone or the door unlocked after 10 p.m., to "ruining the servant girl in the summer of 1892". One landlady was seen by the proctors "drinking at the Lion Hotel with her daughter and undergraduates", and her house was "generally unsatisfactory" – her licence was not renewed.

The present office housed in the Department of Land Economy was at one time a lodging house. In the 1880s, the Master of Pembroke had reported to the Lodgings Syndicate that one room in the house was occupied by boy and girl servants. An inquiry showed that Mrs X had servants sleeping in the house and that the accommodation was insufficient – two sons, aged 13 and 11 had occupied the same room with the servants, who were several years older. The landlady was severely reprimanded by the chairman of the Syndicate but the licence was not taken away. In the old days, licences were signed by the Vice Chancellor. In 1858, a lodging house keeper with two sets of rooms could expect to get 16 shillings a week for the first set, 10 shillings for the second.

Among the shops and commercial enterprises that used to be in Silver Street was a well known fruiterers and florists called R. M. Jones & Son, which opened at No. 19 Silver Street in the 1890s. Mr Jones had

Looking after the housing of students at the Lodgings syndicate: Jillian Hotchkiss (left) and Margot Holbrook.

a daughter, Madeline, who later became Mrs Madeline Reynolds. It was Mrs Reynolds who started the Garden House Hotel after the First World War. When I interviewed her on her 90th birthday on 12 September 1972, Mrs Reynolds told me that she had been born in the gardener's lodge at Queens' College. Her father had used the frontage of the Garden House, in those days a private house, for his market garden. "My father had one of the first cars in Cambridge, and also one of the first punts", she told me. She remembered the great big grain wagons which used to roll down Mill Lane and the horse-drawn barges.

For about 160 years, Haslop's the butcher's has occupied No. 4 Silver Street, although the business was founded by John Haslop in High Street Chesterton. His slaughterhouse was a few yards away. For all those years, it has been owned by members of the same family. Its present owner is Mr Christopher Haslop Butler. Christopher Haslop Butler's father, Mr Albert Haslop Butler, remembers when his great aunt, Mrs Elizabeth Haslop died in 1934: "My father was made executor. He went to the Bursar of St Catharine's and sold the property to him for £1,600. We were given a 21-year-lease on the shop." Albert Haslop Butler, who was in the Queens' College choir when he was a boy of eight, remembers the tethering posts outside the shop and the horse troughs further down the street.

Mrs L. E. Burrows, of Milton, is the granddaughter of John Haslop. She remembers that the business was subsequently handed over to his son, her uncle Tom, and his wife, her aunt Lizzie (née Unwin). "My mother Emily Jane, third daughter of the said John, was the sole remaining member of the Haslop family who died 20 years ago, aged 92 and a half." The Haslop family all had good memories. A favourite shop with the Haslop Butler family was Miss J. E. Asplen's cake and sweet shop across the road at 21 Silver Street.

Silver Street is university and colleges territory. Four colleges have a stake in it: Queens', St Catharine's, Corpus and Darwin. The University started to get a foot in there in 1665, when John Field, who became University Printer in 1655 established the University Press at the corner of Small Bridges Street and Queens' Lane on ground rented from Queens' College, on part of the land now occupied by the Master's Lodge of St Catharine's College. This remained the University printing-house until the early nineteenth century. But it was not until 1762 that, by the purchase of the White Lion on the other side of the same street, the University started to acquire the present site of the Press. The colleges, with the exception of that new boy, Darwin, founded in 1964, are much older landowners than the University. They obtained the greater part of their present sites in the fifteenth century.

On the north side of Silver Street, in the parish of St Botolph's, Queens' and St Catharine's have been neighbours since 1475. "Catz", as St Catharine's is fondly known, was founded nearly 30 years after the foundation of Queens'. The two colleges, however, haven't always been the best of neighbours. In the archives of Queens', there is a letter from Sir Isaac Newton backing up a claim by the college that a building by St Catharine's would obscure Queens' light. Again, in the nineteenth century when Queens' was building a chapel, St Catharine's wanted it moved away from Queens' Lane because it would obscure its light.

But the two colleges have also done deals with one another. In 1836, Queens' sold to St Catharine's land on which stood almshouses, a few yards to the east of the corner of Queens' Lane. These almshouses had been established by Andrew Doket, rector of St Botolph's and first president of Queens' who had bought property in Silver Street to provide accommodation for eight poor women. In 1838, the almshouses were moved into Queens' Lane. They were finally pulled down to make room for the Doket building of Queens' in 1911, when the charity was converted into pensions.

Queens' is the college we all associate with Silver Street. For many visitors to Cambridge it is the first college they see as they are deposited by Silver Street bridge. Queens' bridge – that handsome teak structure put up in 1904 – was modelled on the original bridge built by James Essex to the design of William Etheridge in 1749 and later rebuilt in 1867, and is very often the first part of the college that visitors see when they arrive in Silver Street. Each year, 18,000 people then go on to visit Queens' College, which is the one college to charge an admission fee of 25p.

When I called on the Junior Bursar of Queens', Dr Robin Walker in his Rapunzel turret over the gatehouse in Old Court last week, in the tower that until the mid-1960s used to be the Strong Room, we talked about the so-called Mathematical Bridge. "There are so many lies told about the bridge," he said. "There is no truth in the legend that Newton, who died in 1727, was involved in the design of the bridge, nor that it was first built without bolts. Early prints show the bolts clearly, and even the model has pins at the joints." Visitors from Oxford may know that the design of Queens' Bridge was copied from a foot-bridge across the Thames at Iffley Lock, near Oxford.

Dr Walker, a mathematician who has the history of the college at his finger-tips, is quite a one for nailing legends about Queens'. "Did you know that the half timbered President's Lodge is a twentieth-century fake?" That shook me. I'd always thought of Queens' President's Lodge as Cambridge's bit of Stratford-upon-Avon – real Tudor black and white. "No, those timber frames were never designed to be exposed. It was originally an East Anglian plaster building with the timber frames encased in the plaster lining. No one, is quite sure when it was built, although the style is that of the 1590s, but we know that some building of some sort went up in the 1540s.

"The Lodge was restored in 1911, and a consequence of the restoration was that they plastered in between the beams and not on top of them." Why? Dr Walker thought this was a "nice bit of Edwardian nostalgia". They put on little curly bits round the window frames and restored it to a Tudor-looking style.

Queens' Mathematical Bridge in winter in the 1880s.

"They may," he said "have been under the misapprehension that that was its original style." After its Edwardian face-lift, perhaps the worst thing that happened to the President's Lodge was when a snowball was thrown through a medieval stained glass light in an upper window during the student riots of 1968.

Fragments of stained glass, believed to come from the Carmelite Monastery which stood on part of the site of Queens' College until the Dissolution of the Monasteries in 1538, are to be found in a window in the college library. Medieval reading desks with their Tudor, Jacobean and eighteenth-century extensions furnish the Old Library founded in 1448. In Tudor times, there would have been an iron rod going through the bookshelf from one side to another and the books would have been chained to it. Stealing books is obviously not just a modern phenomenon.

Queens' Hall, built in 1449, is a mishmash of styles. It is a medieval room with classical panelling. In earlier centuries it would have had a flat roof, but the Victorians came along and introduced the Arthurian banqueting hall effect. The decorations are a gloriously colourful Victorian extravaganza. The hall is now used for special functions, private dinners and feasts. During term time, the college members eat in the new dining hall in Cripps Court (built on the site of the old Fellows' garden and which has just picked up a commendation in the RIBA 1982 awards).

The Fisher Building, built in 1936 to the designs of G. C. Drinkwater at a cost of £50,000, stands on the site of a group of houses and cottages, which were demolished in 1936 to make way for the building. These pretty cottages included

Silver Street in 1890 looking towards Queen's Road.

Butler's and Shoeblacks Cottage where college servants use to live. The Head Porter's house was there too, also Coulson's Yard, originally Flack's Yard. Flack, who died in 1925, was a builder who used to do quite a lot of work for Queens'. Now we have the Fisher building which, during the Second World War, was billeted for the purpose of the London University Medical School. Incidentally, Pevsner thinks it looks like a block of flats in Pinner!

At the beginning of the article I said that two other colleges had a stake in Silver Street – Corpus Christi and Darwin. The University Press owns all the ground between Silver Street and Mill Lane, Trumpington Street and the river, north, south, east and west but it doesn't own the site of the Anchor Inn and boatyard, which still belongs, as it has belonged for many centuries, to Corpus.

Joan Last of 59 Fallowfield, Cambridge was born nearby in Granta Place, where the University Centre now stands. "I well remember the Old Mill before it was pulled down, and also remember it being pulled down. Laundress Green was our playground, and I remember the small island which is now part of Darwin College being a mass of buttercups. The cows used to cross the river from the Granta pub and were put on this island to graze. I also remember the houses which were on the site of the Fisher Buildings. I used to play there with Edith Bremner who lived in one of them. I also used to climb the tall tree nearby."

Another of her memories was of the dairy which was behind Miss Asplen's shop. "There was an archway between her shop and Mrs Jones's fruit and veg shop. We used to fetch milk in a jug from the dairy, but from the Mill Lane entrance which was next door to my aunt, Mrs Barker's house. Their house and Mrs Ludman's were pulled down to build the University clubrooms and car park."

The site of Darwin College, founded in 1963, has a fascinating history. Margaret Keynes (née Darwin), in her account of Newnham Grange *A House by the River* explains that, whereas now Newnham millstream flows down past the college to join the main river at Laundress Green, in former days it diverged into another branch before reaching the Mill Pool. Apparently this was at a point about 80 yards to the west of the present bridge, near the east end of the Old Granary. "Here at one time, the stream crossed the line of the present road to the north-west. Nothing now remains to be seen of this ancient branch of the Cam, except the Queens' Ditch which, after making a loop westwards towards Queen's Road, runs north-east to rejoin the main stream of the river at the King's Bridge."

A medieval hermit who collected tolls, corn and coal barges being unloaded at the nearby wharves, and a riverside garden which was a magical playground to young Victorian children, are just some of the romantic associations which are attached to the site of Darwin College at the south western end of Silver Street. John Hamond's map of 1592 shows no buildings on the river bank between Queens' and Newnham Mill, but on a little island, now part of Darwin College there appears a small building, which is believed to be the remains of the hermitage and chapel.

According to Cooper's *Annals of Cambridge*, the bridges and causeway between Cambridge and Barton were in such a state of disrepair in 1399 that King Henry IV granted to John Jaye, the hermit, certain duty on saleable articles passing along the bridges and causeway, in return for his maintenance of the area. In 1406, a similar privilege was given to another hermit, Thomas Kendall and in 1428, the Corporation granted the willows on the causeway to the hermit for the repair of his house and the "slippery and ruinous way near the aforesaid bridges and causeway".

In 1549, the old institution of the hermitage was brought to an end, and the accounts of the town record the sale of the chapel for £11, a "sylver Challys" for 40s, and "the Wyllowes at the Armitage" for 20d. The name Armitage was retained for the strip of ground by the river adjacent to the Small Bridges, and it occurs in many corporation documents from the seventeenth to the nineteenth century, says A. W. Goodman in *A little history of St Botolph's, Cambridge*.

After the hermit left, there is no trace of any building upon the land to the left of the road leading to Newnham Mill until late in the seventeenth century. In 1672, the Corporation leased to Richard Dickenson "the Armitage and void ground beyond the holt towards Newnham Mill" for 21 years.

A. S. Goodman, in 1922, writes that: "from this time onwards there is a constant succession of leases of the two pieces of ground. This part of the river bank gradually became busy with barges, and it is only within living memory that pleasure boats have superseded the freights of coal and corn, and that white flannelled undergraduates have taken the place of grimy barges. When railways came to Cambridge, the action of the university prevented the London and North-Western from building its terminus where Newnham Terrace now stands and the Great Northern from discharging its goods and passengers at the foot of Mill Lane."

A plan of 1698 by David Loggan shows a house, and a small building near it, where Newnham Grange and the old Granary now stand, and early in the eighteenth century rates were paid for "the Causeway house". Further to the west there appears in Loggan the little clump of trees described in Corporation leases as "the holt".

On 17 June 1790, Mr Patrick Beales advertised in the *Cambridge Chronicle* that he had entered on Merchant's Yard at the Small Bridges, lately occupied by Mr French and formerly by Mr Lord, and after holding leases from the Corporation of the whole of the river bank from the bridges to the mill pit, the Beales family were allowed in 1839 to turn the Armitage and land beyond it into freehold. The Armitage was eventually bought in the 1880s from the Beales family by Sir George Howard Darwin, the astronomer son of Charles Darwin.

The memory of the hermit has been preserved in the "Hermitage", the name given to the large house which a Dr Parkinson built at the holt and bequeathed to St John's College. For several years the Hermitage provided temporary accommodation for New Hall before their move to their new building on Huntingdon Road. Now the Hermitage is an integral part of Darwin College.

Before New Hall was based there, the Hermitage next to Newnham Grange was a guest house from the late 1940s until about 1954. This is the last year that Miss Lucy Cragoe was listed as living there and she was the proprietress of the Hermitage Guest House in the 1948 and 1953 Kelly's directories.

Christine Courtney of 9 Shelford Road, Trumpington, lived there for three months when she first moved to Cambridge in February 1949. She remembers that: "The Hermitage was crammed with interesting characters, both town and gown, including two eminent university researchers named Smart and Daft. Many of the guests were accommodated in rooms along Granta Terrace, and only had meals in the Hermitage dining-room which was packed to capacity. Mrs Courtney says that it was after the closure of the hotel that the Hermitage became New Hall.

When Sir George Howard Darwin bought the family house and business place of the Beales, his daughter Gwen Raverat recalls in *Period Piece* that "the house had no name, nor had the road. All that part of Cambridge was simply called Newnham, so my father named it Newnham Grange." Raverat felt that the house was a good investment, but she was sure her father really bought the place because "he fell in love with it and all its romantic associations".

Lady Darwin took to the place with enthusiasm, which was "characteristically brave of her for most mothers would have thought the situation damp, and the river both dangerous and smelly". When the Darwins moved in to Newnham Grange, both the mills were in use. Gwen Raverat said she still now felt there was an unnatural gap in the landscape, where Foster's Mill used to stand before it was pulled down.

We used to spend many hours watching the fat corn-sacks being hauled up by a pulley into the overhanging gable, sometimes from a barge. But more often from the great yellow four-horse wagons, which stood beneath the trapdoor.

Among the numerous incidents remembered by Gwen Raverat about her childhood were the floods that frequently came to Silver Street.

Once, I was taken out of bed and carried down to the front door in my nightgown to see the water covering the road and the Green, when a flood had risen suddenly one night.

(from Gwen Raverat *Period Piece*, Faber & Faber, 1952)

When Gwen Raverat was about nine her mother decided that the one big empty granary remaining on the site should be put to a more useful purpose. It was converted into living accommodation, and named the Old Granary. One of the rooms in the Old Granary is called The Painted Room. It was where Gwen Raverat used to draw and paint. The room is now a Darwin research Fellow's office, but well preserved on the walls are murals by Gwen and her husband Jacques Raverat, a rather fine group of the personalities and dignitories who used to come and visit the house.

Among the tenants, who rented the Old Granary from the Darwins from August 1895 until 1944 when Lady Darwin wanted the house back as a home for her daughter Gwen, were Arthur Christopher Benson, son of the Archbishop of Canterbury and elder brother of E. F. Benson, the novelist. Bertrand Russell also lived there for a while and Louis Clarke, the distinguished archaeologist, made his home there from 1927 to 1938. He was succeeded by Henry Morris, the late chief education officer, who was heart broken when he had to leave. He had furnished the place beautifully to reflect his concept of "gracious living".

Before Darwin College was founded, the family of Richard Pettit, the builders of 50 Halifax Road, did the maintenance and building work for the Darwin family over a number of years. The building business was started by Richard Pettit's late uncles, W. J. Mathie and F. H. Pettit in about 1904. Richard took over their business in 1944. Mr Pettit worked for the late Lady Darwin long before her son, Sir Charles, took over Newnham Grange.

He worked for Gwen Raverat too, and when they did repairs on the riverside of the Old Granary they had to hire a flat boat to stand their ladders on to get to parts of the house. He remembers, too, when Gwen Raverat was seriously ill, he made a contraption for her to pull herself up in bed: "Lady Darwin had a girl student who went berserk while studying and set a fire alight in the middle of four rooms. These fires were put out quickly and we had to make good the damage by redecorating."

After the death of Lady Darwin, Mr Pettit altered Newnham Grange for Sir Charles, Lady Darwin and their family: "One of the rooms was redecorated in gold paint, where all ancestors of the Darwin family were in gilt frames, and above the picture rail in this room was a Wedgwood pattern which we had touched up by a firm of artistic writers."

Three colleges were involved in the foundation of Darwin College: Gonville and Caius, St John's and Trinity. They had announced their intention to found Darwin College in a report by the Council of the Senate of the University of Cambridge in June 1963. Nearly six months before, on 31 December 1962, the death had occurred in Cambridge of Sir Charles Darwin, grandson of *the* Charles Darwin. His home, Newnham Grange and the Old Granary became available because remaining members of his family decided to move from Cambridge.

The plan to acquire the property received the blessing of Lady Darwin, and by the time details of the foundation were announced, the new graduate college had a name and a site. It now has 300 graduate students, of whom one third are women and 40 per cent come from overseas. The college has been physically fashioned out of three houses with some careful in-filling. Some of the best features of the Hermitage and Newnham Grange have been preserved and it is possible to recapture the atmosphere of Darwin family life in some of the college quiet rooms, which have preserved the dignity of the drawing room. The gardens by the river are a delight.

Revisited

Thirty years on, and I am back at Queens' College to talk once more to Dr Robin Walker who supervises computer science students at the College. However, although he is due to retire as Junior Bursar and Director of Studies in Computer Science at the end of September 2014, he will be taking on the role of part-time Estate Bursar, responsible for the major building projects for the College estate.

He is still wearing his Junior Bursar's hat, only this time he is no longer in his Rapunzel turret over the gatehouse in Old Court, having moved to a large office in a building dating from 1756 overlooking the river by the Mathematical Bridge.

It is not a quiet spot. Double glazing fails to drown out the screams and shrieks of the young visitors attempting to punt up and down the river, poles flailing beneath the windows as they barge into each other. Dr Walker and his secretary Lorraine Loftus seem immune to the noisy chaos.

What have been the changes? "Well", says Dr Walker, coming straight to the point, "On the south side of Silver Street, east of The Anchor there is almost no life now. The Anchor and the Café Aristo, the latest incarnation of the coffee shop at the corner of Laundress Lane are the only signs of life!" At the other end of Laundress Lane a sign on the wall nearest the river says: "No thoroughfare for carriages and horses 24 March 1857."

Dr Walker as a first-year undergraduate at Queens' experienced the lodging house system first hand. He was in lodgings with a lady in Thoday Street, off Mill Road, and paid her two shillings to have a bath! Unlike Peter Watson (see Adams Road chapter) who lived close by in lodgings in Newnham, when he was an undergraduate, and came into college for a bath in his dressing gown on the bus – that would have been too far for Dr Walker!

Dr Robin Walker, junior bursar of Queens' College, photograph taken by the Alumni & Development Office at their Alumni Weekend in the summer of 2014. There was a dinner later that evening at Queens' in honour of Dr Walker's retirement.

Queens'
President's Lodge
– originally an
East Anglian
plaster building
with the timber
frames encased
in the plaster
lining.

Dr Walker concludes that from the late 1970s a lot of things changed in Cambridge: "The Cambridge Phenomenon and the development of the Science Park resulted in young, relatively wealthy people moving into the city and squeezing people out. A lot of properties that had been in the rental market were bought up, and the rental market dried up. The University abolished the lodging house system in 1992." The former Lodging Houses Syndicate offices, together with the buildings right up to what used to be the Pitt Press are owned by the University. Nos. 16–21 are occupied by the University's Department of Land Economy.

The Department of Applied Mathematics and Theoretical Physics (DAMTP), was housed in the Pitt Press building, which used to be the warehouse of the Cambridge University Press Printing operation. But they moved to the Centre for Mathematical Sciences (CMS) in Clarkson Road in 2000, along with the Department of Pure Mathematics, which was based between Silver Street and Mill Lane. When the academics moved out, the University spent a lot of money refurbishing the building for their administrative staff. Then a hotchpotch of small University administrative offices and departments moved in to what is now called No. 17 Mill Lane.

Dr Walker explains: "You are seeing a general shift by University departments from the city centre into west Cambridge. Material Science has moved out to the very end of the West Cambridge site, beyond the Veterinary School. Microsoft Cambridge has moved to Station Road, and the building they have vacated on the West site has been taken over by the Computing Department, formerly in Corn Exchange Street."

Dr Walker asks his secretary and me: "What happened exactly ten years ago, 6 August 2003, in fact?" I start thinking of the Iraq war … No, what he had in mind was the installation of the bollards in Silver Street! Clearly it was a bad day for Queens' College staff. "It makes it more difficult for us to get in and out of college. We now have buses running up and down Silver Street. The University subsidises a bus service, the UNI 4 which runs between Madingley Road Park and Ride through the West Cambridge site down Grange Road, along West Road, Silver Street and on to Addenbrooke's. But there are in fact two No. 4 buses, as another No. 4 runs from some outer villages into Cambridge." Confusing!

Queens' Mathematical Bridge in winter.

Whereas in the past, before the advent of the bollards, the coaches bringing tourists to Cambridge used to pull up opposite Darwin College, discharging the hordes beside Queens' Green. Now they park on the Backs. The tourists beat that well-worn path up Silver Street past the new Queens' Porter's Lodge, opened Easter 2013, before stopping to take photographs of one of the most iconic views of Cambridge, the Wooden Bridge and the oldest building on the river dating from 1460. The "Please Keep Off" sign on the new flowerbed by the railings does not deter them. They are determined to get their camera lenses through those railings!

What used to be the Porter's Lodge in Queens' Lane, is now the visitors entrance. The admission charge is £2.50 (30 years ago it was 25p!) and there is now a souvenir shop attached. Building a new Porter's Lodge fronting Silver Street, and restricting the old one to the visitors' entrance, has enabled the college to control the flow of visitors, but will an entrance fee deter those who just want to wander around? "It doesn't make us much money," said Dr Walker.

A feature of the new Lodge is a wrought iron, bronze screen by the letter cutter Lida Kindersley, the widow of the letter carver and typeface designer David Kindersley. Other new buildings at Queens' include an entirely new floor on top of Cripps Court, and Lyon Court which was opened by the late Queen Mother in 1989. I was at the opening of Lyon Court, and remember the Queen Mother's endearing faux pas as she pulled the cord to unveil the plaque: "I declare this Town Hall open", she said. Nobody batted an eyelid!

When refurbishing work was carried out on the College's dining hall, the main task involved cleaning off the nicotine!

Out on the narrow pavement, on the north side of Silver Street, keeping a prudent eye out for cohorts of tourists, whizzing cyclists and buses, including the topless tourist ones, we reach Mr Polito's, the smart barber's, who have occupied

Darwin College: the Old Granary and Study Centre at night.

for twenty years what was Haslop's, the butchers. Proprietor Reno Polito claims it has the feel of a gentlemen's club: "I do believe we have the best barber shop in Cambridge!", he claims on his website. I think there might be other contenders! In addition to traditional cuts, other services at Mr Polito's include beard trims, complete restyles, and even a cut-throat razor shave if you're getting ready for an extra special occasion – sounds like Sweeney Todd! The shop feels cosy though, and you don't have to book.

Dr Walker leads the way to Ede and Ravenscroft, founded in 1689, the classic menswear and bespoke tailor's shop at 70–72 Trumpington Street on the corner of Silver Street. He points out the Queens' College coat of arms picked out on the building in bright colours. This is a property that no longer belongs to Queens'. But it is the heritage that counts. After all, Queens' would have started in Trumpington Street in 1446, if the other site had not become available.

Darwin College, 50 years old this year, and twinned with Wolfson College, Oxford, has in the manner of a game of Monopoly, put together a great collection of quality, period buildings, including eighteenth-century industrial buildings and nineteenth-century townhouses mostly on its main site in Silver Street. To these it has added some award-winning twentieth-century buildings. Its latest new building is the Study Centre and Library, built in 1994 with a wonderful view of the river. It claims to have one of the longest collegiate riverfronts and it has two private islands. What more could you ask for!

Of its fine collection of portraits of the Darwin family, and the college's Masters and benefactors which hang on the walls in the heart of the site, my favourite is the portrait of Charles Darwin painted in 1875 by the artist Walter William Ouless. You could mistake it for a Rembrandt, such is the depth of his musing gaze. I keep finding excuses to nip into the college to look at it!

Dr Mary Fowler, Master of the college, pays tribute to the Darwin family in the article "Looking Back", her contribution to *Darwin College: a 50th anniversary portrait*:

"As a college, Darwin is extraordinarily fortunate to be formed on the basis of the Darwin family home, and we are most grateful for the generosity of the Darwin family and their strong support for us. Ever since Professor (Sir) George Darwin purchased Newnham Grange as his family home, this has been a place to think and enquire."

Her great-grandparents lived just across Queen's Road in Newnham Cottage, and her grandfather, Sir Ralph Howard Fowler, worked very closely and was good friends with Sir Charles Galton Darwin.

Portrait of Charles Darwin, painted in 1875 by the artist Walter William Ouless.

"My father and siblings could almost claim to be amongst the first Darwin students, for in the late 1920s some went to school in the Malting House, now part of our college. Teaching methods were somewhat unorthodox – my very young father seems to have spent most of his time with a bunsen burner! His school report approvingly describes a pyromaniac, while an aunt recalls gardening and dissection. The school's founder, the extraordinary Geoffrey Pyke, had advertised in *Nature* for a teacher, so it's not surprising that science was encouraged.

My own arrival at the College was – it feels only yesterday – just over 40 years ago. Darwin seemed a very exotic place to me, a shy 22-year-old having seen little more than the inside of a maths lecture theatre, and not knowing anything much at all about the earth sciences prior to starting my Ph.D. in the Department of Geodesy and Geophysics.

This was a college of people who walked barefoot across Greenland or quoted Gladstone on Homer's wine-dark sea. I was rapidly shipped off to a research ship in the eastern Mediterranean, and then, on my return, ordered to write a 'News and Views' for *Nature* about a completely different area, the Philippine Sea. Nowadays, all that seems extraordinary – both health and safety, and the intense competition to get into *Nature* prohibit!

Science, then in the troubled economy of the 1970s, had not much money. I recall one problem: we didn't know the orientation of the seismometers when they landed on the ocean floor some three kilometres down. Spending substantial amounts on equipment to work at those depths was impossible, so I simply poured boiling hot jelly ('jell-o' to North Americans) into a cylinder containing an exposed compass needle. When it set on the sea floor, the direction was recorded. As has often been said of British science, we hadn't got the money, so we had to think!"

The grounds of Darwin College in early September.

NEWNHAM ROAD

12 March 1981

"I love Newnham better than any part of Cambridge," says Newnham resident Mr H. E. Askham when speaking of the Margaret Rose sweet shop in Newnham Road.

Such an affectionate outburst would strike a chord in the hearts of many of the elderly residents who grew up in the rural rides round old Newnham village, built on that historic stretch of meadowlands which includes Newnham Mill, itself one of the focal points for the vital commercial activity of Cambridge in those days before the railway arrived.

The Newnham Mill flooded in 1947.

Driving along
Newnham Road
in the floods of
1947.

James Owen, vicar of Little St Mary's whose vicarage is at 4 Newnham Terrace, tells a little of the Newnham story: "This is a very ancient part of Cambridge. A medieval hermit had the right of toll on the small island of what is now Darwin College. For an anti-traffic man, who rides a bicycle across the Fen to his church, it is appropriate that James Owen should tell how the station nearly came to Newnham.

"In 1842, they wanted to build a railway. Two local sites were proposed. One suggestion was Granta Place, where the Graduate Centre is. The alternative was Newnham Terrace. They were going to run the trains along the Backs – an appalling thought – but it was logical because the commercial centre was located round Little St Mary's and the Mill Pool. But the University resisted the idea and the station was sited further out and denied a second platform."

The trains didn't come to Newnham, but the horse-drawn trams did. And horse-drawn tram travel was a dashed slow business, according to Gwen Raverat, granddaughter of Charles Darwin in *Period Piece*.

When her mother, Maud Darwin, returned to Cambridge from shopping trips in London, she used to come back from the station in the slow old tram, which went swinging and clanking along behind its one ancient horse. What with changing "at the Roman Catholic" and waiting there for the other tram, she could well have walked home in the same time. "Racing the tram was a Cambridge sport; a running child could beat it easily", she wrote.

Later of course, Gwen Raverat took to driving around in a small car, as Mrs Gladys Futter who runs the shoe shop in Newnham Road vividly recalls: "As a small child I remember seeing Gwen Raverat driving down from Barton." After her stroke Gwen Raverat used to sit out sketching on the Fen, and was a familiar sight to Newnham residents.

Ludovic Stewart, the former county music advisor, whose family has been associated with the Malting House in Newnham Road since the early 1900s, recalls how annoyed his father, Dr Hugh Stewart, was when those trams were removed. "The tram used to take him across to Trinity where he was a don."

The Malting House, a late 18th century structure, was originally a malthouse, oast house and small brewery, owned in the 1830s, by the Beales family – a well-known Cambridge trading dynasty. The brewery only lasted 30 years, one of 12 breweries in Cambridge which vanished in a relatively short space of time. The Newnham Malting House was then converted into a granary. In 1903, the Rev. H. F. Stewart, then Dean of Trinity College bought the buildings and converted most of them into an Arts and Crafts house to the designs of architects Smith and Brewer.

In more recent times, cultural history has been made at the Malting House, where a glimpse at the Stewart family's visitors books show that a stream of European intellectuals – composers, poets, philosophers visited the house. The famous German violinist Joseph Joachim was one of the first visitors. He was staying with the Pemberton family at Trumpington Hall, and came to plant a tree in the garden of the house that came to be renowned for its patronage of the arts, and music in particular.

Before the famous playroom was turned into an assembly room in 1912, and thereafter used by the Quakers, who licensed it for weddings, it was used by Morris dancers, and latterly the School Holiday Orchestra. It was also lent to the Archaeological Museum for the storage of Egyptian mummies and housed the Welsh Guards during the First World War. In 1918, it was converted into a concert/recital hall where much of the University's musical life took place.

Other eminent visitors included Albert Schweitzer who lectured there, Alban Berg, Zoltán Kodály (several times), Vaughan Williams who, like other visiting composers, signed the book with a few bars of music, and T. S. Eliot, whom "Granny Stewart" drove over to Little Gidding.

Under the Stewart family ownership, the building and its garden between 1924–7 became the Malting House School, founded by Geoffrey Pyke who wanted a childhood and education free of trauma for his only son, David. He appointed the educational pioneer, Susan Isaacs to run the school. She had answered his advertisement which said: "WANTED – an Educated Young Woman with honours for a group of children aged 2½–7, as a piece of scientific work and research."

Perhaps the children who studied and sometimes dissected animals at the Malting House School would have come into contact with the herds of cows belonging to Mott, the dairyman who had his farm at No. 51 Newnham Road. Before they lived there, the Mott family lived at No. 26 Newnham Road, next to the Malting House. Contemporary memories in Newnham have no difficulty in recalling Mr Mott driving his cows down to the Mill Pond.

At the age of 75, Mr Albert Rhodes of No. 51 Selwyn Road, remembers how his eldest brother Fred, "Snowy" Rhodes (they were a family of seven children), used to drive Mott's cows across the Mill Pond.

Wallis Mott's daughter, Mrs Margaret Butler lives in Histon, she and her husband having recently retired from running Haslops butchers in Silver Street. Mrs Butler recalls how she used to help her father with his Newnham milk round: "I used to run around with the old float, and when we brought the cows back across the Mill Pond and up Newnham Road, we used to hold up all the traffic. My ducks and hens used to follow behind."

Ludovic Stewart, who is 73, remembers Mott's when it was at No. 26: "It always had a lovely basket of eggs in the window. Old Mr Mott used to have a parrot". During the First World War, Mr Stewart recalls Mrs Mott coming into the garden of the Malting House to cry on his mother's shoulder. She had just heard that her son had been killed. In recent years, No. 26 has also been a doctor's surgery. Mrs Joyce Stewart worked there for Dr Jennens.

Generations of children have played around the Mill, sometimes with tragic consequences. Mr Rhodes' sister, Mrs Nellie Norris of No. 17 Selwyn Road

The Newnham Road grocer's shop and off-licence.

Newnham Road in 1925 showing the Granta pub and Queen's Garage.

spoke of the time when "one little boy, Reggie Argent, was drowned in the Mill race when he was trying to get his sailor's cap which had fallen in".

Among the vanished sites of old Newnham village, which has preserved some of its magic in spite of the traffic that has scythed through it, are two local pubs which locals remember: the Coach and Horses on the corner by the Causewayside flats on Fen Causeway (the landlord was a tiny little man called Ben Clark) and the Tally-Ho right next to where the school used to be.

Flourishing local shops include Rhodes the florists and Natural Gems Ltd., where for a bit of pocket money children can buy beads and stones and make their own necklaces and rings. The manageress, Mrs Barbara Parker, will show you how!

Although old Newnham, or Newnham proper as one might call it, never had a parish church or a squire to make it easily identifiable as a village (it has been shared between the parishes of Little St Mary's and St Botolph's until parish boundary reorganisation in 1940 brought it under the wing of St Botolph's), there has always been some confusion in people's minds as to what is really Newnham.

Until 1925, it had its own infants' school on the site of Cocks' filling station. The Rhodes family all went there. Albert Rhodes recalls: "It was run by the two Miss Brittains. There were three classes in what was an L-shaped building."

His sisters say that the school was very strict, and they remember that one day one of the teachers tied a boy to a chair and his mother came to complain. If you wanted a drink of water you had to ask for the key to turn the tap. Albert

Rhodes must have been a robust little boy. He still remembers going across to the Newnham Mill and climbing up the trees to get the swallows' eggs.

Today, Sweeney Todd's – the pizza parlour at the Mill – have made the Mill race a visual feature of the establishment. Next door at the Jolly Millers public-house, history was made centuries ago when Queen Elizabeth I changed horses there, when it was the millers' house, on the occasion of her visit to Cambridge on 5 August 1564. She had spent the previous night in Haslingfield in the house of one of her Gentlemen Pensioners, and rode into Cambridge through Grantchester and Newnham.

Miss Gladys Barton, aged 75, who lives in the Perse Almshouses at No. 5, is a lifelong Newnham resident, and former pupil of the school. She remembers Miss Brittain's black velvet handbag full of the jelly sweets she liked to eat. Miss Barton was friends with the school cleaner and they used to hunt for dropped jelly sweets underneath the desks.

Another Almshouse resident at No. 2, is Mrs Maud Neal, who used to work in the linen room at Gonville and Caius College. Now, so Archdeacon Long, rector of St Botolph's, tells me: "she washes our purificators (church linen)". The Longs

Newnham College staff in 1896.

live right by the Almshouses in St Botolph's Rectory, built in Summerfield, off Newnham Road, on the site of the old orchard in 1934. The rectory wasn't used for many years as Archdeacon Long explains: "When the Rev. C. T. Wood was appointed vicar in 1940, he had been Dean of Queens' and had his own house in Brookside, so it wasn't used as a rectory until 1960 when it became the residence of the Archdeacon of Ely, Michael Carey."

The Summerfield corner with its rural outlook is a popular Newnham spot. The folk in the Almshouses enjoy looking across to what is now known as the Lammas Land recreation centre. Kite-flying, bowls, tennis, paddling, picnics and homing pigeons – all the country pursuits take place there.

If you amble up Summerfield, peep into the rectory garden and admire the crocuses and snowdrops in the springtime, then follow round past the Gonville and Caius playing field where the clock on the pavilion will always keep you right, you can then walk along Church Rate Walk, where once, the children – now men and women in their 70s – used to play in what they called "The Trees".

At Kingfisher Cottage in Church Rate Walk, Mr Leonard Hoskison gave us an impromptu piano lesson and a session in wildlife. My children were thrilled by his collection of kingfishers – stuffed, on tea towels and on paper weights. Local birdwatchers know that kingfishers are to be seen on occasions: streaks of turquoise flashing down the Backs and through Newnham.

Turn right at the end of Church Rate Walk and you find yourself in gaslit Malting Lane, leading back down to Newnham Road. Previously known as Froshlake Way, it was originally the main route that led towards Coton across the west fields owned in the main since medieval times by the colleges. This was the main track in and out of west Cambridge, as can be seen on early maps of the area. On the Corpus Terrier[3] of circa 1360, it is shown as Froshlake Way and the Coton Path. The Baker Map of Cambridge 1830, shows it as a "Foot Path". (Etymologists will know that "frosh" has two meanings: it is the Dutch word for frog, and is slang for a college freshman!). Were the Dutch, the later drainers of the Fens, living here in the Middle Ages and that is how it got the name "frosh"?

Turn left at the end of Church Rate Walk and you will find yourself in Newnham Walk, which leads to what used to be the main entrance of Newnham College. A public footpath, running from the end of Malting Lane through to Grange Road and enshrined in the Enclosure ward of 1805, bisected the college site.

The construction of Sidgwick Avenue was the result of a campaign by Newnham College to close that public footpath. This footpath was highly inconvenient for the college, and could only be closed if an alternative route were offered. There was apparently considerable local and collegiate opposition (Fellows losing parts of their gardens, that sort of thing) to the plan to build Sidgwick Avenue; local residents opposed it vehemently, and it was fiercely debated in the local paper. It was eventually built, however, in 1893 – Newnham College chipping in towards the cost.

---

[3] A terrier is a record system for an institution's land and property holdings.

A Newnham College student's room in 1890.

The original entrance to the college was through the Pfeiffer gatehouse at the end of Newnham Walk. Peep through into the grounds and a great visual treat will await you. It is like coming upon a secret garden.

It is where, between 1874 and 1910, the college architect, Basil Champneys designed, in the words of Mark Girouard, "a series of 'Queen Anne' buildings of delicate and intimate prettiness, grouped with comfortable informality round an immense tree-studded lawn." This quote is taken from Girouard's book *Sweetness and Light – The Queen Anne Movement 1869–1900*. This lyrical description captures to a tee the beauty of the grounds of the college with its red brick Champneys buildings on three sides. Curving bay and oriel windows stacked on top of each other on some of the buildings, and curly pedimented gables together with the steep roofs on others are among the eye-catching feature of the Newnham architecture,

In *A Room of One's Own*, Virgina Woolf describes how "The gardens … lay before me in the spring twilight, wild and open, and in the long grass, sprinkled and carelessly flung, were daffodils and bluebells, not orderly perhaps at the best of times, and now wind-blown and waving as they tugged at their roots. The windows of the building, curved like ships' windows among generous waves of red brick, changed from lemon to silver under the flight of the quick spring clouds." What a gorgeous description of the Newnham College gardens.

And that is just the colourful gardens! What about its blue-stocking students? One generation after another, since 1871 when the college was founded, have achieved greatness in so many fields.

When I visited Newnham ten years ago, on the occasion of the college's centenary celebrations, I wrote in an article published in *The Times* on 4 October 1971, that: "The young, liberated women undergraduates of Cambridge who sport Pocahontas hair-dos and belong to Scarlet Women, the Newnham College based women's lib cell, might think very eccentric and comic the restrictions placed on their Victorian and Edwardian counterparts. But some of their predecessors who were 'up' in the early part of the century with unclouded memories of cycles and chaperones, recall that they did not feel restricted, but rather more excited at being able to come up to the university at all." Surely, that is the key point about the history of Newnham.

Scholastic prowess at the College dates back to the early days when women were first informally admitted to the tripos exams, but long before they could claim degree status. That came in 1948.

As I wrote in 1971: "it has been said that the 'death blow' to the doubters who cast aspersions on the academic ability of women, was struck in 1890 when the name of a Newnham student, Miss Philippa Fawcett, was read in the Senate House as 'above the Senior Wrangler,' the top mathematician in the mathematics tripos.

"The event was celebrated by a dinner in Hall and afterwards the student friends decorated the doorway with lamps, lit a bonfire at the western end of the college grounds and carried the brilliant mathematician around it. Her tutor was called upon to make a speech.

"The name of Philippa Fawcett, who subsequently went out to help organise education in the Transvaal would come to mind as one of the best known scholars of the college. The college itself would select also Jane Harrison, a classical scholar as pioneer of myth, Rebecca Saunders, the botanist and geneticist, Marjorie Stephenson, one of the founders of microbiology and Dorothy Garrod, the archaeologist and first woman professor in Cambridge."

NEWNHAM ROAD

Revisited

I f you hadn't been back to Cambridge for 30 years, and found yourself standing by the Mill Pond in Newnham Road looking across the fenlands, your heart would surely lift, and you would experience a sense of well-being. Why? Well, because the uninterrupted view of rural, bucolic Sheep's Green and Coe Fen, where the cattle still graze, has not changed since you were last here – there is something timeless about this vista.

The Residents Association of Old Newnham (RAON) plays its part in helping to preserve these priceless green open spaces and the uninterrupted view (when the trees are not in full leaf), across to Peterhouse, which forms a boundary to the city. Together with other campaigners, including Professor Stephen Hawking and comedian and television presenter, Griff Rhys Jones, RAON won their fight to block construction of a three-storey extension to the Double Tree Hilton Hotel in Granta Place (formerly the Garden House Hotel). The original application was for a four-storey building, which was turned down the first time round in July 2010.

More than 800 petitioners opposed the second application, a three-storey extension which would have included 31 extra bedrooms and a new leisure centre at the hotel, which was eventually rejected at appeal. Planning inspector Simon Berkeley said the extension would block views of Cambridge from Sheep's Green and Coe Fen, detracting "from the pleasure to be had by lingering to appreciate the more panoramic views of the historic centre. Protruding substantially into an area otherwise largely comprising green open space, it would stand out and appear intrusive."

Jane Singleton, chairman of RAON, said at the time of the appeal that the hotel's extension would have blocked the view – effectively drawing a heavy curtain – between Coe Fen and Sheep's Green. "These two ancient fenlands are an integral part of the fingers of green which penetrate the city. They are not parks, but are uncultivated areas which bring the country – and the cows – right to the city's centre."

The inspector rejected the appeal more than a year ago, but the Double Tree Hilton Hotel refused to take no for an answer, and submitted a further application to expand the site. Residents voted overwhelmingly to oppose this latest hotel application. Many have written letters to the City Council's planning department. A petition was signed by among others, Julian Huppert MP, who also wrote a letter of objection. The City Council Planning Committee has since turned down this latest application.

Artist and architect David Owers lives and works in the Oast House in Malting Lane. Also a RAON member, he challenged the hotel's plans from the outset. He

View across the Mill Pond to Sheep's Green.

tells me that during the first three months of 2010, he was concerned to shift the debate from the already chequered history of the appearance of the hotel to the wider issue of its river setting. He lobbied widely then to raise the level of awareness that the tranquillity of the meadows and the flood plain landscape were at stake, plus the relationship between Sheep's Green, Coe Fen and the unique city edge, formed by the ancient walling of Peterhouse. He added: "It remains of overriding importance for the future to actively conserve and monitor approaches that lead into the heart of the city."

David Owers came to Cambridge in 1964 to join the architectural practice of the University Professor of Architecture, Sir Leslie Martin, and later he and a colleague became partners, staying with Sir Leslie for 12 years. They then set up a new partnership in 1976 and looked around to find new premises. Two years later, the Malting and Oast House came on the market, and Owers and Lumley Architects bought the Oast House from the Stewart family, converting the building into studios for their practice. In 1989, the practice became David Owers Associates and then, at the millennium he began to concentrate more on his oil painting.

View up Maltings Lane leading to Newnham Walk.

He and his wife Jan have lived "over and under the shop" as it were, since 1991, in premises that had been part of the former brewery and later a granary. An overhead gantry ran from Newnham Mill, allowing flour to be ferried across. You

can see the marks on the wall openings where the beer once loaded into barrels was hoisted out of the lower ground floor. The massive pine beams supporting the middle floor were probably shipped in from Norway, he thinks, and an early hand pump for sludge clearance can also be seen. Outside there is a secluded garden enclosed by a fine crinkle crankle wall, with the distinctive concertina look of such walls and having, he believes, solid East Anglian origins.

Half of the architectural office is now leased to the architects Moses Cameron Williams; it is part of the space where Susan Isaacs had run the Malting House School from 1924 until the financial crash of 1929. David Owers pointed out the gallery where the school's stenographers had sat recording every exchange between the young pupils at the school as they dissected animals, played with fire, and carried out basic experiments off their own bat, experiments designed to foster their intellectual growth through discovery, reasoning and thought. Everything they said was noted down – later to be the basis for Isaacs' two significant books in the 1930s. It was all part of the Montessori-type ethos of the place.

He also tells the story of how in September 1984, the organisers of the Mont Pelerin Society's biannual conference announced that it was to be held that year in Cambridge at Queens' College and asked if he and his partner would host a small sherry party at the Oast House for the conference's senior delegates. Among the guests was Professor Friedrich Hayek, the most distinguished economist of his generation who in 1940–42 had lived at the Oast House and written his seminal book *The Road to Serfdom* there. Whilst standing centrally with colleagues in the studio, sipping the Owers' sherry, and tucking into the nibbles, Dr Hayek recalled how: "My library and desk was over there and beyond, under the gallery, there was my bed. I would lie down occasionally and visualise Adolf Hitler strung up from the roof tie rods. It spurred on my writing!"

But let's revisit Newnham College up the road. Reel forward from those early days to the inter- and post-war eras, and you find Newnham graduates continue to be household names. Take just those endowed with literary and journalistic talent such as Margaret Drabble and her sister A. S. Byatt, Sylvia Plath, Emma Thompson, Germaine Greer, Katharine Whitehorn and Clare Balding to pluck just a handful out of the academic ether. And on the science side, one cannot miss out Rosalind Franklin, the famous X-ray crystallographer. A college building is named after her.

As Frances Hazlehurst, the College secretary tells me over a cup of tea in the Senior Combination Room, beautifully decorated with Watts & Co. wallpaper: "Newnham was founded as a college for the education of women with an all-female Fellowship. The college provides an extremely supportive environment where students are encouraged to aim high. Students see that as a great source of strength. They are also genuinely involved in the running of the college, working together with senior members."

And what is the ethos of the college today? How much has it changed? Let the authors of *Newnham College – the alternative prospectus* set out their stall to would-be undergraduates of whom there are now 400, plus 240 graduate students.

Newnham College gardens in the spring showing Sidgwick Hall in the foreground with Clough Hall behind. Peile is just visible lower left.

Things to do and not to do at Newnham. They list 15. Here is a selection:

Do not have an essay crisis whilst sunbathing;
Don't suggest making the garden into a car park;
Do fall asleep on the window seat in the library;
Do watch fireworks from Strachey roof;
Don't ride a motorbike down the corridor saying – Emma Thompson did it!;
Do go punting at midnight; and Do whatever you like – this is Newnham!

Back now to old Newnham to talk to another active campaigner. He is Michael Nedo, the German born director of the Wittgenstein Archive, in Cambridge. He has lived in the house called "Church Rate Corner," since 1986. His home was built in 1924 for Marjorie Wilson Duckett to the design of the architect Baillie Scott (see Storey's Way) and is one of the last in the style of his Arts and Crafts period. It is Grade II listed.

The story goes that Marjorie Wilson Duckett grew up at the top of Storey's Way when she met Baillie Scott as he was building No. 83. When she married a Fellow of Queens' College called Sewell she commissioned Baillie Scott to build the house for them. Their two children were born there. Later the Bennett family lived there. He was H. Stanley Bennett, his wife Joan Bennett was a fellow of Girton and they were both members of the English Faculty.

Church Rate Corner is a beautiful period house with Cotswold style gables. It faces south and is surrounded by an enclosed garden on three sides which was also planned by Baillie Scott. To the east is the original orchard walk now lined with hazels. A narrow raised stone terrace along the south of the house is edged with a wide herbaceous border beyond. On a summer afternoon, the lavender and roses in the garden contribute to an atmosphere of paradise!

Dr Nedo, who is a veteran campaigner against building developments not in keeping with the character of the area, sees himself as "a custodian – not so much the owner of Church Rate Corner". One of the battles which he lost was against the diocese of Ely who wanted to, and succeeded in, building a mock-Baillie Scott house, now the new Vicarage of Little St Mary's at the bottom of the back garden of Summerfield Rectory, right up against the garden wall of Church Rate Corner.

There is some evidence that Sylvia Plath and Ted Hughes used to meet in that part of the garden, which was a bit of a wilderness, for trysts from time to time. Ted Hughes often stayed in the Rectory garden as his friend, fellow American Lucas Myers lived in a hut there. As told by Elaine Feinstein in *Ted Hughes: The Life of a Poet* (Phoenix Paperback, Weidenfeld and Nicolson, 2001), the story goes that Myers had advertised in the University newspaper *Varsity* for some kind of shed and had been answered on 19 February 1955 by Mrs Helen Hitchcock, the widow of the former rector of St Botolph's.

"She had been allowed to remain in the rectory after the death of her husband and lived by letting rooms to four or five students and an au pair. She was able to offer Myers the hut in her garden rent free, with light, an electric fire and a radiator, in return for the stoking of two fires – an Aga cooking stove and a Sentry

Church Rate Corner, the house designed by the architect Baillie Scott.

boiler." The hut had once been used as a chicken coop and the smell, in spite of washing and painting, had never quite gone away. "The first time Hughes stayed in the hut, he insisted on sleeping on the floor. He admitted no discomfort at the time, but later spoke of the impossibility of getting the smell of chicken droppings out of his green jumper." On a subsequent visit to Cambridge in 1955, he bought a tent and pitched it in the large Rectory garden filled with fruit trees.

Church Rate Corner was built in the orchard of what was a large house and estate called "Plas Dinas" in Malting Lane. Built early in the nineteenth century and enlarged later in the mid-1800s, Plas Dinas and its substantial gardens and orchard are shown on a map related to a sale in about 1880. Before that, according to Michael Nedo, it seems that these grounds were an orchard to the nunnery on the site of what is now the Sidgwick site in Sidgwick Avenue.

The Spalding Street Directories show that in 1884 the Reverend Thomas Herbert Orpen, late Fellow of Pembroke College and vicar of All Saints was living there; by 1887, it was the home of Henry Chester Goodhart, a fellow of Trinity College. Originally one house and stables, it was later divided into three properties consisting of "Little Newnham", "Frostlake Cottage" and "The Loft", originally the stables of Plas Dinas, the big house.

By 1907, Richard Dacre Archer-Hind, Greek scholar and Fellow of Trinity College, lived in Little Newnham, the part of the original house facing south towards Church Rate Walk. He loved his garden, and kept an exact record of the rare plants which it contained. After her husband's death in 1910, Mrs Laura Archer-Hind continued to live there for many years. The street directory for 1935 lists her there, but by 1938 the Bursar of Corpus Christi College, Patrick Charvet, was in residence. For many years, the house continued to be the home of senior members of Corpus and their families.

Little Newnham is no longer a family home for Corpus dons. Like many houses in west Cambridge which were once homes for academics and their families, it has been divided into two flats: Little Newnham 1 and 2.

However, a plan by the college to sell off part of the grounds of Little Newnham to a developer, who planned to build a house on the site, was turned down on appeal by the planning inspector – much to the relief of local neighbours, who had made their views known in a trenchant manner.

Another development which brought local residents of Old Newnham together in campaigning mode when it was first proposed, was Clare College's scheme for postgraduate accommodation on Newnham Road in Cambridge's Central Conservation Area. The first set of proposals were turned down; amendments were then made and the revised scheme was approved unanimously by Cambridge City Council in January 2011.

The approved scheme has seen existing poor quality buildings demolished on what was an abandoned brown field site with derelict cars and lock-up garages, and replaced by a new terraced garden building to the rear of the site and an extension to the Victorian terrace, Nos. 46–52 which fronts Newnham Road. Altogether, there will be 32 graduate student rooms and flats on the site.

There seems to be general agreement among local residents that Clare College listened to their concerns about the development and met some of their objections. David Owers liaised with the college and architects employed on the scheme. His garden is relatively close to the new buildings, but shady trees will give protection.

Sitting with Lucy Adrian in the garden of her home, "Frostlake Cottage" (which she says was the "back quarter of Plas Dinas"), looking across to the roof of the new Clare garden building, you can see that the reduction of its height from the original plan has made quite a difference. No longer a big warehouse shape rearing up and dominating the south facing view, it has been reduced to two storeys at the west end, and it tapers down into a much less obtrusive building. To Lady Adrian's relief, the college has maintained a substantial ash tree on the site, which provides shade to her enclosed garden. Cooperation and sensitive compromise appear to have won the day with the handling of this scheme by Clare College's Bursar, Donald Hearn and his team. It doesn't always have to be a full-scale battle then when it comes to developments in west Cambridge!

Those interested in archaeology will be intrigued to know that preparatory building excavations for the Clare scheme, behind Nos. 34–38 Newnham Road during February 2006, found evidence of a medieval pond in the backyard. At different levels beneath No. 36, excavations exposed the foundations of what were probably a series of 17th century tenements fronting Newnham Road. Going deeper, according to a report by Cambridge Archaeological Unit, "there were traces of a sixteenth-century (or earlier) timbered house. Below this, a layer of garden soil containing shards of fifteenth-century coarse ware suggested a still earlier phase of intensive backyard cultivations, perhaps connected with medieval dwellings on Malting Lane and Elde Newenham Weye (Newnham Road)."

Perhaps Ludwig Wittgenstein sat out in the garden of Frostlake Cottage in the early summer of 1929 when he was living as a lodger with Maurice Dobb and his wife. He was friends at the time with the famous literary critic F. R. Leavis, and working desperately hard apparently, and was chronically short of sleep. On one occasion, when they were out walking together until after midnight, Wittgenstein was so exhausted that on their way back to Malting House Lane he could hardly walk without the support of Leavis's arm. When they finally reached Frostlake Cottage, Leavis implored him to go to bed at once. "You don't understand", he replied. "When I'm engaged on a piece of work I'm always afraid I shall die before I've finished it. So I make a fair copy of the day's work, and give it to Frank Ramsey for safekeeping. I haven't made today's copy".

Fellow Emerita of Newnham College, Lucy Adrian has lived at Frostlake Cottage since 1992 when her husband, the late Lord Adrian, retired as Master of Pembroke College. They had bought Frostlake Cottage in 1982 from the family of Stephen Roskill, the naval historian who died in Cambridge that year. Before that the Adrians had lived at No. 3 Adams Road.

Norwegian born Erin Page from Oslo, who has lived at Ashton House in Newnham Road since the 1960s, is the widow of Professor Raymond Page, who died aged 87, in 2012. He was the Emeritus Professor of Anglo Saxon at the

University of Cambridge and was the world's leading expert on, and decipherer of, runes, the angular lettering originally used by Germanic tribes on the edge of the Roman Empire.

While at Corpus he served, from 1965 to 1991, as Fellow Librarian of the college's Parker Library, which houses the outstanding collection of medieval manuscripts and early printed books, bequeathed by the sixteenth-century Protestant Archbishop Matthew Parker. Parker had stipulated that his legacy to Corpus be audited annually and that if "six large, or 12 small" books were found to be lost, the entire collection was to pass to Corpus's rival college, Caius.

Representatives from both colleges gather every so often to conduct a ceremony of inspection and, understandably, Page was determined not to see the manuscripts fall into the hands of eager librarians at Caius.

He established a conservation studio, which made the library a flagship for new techniques and led to the setting up of a Cambridge Colleges Conservation Consortium. His duties also included accompanying one of its most precious manuscripts, the sixth-century Gospels of St Augustine, to Canterbury so that it could be used during the swearing-in ceremonies of Archbishops Coggan and Runcie.

Looking back on 60 years living in Old Newnham, Mrs Page thinks there have been very few changes. "I have loved the traditional way of life we have lived here." She is sorry though about the loss of the little shops in Newnham Road, including the corner shop and the cobbler.

Next door to Mrs Page is Newnham House, built in 1820 at the junction of Newnham Road and Malting Lane. It is another fine townhouse, which has been turned into a hall of residence for Corpus postgraduates.

Superficially then, Newnham Road and the immediate vicinity has only changed for the better. Like many gentrified inner-city areas it is tidier, smarter, with brighter street lights, cleaner curtains and fresher paint. The increase in traffic however, is a constant irritant, and there is no local parking.

Probe a little below the surface, however, and the changes are profound. The area has lost many of the old shops, although there are several thriving restaurants now. In 1970 this was a diverse, mixed community, with a wide social mix, a local factory (now the Bella Italia), several other business premises, a doctors' surgery, and two rather down-at-heel pubs, facing each other across the pond in resentful competition, and each with a dedicated clientele who would never dream of entering the other, as one local resident put it to me.

The short stretch of Newnham Road, between the Mill Pond and the roundabout at the end of Fen Causeway, had a wide range of useful shops: a proper grocer, an off-licence, a newsagent, a cobbler, a florist, a women's hairdresser, an antique dealer, and a confectioner and café – the Margaret Rose. It was a picture of 1930s suburbia translated to the fringe of the university, so I am told. There was even a local bus service, every twenty minutes or so to and from King's Parade. Doubtless the inhabitants of the Grade II listed Perse Almshouses (built in 1861) by the roundabout would have made use of those buses. Now, these almshouses have all been sold to private owners.

Domenic, the barber

Another successful business in Newnham Road is Domenico Di Martino's, the Gentleman's Hairdresser at No. 45, run by the man known to his many clients as Domenic. He has been working as a hairdresser in Cambridge for 43 years, having come to Cambridge in the 1970s from Caserta in southern Italy, near Naples. He came here to join his sisters who had both married Italians.

He started running the hairdressing salon in what used to be Joshua Taylor's in 1970. In 1975, he opened his first shop at 25 St Andrews Street above what was Barratt's China Shop. When Robert Sayle took over the site for its television and toy department in 1979, he went back to Joshua Taylors. Between 2004–8, he ran the third Domenic's at Friends Meeting House in Jesus Lane. Since 2009, he has been a tenant of Darwin College at 45 Newnham Road, having trained many of the city's experienced barbers! Domenic employs two members of staff at the salon, Svetlana from Russia and Yannis from Crete. "I have achieved everything in Cambridge, and have worked hard. All I had was honour when I came here."

In the barber's chair. Domenic cutting the hair of Chris Smith, his client since 1977, and in the foreground, Yannis Kadianakis and client, James Robinson.

With the loss of the amenities listed above, locals will tell you that the atmosphere of Old Newnham has changed, although this is not immediately apparent from the street. The area is now almost wholly given over to university lodgings of one kind or another, and the social mix and the shops it sustained have gone.

Someone who is, perhaps, not pessimistic about the changes to the area is Lawrence Austen. He has run the Granta Canoe and Punt Hire Company for the last 20 years from moorings on the Mill Pond, by the Granta Public House. He used to cycle past what was a piece of waste land which led to the ford across the pond, where the cattle used to be driven to graze on the Fen opposite (you can see the muddy slope on the bank where the cattle used to scramble up onto the grass). The willows that grace the bank on the opposite side were planted by Ludovic Stewart's (mentioned in the earlier section) mother.

"There were no boats there", says Lawrence Austen, "just the odd college or private one, so I approached the Greene King brewery which owns the Granta, about establishing a punting business there". He leases the pub's mooring, and land from the city council on the bank next to the pub. "I started with four ex-college boats, which were repaired and maintained at his workshop in Grantchester (part of the Pemberton Estate)". He is in business all the year round employing and training his crew of students and Perse school boys; much of the business comes from corporate clients, as well as passing tourists and locals. And it is a popular local enterprise, "We are like Switzerland. We are very neutral and tend to get on with everybody." His is a thriving business.

If you are feeling peckish, there is no shortage of excellent restaurants in Newnham Road to tempt your palette: pub grub at The Granta, the full range of Italian meals at Bella Italia, Indian food at India House, formerly the Jolly Millers, once a rather raffish pub. Next door at No. 35 on the site of what used to be a garage, is the Thai restaurant, Sala Thong, which pioneered Thai cooking in the city long before mass travel to Thailand. What used to be an excellent oriental supermarket next door at No. 37 is now the Rice Boat, a restaurant specialising in food from Kerala in south-west India, the land where the spice trade originated.

No. 45 is one of many properties owned by Darwin College in that part of Newnham Road near the roundabout. Others are Nos. 45A, 49A and the Cambridge Book & Print Gallery at No. 49. The Gallery specialises in fine art and rare books. On the same side, at the other end of the road, Darwin now owns the whole of Newnham Terrace, built during the 1850s. These are typical mid-Victorian townhouses, which would have provided spacious accommodation for families and their servants, together with students who might have lodged there. Over the years, several of these buildings came into the ownership of King's College. Gradually, Darwin College has bought up almost all of these houses and converted them into accommodation for graduate members of the college.

No. 1 Newnham Terrace was, for many years, the home of Professor Richard Gooderson and his wife Marjorie. Professor Gooderson was a Reader in English Law in the University from 1967. He was a Fellow of St Catharine's College from 1948 and a Recorder of the Crown Court from 1972. After his death, his widow carried on living at No. 1 before moving later to Pinehurst. At which point Darwin, who had built a glass door leading from their dining hall facing across to No.1, seized their chance to acquire the property, and to build a bridge linking the main college with its new acquisition. (Marjorie Gooderson died at the age of 101, in July 2013.)

Then followed further opportunities to acquire eventually all the houses in the terrace. No. 2 was once a guest house, and No. 4 was Little St Mary's Rectory. Nos. 9–12 were purchased in 2000 from King's College with a grant from the Rayne Foundation. So, after fifty years of development, the only part of the original triangular site that does not belong to Darwin College is the Granta pub!

A particular attraction of Newnham Terrace is the series of gardens at the back, which stretch down to the river. The decision to retain part of the original dividing walls of the gardens means that some of the original character of each house has been kept, while still being able to wander through the whole garden on this beautiful site.

At No.12, students have made an allotment where they grow vegetables, and they have hauled up into the garden an old punt that was beyond repair. It is now used as a raised bed for vegetables! Students practise T'ai Chi in the gardens, at the same time as looking across to where swans nest on the Darwin islands.

But to return to the story of the College's acquisitions, which have continued their onward march along Newnham Road and elsewhere! When the Malting House came on the market, Darwin took advantage of the opportunity (not the most popular decision among local residents!), winning a competitive tender for the purchase of the famous Grade II listed building in 2003. Graduate members moved in later that year. The College now has an additional 14 bedsitting rooms for its graduate students, together with a seminar room which the College describes as a sort of common-room for research Fellows.

And then there is Gwen Raverat House built by Darwin College in Anderson Court, off Newnham Road, where in 1884 according to the Spalding Street Directory there were eight dwellings, home to two laundresses (all that college laundry!), two gardeners, a photographer, a groom and printer.

Gwen Raverat House, opened on 2 December 1996, has 54 bedsitting rooms and on each of the three floors, there are three kitchens and bathrooms. I wonder what the great lady, Gwen Raverat herself, would think to see her name on the wall of a building that has the slight feel of a Travelodge hotel.

In 1993, Darwin bought a plot of land belonging to Newnham College in Wordsworth Grove and built accommodation for 28 graduate students. The new building is named Frank Young House in honour of Darwin's first Master. The houses in Wordsworth Grove are predominately of the late Victorian and Edwardian period.

The front of the Frank Young building reflects its traditional setting, whilst the elevation looking out over the Gonville and Caius playing fields is very modern. It has been remarked that it looks like the sort of house you might expect to find on a beach in California!

Darwin has also acquired No. 5 Wordsworth Grove and No. 2 Summerfield, together with "Newnham Path" in Church Rate Walk. Newnham Path was the home of the late Helen Fowler, who studied English at Newnham between 1939 and 1942 and afterwards became a wartime intelligence officer. She and her husband Laurence compiled *Cambridge Commemorated* published by CUP in 1984, an anthology of portrait and word pictures of Cambridge and Cambridge life over the centuries.

FEN CAUSEWAY

18 July – 1 August 1985

Fen Causeway, formerly Coe Fen Lane and before that the romantic sounding Love Lane, was constructed as a road across Coe Fen, linking Newnham village with Trumpington Road in 1926 after fierce opposition, a public inquiry, alternative schemes and the sort of horrified protests worthy of the letters column of the *Cambridge Evening News* today. Before the bridge was built, the links between the rest of the town and west Cambridge were only by the Silver Street and Magdalene Street bridges – otherwise people walked or cycled.

One passionate protester against the building of the new road turned to poetry in his distress. *The Coe Fen Road* by Quentin Nelson was a rapier sharp attack on the City Council for their road plans. The poet, in casual conversation with a workman wielding a theodolite on the fen finds out that "We are going to build a road." He is devastated and in the spirit of King Lear he cries out:

> "Every frog," I said, "and every toad
> Will croak damnation to your soul:
> Every shooting willow-bole will shake his knotted jowl:
> That pair of paddling waterfowl
> And quick wagtail no longer beat
> The pools and grasses with their feet.
> The rooks, that waddle on the green,
> Will leave the places, where they've been.
> And caw their cursings poplar-high:
> The kingfisher will fade and die."

The workman explained the scheme:

> "The road" he said, "will be straight and grand,
> With cast-iron railings on either hand,
> Concrete conduits, and bridges wide,
> With faked stone walls on either side."

It was a knife through the heart. Nelson "shuddered to think of the changing fen. God! What shall we do with these wicked men?"

The final stanzas of *The Coe Fen Road* are heavy with prescient cynicism

See how the motor-lorries go
Heavily laden to and fro. Earning money for business men:
What do they do with the money, then?
Joys can only be bought in a shop:
Sheep aren't sheep; they're mutton chop.
All the delicate things on earth
Are trampled down with their growing girth.

They have turfed the banks of the road with green,
Because the banks of the road are easily seen,
When the summer comes, and the river is gay
With punts and skiffs on a sunny day;
And the painted folk that pass that way,
Are brothers and sisters — so they say!

Coe Fen in its virgin state with wildlife and an artist's impression of the traffic that would soon build up on the road that City planners proposed. Drawings by Adrian Graham from the prose poem *The Coe Fen Road* by Quentin Nelson, Mercury Press, 1929

Contractor of imagination
Of our aesthetic generation, When you had done with bricks and lime,
'Tis good to think you still had time,
To plant a timely sod of turf, that we who loved the fen might know,
That you, who have defiled it so,
Knew 'twas a wicked thing to do,
Even if you were ordered to.

(Quentin Nelson *The Coe Fen Road*, The Mercury Press, 1929)

Like the city's other commons – Stourbridge Common, Midsummer Common, Coldhams Common and Donkeys Common, Coe Fen has been common land since time immemorial. Also known as Cow Fen it has always been grazing land. A pinder[4], employed by the council to look after the horses and cattle on the city's commons, keeps a regular eye on Cow Fen, which appealed to the hunting, shooting and fishing brigade as long ago as the eighteenth century.

Henry Gunning in his *Reminiscences of Cambridge* from 1780 to 1884 wrote of his passion for shooting: "for which diversion Cambridge afforded the most extraordinary facilities. In going over the land now occupied by Downing terrace, you generally got five or six shots at snipes. Crossing the Leys, you entered on Cow-fen; this abounded with snipes. Walking through the osier bed on the Trumpington side of the brook, you frequently met with a partridge, and now and then a pheasant."

In 1872, undergraduates began to play golf on Coe Fen before moving in 1875 to a nine-hole course on Coldham's Common.

The city had its bathing place on Sheep's Green in Victorian times. An iron footbridge called the Robinson Crusoe footbridge linking the south ends of Sheep's Green and Coe Fen was opened in 1910 to replace the chain ferry taking ladies over to the bathing place in what was called Snobs Stream. People still bathe in the river every day all through the winter. "No modest female approached the town bathing place", wrote F. A. Reeve in *Cambridge* (Batsford, 1964). Ladies who passed in boats opened parasols so that they might not see the naked men and boys. In 1894, a ladder was provided above the iron bridge, for the use of female bathers and this adjoined the men's bathing place; there were many letters in the press supporting or opposing the custom of nude bathing for men and boys. In 1896, an enclosure for women was provided, and Miss Hardy became custodian at a salary of ten shillings a week.

As you cross the foot and cycle bridge to Coe Fen from Sheep's Green you will see a small walled riverside area containing an old boathouse and a roofless folly. This is known as "Hodson's Folly", after the Mr Hodson who built it in the 19th century as a private area in which his daughters could bathe at the ladies bathing place in Snobs Stream.

Coe Fen was one of several commons near the city centre used as drying grounds by Cambridge laundresses who did washing for colleges. F. A. Reeve

---

[4] A person whose job was to impound stray animals

Fen Causeway soon after the road opened in 1926.

records that there were three college laundries in Granta Place and Little St Mary's Lane: "At 1 Granta Place, a widow with two sons and two daughters, helped by several hired women did all the washing for two colleges in their small house. The eldest son fetched the linen in a handcart, and washing was done in the kitchen and a small penthouse. Coe Fen was the drying ground. People put up their own posts, but paid a fee of a shilling a year to the Corporation.

Before the outbreak of the First World War, soldiers were encamped on several Cambridge commons, including Coe Fen. Jack Overhill writes in "Carabineer", published in the *East Anglian Magazine Volume 33*, that when war with Germany came, the soldiers returned to Coe Fen where they had been on manoeuvres in 1912. "War came and one morning a boy told me there were soldiers on Coe Fen. I ran down the lane and there, stretching away to the far end of the Fen, was a row of white bell tents. Parallel with them, over the middle ditch, were horses and wagons. There were no sentries and I peeped in some of the tents where soldiers were sitting and lying, some still sleeping."

These were men of the Royal Army Medical Corps. While they were on Coe Fen, they were inoculated. Overhill said he read no warning of the war. He was only vaguely aware of big battles being waged in France and Belgium. One morning he ran down the lane to the Fen. There he saw only horses, grass, trees and sky. Soldiers, tents, and wagons had vanished. They had come in the night and gone in the night.

The Causewayside flats on Fen Causeway were built in 1934 on land that for many years had been Mott's Dairy and cowsheds. Mott's cows had grazed on Coe Fen and on Lammas Land opposite which occupants of the Causewayside flats, particularly those with young children, regard today as their front garden. Adults call it the "Costa del Newnham". The flats on the site of Mott's Dairy were built

Troops camped on Coe Fen in 1914.

by a firm of London developers in the then fashionable style of the day, with metal window frames (they have warped over the years) and flat roofs. The flats were then acquired by Cambridge University after the Second World War.

Dr Frederick Norton, an emeritus fellow of Wolfson College, who retired in 1972 from his post as a librarian in the University Library, has lived at Causewayside for many years. He can remember the site and the Causeway itself before the flats and the road were built, and has clear memories of walking as an aspirant undergraduate across Coe Fen to take scholarship papers at Pembroke College, where he read modern languages.

He first started his working life as a librarian in what are now the University offices next to King's College, in the Old Schools. The air was impregnated with dust from the books and was not a healthy place to work.

Dr Norton, who will be remembered for starting the modern foreign languages section in the University Library in the days when the library depended on the generosity of dons and professors for the enlargement of its lists, can recall the occasion when the late Emperor of Ethiopia, Haile Selassie came to study at the University Library: "I can remember seeing him in the library. When he got back he sent us all sorts of presents." One thank-you gift consisted of a hundred-weight of the best coffee and a special newspaper printed on gold. Other offerings included elephant tusks. It was his way of saying 'thank you' to the library staff who had helped and encouraged him."

Another distinquished visitor to the "UL", as the University Library is known, in the post-war period was Marshal Tito of Yugoslavia. He apparently turned up rather suddenly one day, flanked by an escort of a dozen police on motor bikes. "We showed him some of our fifteenth-century books about which he knew a lot," said Dr Norton.

Dr Norton has lived in Causewayside for many years. He is one of the oldest tenants, most of whom are connected with the university. Scholars from overseas who may be in Cambridge for a short period of time are among the members of this quiet, self-contained community of academics.

For several years, until her death in 1972, Nora Chadwick, the distinguished English scholar and Honorary Fellow of Newnham College, lived at No. 7 Causewayside. She moved there from her previous home in Adams Road. Her friend and fellow Newnham scholar, Enid Welsford wrote in her "Memoriam" to Nora, how she crammed the flat with her books and old-fashioned furniture, and "lived in much the same way as before, writing at her huge desk or dispensing delightful hospitality, well content with what to other – never to herself – might seem cramped and uncomfortable surroundings."

Some of the flats are leased by the University to Cambridge University Press who house several employees there. Miss Mary Thwaites, who has a basement flat at the Newnham Road end of the Causeway has worked for the Press in their Edinburgh Building as a general assistant for the past six years. She appreciates living in Causewayside. The flats are so central, and Lammas Land is an attractive, open green space across the road.

When Elisabeth Funnell leased the little shop next to Cock's Garage at the head of Fen Causeway, as a warehouse for the beautiful Indian clothes which she has been selling on a wholesale basis since 1977, her friends said: "Why don't you open it as a shop, it's got such a pretty window and front door." That's how Camelios, which has built up a following of customers particularly in the Newnham area, came into existence six months ago. I ask her about the significance of the name: "Well", she says, "Cam brings in Cambridge, and helios is the Greek word for sun. The name as a whole evokes an image of India where I have travelled extensively and seen the clothes we sell being made by women working out-of-doors in the sun."

An Aladdin's cave of a shop

The clothes sold in Camelios: dresses, skirts, shirts, waistcoats and blouses are made from cotton and silk. Some of the clothes are made by her Indian tailor in London under the name Anmol. Mrs Funnell became interested in India after extensive travels there. Camelios is an Aladdin's cave of a shop, full of richly coloured silk fabrics and delicate Indian ornaments.

Books about the subcontinent, its history, religions and literature, fill the shelves by the changing area. It's all a contrast to the spotlights and pop music to be found in many other shops in the city. But then the shop has an interesting past. At one time it was a little pub called the Tally-Ho. It had extensive cellars with vaulted oak arches. When Mrs Funnell's husband was excavating at the back he found the original cobbled yard of the pub buried eight inches below the surface. He dug the cobbles up and has incorporated them into the present garden, a peaceful spot in this busy part of Newnham.

Scroope House, an early Victorian mansion designed by a former architect of St Catharine's College, was to become 100 years later the nucleus of the university's Engineering Department, a department which today enjoys a prestigious worldwide reputation.

When Scroope House was built on land belonging to Gonville and Caius College in 1837 (the year of Queen Victoria's accession to the throne), Fen Causeway was simply Love Lane, a track that meandered down to that chunk of original land, Coe Fen. A lane visible on R. C. Baker's 1844 map led from Love Lane to the back of Scroope Terrace. Scroope House was occupied for some years by John Willis Clark, the University Registrary who was a godsend to architectural historians on account of his interpretation of early maps of the city centre.

The next occupant of the house (designed by James Walker – William Wilkins's clerk of works at Corpus Christi College in 1826 before he took on the job at St Catharine's), was Warburton Wyngate, Hon. Surgeon to the Volunteer Fire Brigade.

Engineering at Cambridge

It was in 1922 that the Engineering Department, known between the wars as Mechanical Sciences, moved to Scroope House on the strength of a gift of £25,000 from Sir Dorabji Tata, head of an Indian engineering combine. Engineering had been taught at Cambridge from the early years of the 19th century, but the modern department was founded in 1875 in a laboratory in Free School Lane. The first chair was that of Mechanism and Applied Mechanics.

From 1915 to 1918, the Engineering Laboratory had been, to quote T. E. B. Howarth in *Cambridge Between Two Wars*: "largely given over to the manufacture of thirteen and eighteen pounder shells". The professor, Charles Inglis of King's, was "busy designing a transportable military bridge", the prototype of the Bailey. A portrait of Professor Inglis hangs in the boardroom.

There was a dramatic increase in the number of engineering students immediately after the First World War. In 1920 there were three honours students and two others; in 1921, 119 were taking honours. At the end of the war in 1918, there were six teaching staff and by October 1919 the number had increased to 38, and it was then a case of standing room only in Free School Lane. Engineering was desperately in need of more space, which – 60 years on, on a new site – is also the case today.

With its move to Scroope House in 1922, under the direction of Professor Inglis, the department continued to expand. One determined member of the team who had their offices and workshops on land behind Scroope House was the electrical engineer, E B. Moullin, who was a Fellow of King's College.

Howarth notes that he invented an electric torsiometer (a balance measure) with which, as his obituarist tells us: "He crossed the Atlantic in the liner *Franconia*, spending most of his time not in the elegant saloons but in the cramped propeller tunnels in the bottom of the ship, which even the greasers on their inspections left as soon as they could; here he tended his instruments on the spinning shafts and hoped that the weather would be severe enough for the propellors to pitch out of the water."

The first Chair of Aeronautical engineering was founded in Cambridge to commemorate Francis Mond, who was killed flying during the First World War. His father Emile Mond endowed the professorship of aeronautics. Meanwhile the department was expanding again. The teaching staff, which numbered 24 during the Second World War, grew enormously, first in the 1950s and then in the 1960s, in common with engineering departments throughout the country and is now the largest university engineering department in the country.

That major expansion was presided over by Lord Baker, now aged 84, whose name is a byword among engineers. The new Engineering block, which was built in 1952 alongside Scroope House and which was later demolished, is known as the Baker Building. Indeed part of it, a solid E-shaped building, was constructed using Baker's own plastic theory of structures. Residents of Cambridge will appreciate the fact that Baker designed the standard indoor air raid shelter, known as the Morrison shelter, which was so brilliantly successful during the Second World War.

Expansion in the department during the past few years has concentrated on electrical and information engineering – Cambridge is after all the "Silicon Valley" of the Fens. However, the department today has reached the point where, with growing student numbers, research activity at a record level and with enough money to fund day-to-day expenditure, it has run out of space on the main site.

Individual projects are poised to expand, for instance the field of space dynamics – to name just one – but there is nowhere for them to go. "There have been no central funds for large-scale building for the last 20 years. We must look outside Government sources to help us achieve our aim," says Professor Jack Heyman, the current head of department.

Professor Heyman, who wearing another hat helps to prop up the Church of England (he is the only engineer on the Cathedrals' Advisory Board), has plans for a new multi-storey building to replace the old 1924 workshops and laboratories at the Coe Fen end of the site. "We are looking for about £10 million for this building scheme", he told me on the eve of one of his trips to Worcester Cathedral to advise on its ancient fabric.

From medieval structures to robotics and power electronics is a long leap. Professor Heyman is a man concerned both with heritage of the past and the vital importance of planning for the future for his multi-disciplinary department of engineering.

FEN CAUSEWAY

Revisited

Ten years ago, when the bollards were installed in Silver Street – restricting traffic flows in and out of the centre to certain hours of the day – the predictable knock-on effect was to increase the traffic pouring up and down Fen Causeway, a key part of the city's inner ring road. Blot out the busy road though and make your way across to Lammas Land on the south side. It is still one of the city's most popular green and pleasant parks. As Jo Edkins in *Greens, Commons and Pieces 2010* explains: "Lammas was August 1st, observed as a harvest festival in the early English church. Loaves of bread were consecrated, made from the first ripe corn. Areas of green were designated Lammas lands in law, that is they were common lands for nine months of the year, but for the sole use of their owners for the remainder (Lammas Day being the day they changed ownership)."

Families with young children, many of them visiting scholars living in the Causewayside flats across the road, flock to the playground and paddling pool on Lammas Land with their young children. Others take their trikes, bikes, scooters and footballs there, while students practise balancing on slivers of wire secured between the trees. You can play tennis there, eat ice cream, walk the dog or just sit and read.

Geoffrey Skelsey, who was the principal assistant registrar for 30 years has lived at Causewayside on and off since 1982, and remembers the days when he used to have his groceries delivered by Bagleys, the grocer's in Newnham Road, next door to the cobblers. "There has been a big change at Causewayside. The university once offered long-term leases, but now the flats are only let for two years on fixed term tenancies.

"There is a desperate need for accommodation for short-term visitors with families. The place is well run with good and efficient staff, but the social and cultural mix has changed as a consequence of the changes to the tenancy arrangements, although there are still a few tenants living there on long-term leases who have lived there for many years." He is one of them. He recalls that in the 1960s and 70s, there were professors who had been living at Causewayside since 1940, as well as one or two old ladies.

There have been changes too in the administration of the university. His job as principal assistant registrar, the equivalent of Permanent Secretary to the Vice-Chancellor was, as he put it: "speaking truth to power".

"The job was to be the person who received and interpreted communications and put them into context. But there have been changes. The university administration has become more and more obsessed with process, not product. It is less collegiate. When I joined in 1967 (he read English at St Catharine's College), there were about 80 staff in the Registry including typists. Now there are at least ten times that number.

"At Cambridge University, the increase in undergraduates has been modest in comparison with other leading universities, although in the '60s Cambridge was regarded as a big university. However, there has been a huge increase in the number of postgraduate students who bring with them a need for accommodation."

Mr Skelsey thinks the Cambridge "brand" will survive, but it faces three dangers. The first is distance learning, the second competition from other universities. "Fifty years ago Cambridge was pre-eminent in the sciences and technology." The third problem is finance. "Sustaining the tutorial/supervision system is very, very costly." He reminds me that the Government doesn't pay anything for arts and humanities subjects.

After leaving the University Registry, he worked for six or seven years as a researcher and speech writer at Westminster until the 2010 General Election. His personal research concerns aspects of Belgian history, about which he has written five books.

The Causewayside flats on Fen Causeway.

GRANTCHESTER STREET

27 August 1981

Grantchester Street, in Newnham Croft, is part of what they used to call Croft Town in the early part of the century. Building in the area and on the west side of the street was begun in the 1850s and 1860s, as part of a housing scheme, for the employees of the new colleges to be built west of the river. The whole of the Newnham Croft area was at one time an old Saxon burial ground, similar to the one found in Trinity Fellows' Garden.

Although most of Newnham Croft's buildings date from the last 150 years, evidence of ancient tracks survive in the road patterns, and fence lines follow early field boundaries. Ancient hedge lines can still be traced and slight variations in the ground level in some gardens betray the original site of the gravel pits.

The terraced houses in Derby Street and the houses on the east side of Hardwick Street were built at the same time as the west side of Grantchester Street. Tony Dathan's chapter on Newnham Croft in John A. Gray's booklet on Newnham (Hanwell Publications, 1977) tells us that houses were gradually added in Merton Street through the 1880s: "By 1895 this was the extent of the Croft, with a tennis court where Newnham Croft School now stands, and no Chedworth Street, Eltisley Avenue or Owlstone Road." Open land disappeared as houses were built in Owlstone Road, between 1900 and 1904.

The far end of the west side of Grantchester Street, which in 1903 was still called Gravel Pit Lane, was built back towards Merton Street by 1904. There had been a path across the field for some years, leading direct from Gravel Pit Lane, now Grantchester Street, across to the bathing place and houses at the end of Grantchester Meadows. As Tony Dathan says: "By 1903 the Rev Symmonds in the parish magazine was complaining that cyclists were making the path very muddy.

Fourteen additional houses were built in Grantchester Street between 1903 and 1904, while in 1913 permission was given for six houses and one shop – a fruit shop, later to become the butcher's, to be built by J. R. Bennett & Sons of Gwydir Street.

One of the most interesting houses in Grantchester Street is a house called "The Porch", the home of Dr Monica Shutter, who has charted the history of her home back to 1871, the year in which it was built. The house was originally called Barrington Villa, which sounds suitably Victorian and staid. It became known as The Porch when Miss Caroline Stephen moved in there in 1895 and it was her home until she died there in 1909.

Miss Caroline Stephen was the sister of Leslie Stephen, the Victorian writer and father of Virginia Woolf, who was sent down to stay at The Porch to throw off the depressions that used to overwhelm her. Dr Shutter recalls being told that Virginia Woolf preferred to recover from her depression among the bright lights of London. Her visits to The Porch and Cambridge are described in her published *Letters*.

Caroline Stephen, a staunch Quaker and doer of good works, was also the aunt of Miss Katherine Stephen, the principal of Newnham College. She called her home, one of the first to be built in Grantchester Street, The Porch because she regarded it as her porch to heaven. "She said she would settle here until she died", said Dr Shutter. Another distinguished resident of The Porch was Dr W. T. A. Barber, the headmaster of The Leys, who was a missionary in China and later the principal of Richmond College for the training of Methodist Ministers.

Dr Shutter has lived in the house for 32 years. It was sold to her father in 1949 for £4,100. She has found out from the deeds that it was sold in 1896 for £1,040. She is one of many Newnhamites who enjoy "village" life in that rather

Grantchester Street looking towards Barton Road in the 1970s.

pleasant little enclave of Newnham Croft, just ten minutes walk across Lammas Land from the city centre.

Down at the far end of Grantchester Street, hidden among trees and undergrowth on the thickly wooded island called Paradise, is an old house called Paradise House, which was once a public house called the Parrot – a favourite haunt of students according to F.A. Reeve in *The Cambridge Nobody Knows* (The Oleander Press, 1977).

The house was built at the end of the eighteenth century and passed into the ownership of the Pembertons of Trumpington Hall in March 1840. For a number of years it was used as a public house by Hudson's brewery of Pampisford. Later a Cambridge brewery called Dales (sold to Whitbreads in 1955) took it over. Sir Antony Pemberton confirmed that on a damp day the word Dales can be seen on the river side of the house. At one time, the public house was shut down by the proctors because it was being used as a brothel.

At Paradise House, in common with some other houses in Grantchester Meadows, the downstairs flooring was built a good thirty inches clear of ground level to be above occasional flooding. Although the house stands on the highest part of the small island in the River Cam, it was said by F. A. Reeve that floodwater had been heard under the boards in years gone by. The biggest flood since 1947 was in 1977 when the water was six inches under the floorboards of Paradise House.

In the grounds of Paradise House there are the remains of two fishponds, built for keeping fish fresh till required for the table. F. A. Reeve adds another detail: "At the far end of the island", he writes, "where there is a smaller island, a cold bath was constructed for the use of the ladies of Newnham College."

F.A. Reeve tells us that references to Paradise Island go back a long way. "The earliest mention of bathing in Cambridge records that in 1567 the son of Walter Haddon, while at King's College, was drowned "while washing himself in a place in the river Cam called Paradise". It was also in the waters around Paradise that Byron's brilliant friend Matthews became entangled in weeds and was drowned.

Before the locks on Sheep's Green were improved, Paradise House was often completely cut off by floods, writes F. A. Reeve: "In the great flood in 1795 the water in the house was seven feet deep. Furniture washed out of the rooms was found later near Silver Street Bridge, and provisions had to be sent to the house by barge. The house was surrounded by water most recently during the Fen floods of 1947."

From 1906 until 1974, the Griffiths were the tenants. Recent tenants include the Duke of Roxburgh and a South African mathematician called Professor Baumslang, who found Cambridge rather wet and cold.

The Pembertons were granted the fishing rights on the river by King Charles II. To exercise those rights they had to chain the river off, so they bought Paradise Island in 1840.

Along the unmade-up road into the lower end of Grantchester Street, you will find at No. 51 Grantchester Street, in the row of terraced bay-windowed houses there, the home of 92-year-old Miss Mildred Diver. Miss Diver used to help her late sister-in-law, Mrs Cornwall run the sub-post office at No. 21 Grantchester Street. Miss Diver remembered how Mrs Cornwall, who was widowed in the First World War, took over the business in 1918: "The shop used to have a public telephone in it." She says that she and her sister-in-law used to stand behind the counter and say to each other: "they'll never build in Newnham".

What they meant was on the university hockey field, and of course to many people's surprise, they have been proved wrong. The Granta Housing Association is putting the finishing touches on a large housing scheme in just that spot. The scheme should provide much needed homes for the elderly and for single people.

In 1914, the Granta Fruitery was opened on the east side of Grantchester Street, where Jack Cousins runs the butcher's shop now. Originally, the fruit shop was run by a Mrs Fuller and then by Mr C. H. Rogers, but by 1921 Benjamin Freestone was running the business under the name of Granta Fruit Stores. Mr C. Page had taken over by 1928 and turned the premises into a butcher's shop, which was then taken over by Mr C. Cousins in 1929. Jack Cousins who now runs this popular shop with his wife Una started work there with his father when he was 15. The shop has only ever been closed once for a full week in 1976 when the shop front was replaced.

Across the street in Grantchester Terrace, the three properties built in 1874 have housed trades since the expansion of the Croft in the Edwardian era, writes Tony Dathan: "At No. 25 Mr Rumble opened a gentlemen's hairdresser's in 1918.

Jack and Una Cousins, Grantchester Street's friendly local butchers.

On his death in 1926, his wife had the washbasins removed and opened a sweet-shop, which also sold fireworks and tobacco. The shop was well patronised by the children of Newnham Croft School and also the young ladies from the finishing school at Owlstone Croft. Mrs Rumble ran a savings scheme to enable children to save for fireworks for Guy Fawkes' night." Sweet rationing, however, caused the shop to close in 1940 and it has never reopened. It is now the home of Miss Margaret Lewis, a kind Geordie who has had years of experience in the catering business.

At No. 27 Grantchester Street, Mr Stubbens the shoemender ran his business from about 1910 until 1960. Next door at No. 29 Mr "Lucky" Gould had a barber's shop from about 1940 until about 1960. This is now the greengrocer's W. Cooper, a shop which is just as popular as Cousins the butcher. There also used to be a clock repairer's next door.

Mrs Dorothy Buss who ran No. 31 Eltisley Avenue initially as a tobacconist's, established the hairdressing tradition at that shop when she bought a business called The College of Hairdressing and moved it to Newnham Croft. Miss Gerda Meyer is the present owner of the salon.

William Heffer, great grandson of William Heffer (the founder of Heffers Bookshop) and his wife Lesley used to live at No. 31 Grantchester Street which they bought for £9,000 in the early 1970s. Before that they were living round the corner in Merton Street. "We bought the house from two lady professors at London University and started off by living in the top half and letting out the bottom half of the house." He remembers that the house still had plenty of bell pulls. The Heffers' three sons all started off at Newnham Croft before moving to King's College School. Some years later, the Heffers sold their house to Desmond Hirsch and his wife Pam, and moved to No. 41 Barton Road.

No one knows Newnham better than Bert Dring, who has lived most of his life in the area. He and his wife moved into No. 11 Grantchester Street when they were first married more than 50 years ago. Bert Dring was the local builder and undertaker, so he knows all about underground wells, settlement and parish boundaries. He and his wife remember the lime trees that used to flower stickily on the opposite side of the road from their house. They talk affectionately about Bob Brown, the landlord of the Red Bull, and his wife Rosie. Bob Brown was also a cab driver in Newmarket and to boost his income used to sell vegetables and rabbits in the front lounge of the pub.

There have been many changes in Newnham. As Bert Dring puts it: "Most of the Newnham people are dead and gone. I can count all the Newnham people I know on both hands". He'd be glad to know that the newcomers appreciate their heritage.

GRANTCHESTER STREET

Revisited

Turn into Grantchester Street off Barton Road and you are at once in the heart of Newnham Croft. It was designated a conservation area by Cambridge City Council in 1998.

It is a busy street now – much busier than it was 30 years ago, mainly because there are more cars, more on-street parking, more commuter parking and, because the street and adjoining streets are narrow, at times they are completely blocked as cars, taxis and grocery delivery vans get stuck, and have to wait to get through. Mrs Anne Parsons who lives at the junction of Grantchester Street and Newnham Croft Street says her terraced house regularly gets clipped by lorries, and she dreads the sound of reversing vans for fear her brick wall will get another bashing.

More than three times the City Council has asked residents whether they want residents parking, but so far they have always said "No".

Alan Jones, who lives in Grantchester Meadows, says: "The environment of Newnham is less pleasant now. Much higher house prices in Newnham Croft have led to wealthier inhabitants and fewer academics. A number of houses are let to overseas visitors, or to people exploring the possibility of settling in Cambridge."

As for sky-rocketing house prices, in the summer of 2013 a small two bedroomed terraced house with a loft conversion in Grantchester Street sold for £450,000 – it was probably built for a few hundred pounds in the early 1900s! Houses in Hardwick Street, Marlowe Road and Owlstone Croft can sell at between £600,000 – £700,000. No academic could afford those prices.

Mr Jones explains that as a consequence of the house price hike, Newnham Croft School is nowadays less well attended by local children because more parents are choosing private schools. "So you have children flowing in from outside Newnham to the school because fewer local children are going to it, and many local children flowing out to the independent schools, which are conveniently close to Newnham."

Mr Jones does consider though that the community spirit in Newnham is still strong, as demonstrated whenever the environment is threatened. "There is a small conservation group, which is very active as it takes constant vigilance to

Close to town – Grantchester Meadows and the River Cam.

maintain this rather special semi-rural environment, but the idyllic picture of the area needs to be revised slightly."

"The relocation of the post office from Grantchester Street to the Derby Stores was of course very important, and it is another hub of Newnham, with a team we all know well."

The Conservation Area appraisal document, written in 1998, highlights in a fitting way the special character of Newnham Croft which is so precious to its residents. "It is the close juxtaposition of the urban and the rural. Excellent shops lie one street away from snipe meadows, kingfishers and almost impenetrable woods. Most of the buildings are seen against a background of big trees, many of which are left over from vanished orchards or the gardens of big houses, whilst others have sprung up on abandoned meadows and at the bottoms of gardens."

As the Conservation Area appraisal states: "Newnham residents are cautious of major changes to their environment; they care about the quality and scale of development, their predominantly Victorian and Edwardian architecture and their trees, open space and relative quiet. They spontaneously unite (and not infrequently combust) on issues such as the demolition of the former Newnham Croft school or the threat of a fish and chip shop being introduced into a predominantly residential area."

On the subject of fish and chips, however, there may not be a shop, but a fish and chip van does come to Grantchester Street every Tuesday between 5 and 7 p.m. Its customers regularly include college Fellows queuing for their regular fish and chips. A fishmonger from Grimsby sells freshly caught fish there every Saturday morning between 9 a.m. and 12 noon.

When it came to the demolition in 1992 of the original (1915) Newnham Croft School and the future of the site, local residents leapt into campaigning mode. After an extensive campaign by the local community to keep the school's playing fields, the school itself was rebuilt partly on its old site while the rest of the site on the south side of Chedworth Street was developed into modern housing.

As well as the conservation group, local shopkeepers and the many local residents, particularly the elderly, who support them also play their part in sustaining the community. In order to survive, the shops have all had to diversify. Thus Cousins the butchers, at No. 36 owned by Mr and Mrs John Crowther and run these last ten years by general manager, Tony Bales, sells fruit and vegetables, cheese and homemade cakes, as well as meat. "We are a real old fashioned butcher, and cook most of our own pies. We are well supported by locals and people who come in from afar. Newnham people aren't supermarket people", says Mr Bales.

Tony Bales, left general manager and Peter Birch outside Cousins the butchers in Grantchester Street.

The Co-op at No. 3 Grantchester Street is another well-supported shop, patronised particularly by students. As deputy manager Liam Wallis told me, "Students boost sales". But when the Co-op tried to sell morning newspapers, local residents jumped to the defence of the Derby Stores, which is the established outlet for the printed word in Newnham Croft. The Co-op backed down.

For the residents of Newnham, Mrs N. K. Jank's pharmacy and shop is the place to find excellent knowledge, service and great kindness. It is one of the main focal points of this special community and Mrs Jank is a mother figure to many. As one resident wrote about the shop on a pharmacist's website: "Mrs Jank's shop is a haven of delicious scents, attractive merchandise and Mrs Jank's excellent advice when asked about problems ranging from teething pains to malaria prophylaxis. Invariably smiling and helpful when it comes to organising a repeat prescription or ordering a special soap – and she makes the prettiest parcels in Cambridge! We are very lucky to have her!"

Mrs Jank, whose parents came to the UK from Kenya, has been running her chemist's shop in Eltisley Avenue since 1982. She owns the premises which originally used to be a shop that mended clocks. "When we bought the shop and opened the business it was quite a big risk. There was no Newnham Walk surgery then, and it was a big gamble to open a pharmacy without a surgery", she said. Her fears have proved unfounded. Mrs Jank and her husband don't live over the shop; they live at Cambourne instead where at least they are able to park their cars in the front drive! No hope of doing that in Grantchester Street or Eltisley Avenue. The residents of Eltisley Avenue held a street party in the summer of 2012 to mark the centenary of the completion of their street which was built in two sections, the south side between 1902–1912 and the north side 10–15 years later.

Next door to Mrs Jank, the hairdressing salon, owned by Rod and Jenny Widdowson, is as popular as the pharmacist.

Paradise House on Paradise Island – a glorious place to spend a childhood.

At the far end of the street, the garage G. P. Motors Ltd is still run by the Palmer family who founded the car sales and service business 20 years ago. It is another local business which is well supported by Newnham residents.

Dr Shutter, who used to live across the road from the pharmacy at The Porch, now lives round the corner in Hardwick Street. She moved in 1990 when she retired from general practice, having qualified as a doctor in 1948, in the same month that the National Health Service started. Her daughter and family moved into The Porch in her place, keeping up the neighbourly spirit of the area by leaving windfall fruit on the wall outside.

Dr Shutter may have retired, but she, like so many of the retirees in Newnham, is still very active. One of her contributions to the community is to run the Thursday lunch club in the Community Room at Newnham Croft Community School. Up to 18 senior citizens attend regularly, paying £2.50 for a good two-course meal followed by tea and coffee. They assemble at 12.30 p.m. after the Kindergarten session has finished at 12 noon. The lunches are cooked at The Leys School: "Four or five drivers head over to the Leys School and pick up the lunches which are packed into heat controlled boxes", says Dr Shutter.

Dr Shutter also tells me of the bus service that goes once a week from the Pinehurst flats in Grange Road to Newnham Croft where it picks up and takes passengers into town before bringing them back two hours later. Local shop keepers contribute to the running of this service.

What used to be the local Granta Housing Association development in Grantchester Street, which provided homes exclusively for the elderly, is no

Off the beaten track and into a little jungle! The Paradise Local Nature Reserve linked to Lammas Land, Sheep's Green and Coe Fen is a dense patch of woodland by the river. And it is a short walk to the city centre!

Cows grazing
on Grantchester
Meadows in full
view of the city's
spires.

longer a local housing scheme. It is run by the Metropolitan Housing Association
and is for mixed use, not just for the elderly.

For nearly 20 years, from 1980, Sir Michael and Sally Oliver lived at Paradise
House as tenants of the Pemberton family. Sir Michael became Lord Mayor of
London in 2001 and they moved from Paradise House into the Mansion House.
They have many vivid memories of their time in Paradise: "Just as F. A. Reeve
says in *The Cambridge Nobody Knows*, we too could hear the water under the floor
boards every time the garden flooded", says Sally Oliver.

She recalls that the lawn at Paradise House used to flood at least four times a
year: "The water would creep up slowly from the far end of the garden until it
reached the balustrade at the edge of the driveway. It was beautiful, resembling
a huge, still lake with gracious trees surrounding it. One year, a really big flood
came and the water came right up to the three steps leading up to the front door,
and we tied a rowing boat to the door so that we could row out if necessary!

"Our over-excited children of ten and eight begged to be allowed to hang
hammocks in the trees that were now in the middle of a lake, and sleep out over
the water. That evening they waded thigh deep out to the trees, hung the hammocks, and snuggled down to sleep. At about 3 a.m. we heard them wading back
again frozen with cold. Sleeping over water is far colder than sleeping over land!"

Paradise Island was for the Olivers the most glorious place to spend a childhood. For several years they hung a rope on a huge willow tree that overhung
the river. All the children in Newnham came to swing on it, making huge arcs
over the water. Sometimes they would "bomb" passing punts to the fury of those
drenched in the spray. Word of the rope got about and soon many punting parties
would also stop for a swing. Sadly they were warned that they had better have
really good liability insurance as someone was sure to be hurt at some point. With

great regret they removed the rope and for the rest of that summer people would ring the doorbell asking them to put it back!

There was never any evidence of a ghost at Paradise House except just once. The Olivers were away but a young man called Tom was housesitting for them. "We had converted the mezzanine bathroom into a kid's bedroom by building a bed over the bath. Tom was sleeping in this room (the oldest part of the house) when he became absolutely terrified. He knew there was someone very angry in that little room with him. Whoever it was did not like him. The presence remained in the room all night too near the door for Tom to get out, so he just lay in bed praying for dawn to come! He refused to ever stay again!"

It was while living there that Sally and the late Lesley Heffer started Daisy Chain Jewellery in a little glass greenhouse in Paradise garden.

Another young family is now renting Paradise House. Chris Pratten, who works for a fund manager in the City and his wife Rita Langan, a chartered accountant, chose the house so that their two young sons could go to King's College School, and roam free in the garden with its massive trees and that wild wooded feel so beloved of the Olivers. They, like the Oliver children, hide away here in the Paradise garden in the manner of the boys who hid out in the woods in *Brendon Chase*, that great children's novel by Denys Watkins-Pitchford writing as "BB". Wildlife roams freely too in this garden – foxes, muntjac deer, etc.

Chris says that it is like living in a wood, and it can get very wet. "Last Christmas was very, very wet and the whole of the garden was flooded." No wonder the floors were raised two feet off the ground when the house was built! The bridge leading across the river to the island was in a state of disrepair and is currently being strengthened, and the house has been extended in a seamless manner to

On the swings and roundabouts at Lammas Land.

provide more living space. It is only the different colour of the bricks that reveals that the house was once smaller. A condition of the lease is that tenants must mow a six foot wide strip of lawn to maintain access to the end of the garden, and the river.

Rita recounts how the boys have fun at Halloween: "Halloween is a great time in Newnham. If you leave a pumpkin on your doorstep, it means you are open for trick or treating." And there certainly are a lot of children living in Newnham, particularly in Marlowe Road which is a dead end, so that playing out in the street is very safe. And of course, it is great for street parties, often arranged on an impromptu basis! Residents of Newnham must hold the record for throwing street parties.

Not quite a street party, but at Christmas, the nativity is enacted in the area outside the butcher's shop. A local newborn baby is cast as baby Jesus, and local merchant bankers have been spotted in the roles of the three Kings, so I am told!

The sculptor, Christophe Gordon Brown has a tiny studio in a small brick building that used to be a delicatessen run by the Bliss Brothers, just beyond the junction of Grantchester Street and Eltisley Avenue. You can't miss it, because there is a big sign outside saying "The Studio". Christophe started off as a goldsmith, and used to work with Bill Powell in Workshop Design on Magdalene Street Bridge in Cambridge. He came to the Studio in Grantchester Street 18 years ago and worked as a jeweller for about four years.

"Trinity", a bronze sculpture by Christophe Gordon Brown.

Then disaster struck. "I had a robbery. They took everything. I lost £12,000 of stock and I wasn't insured, so I turned to sculpture. But if I were to meet those thieves now, I would take them out to lunch because I was getting a little bit bored with jewellery making and perhaps needed help to make the change." But to begin with, after the robbery (the criminals were never caught) he needed to pummel a punch bag in a friend's gym to get rid of his anger at what had happened. He felt much better after that.

Then in one of those acts of generosity that restore one's faith in human nature, a local person posted an anonymous cheque for £2,000 through his door accompanied by a note saying: "Here is something to help you." Two weeks later a customer called in, and commissioned a sculpture from him. "I designed it for her and we agreed a price of £600. I was off on my new adventure. The whole thing was providential, but the first six years working as a sculptor were very hard."

Christophe, whose father Gordon was a painter, works mainly in stone and marble. He recently won a competition to design a sculpture for the front of the Varsity Hotel in Thompsons Lane. "It was a big commission involving a carved helix spiralling into the building, covered in French gold leaf, embedded in four tons of polished, curved concrete." It is a beautiful piece of sculpture standing 12 feet high. His core principle and philosophy of art and design is that "beauty is the aim". He says that the challenge is to get the balance between the straight line and the curve. "The curve symbolises dynamic change and movement and the straight line symbolises structure and order. You have to get the right balance." A fine example of this philosophy of the balance between straight line and curve was on display in the tiny studio in the form of a stone sculpture of two wrestlers, with both bent and straight limbs represented.

It is vital for him to keep creating and being innovative. "The life force pushes through you. An artist needs to keep away from egotism and self importance which can be a trap and which diminishes creativity." Christophe's contemporary sculptures in stone, bronze and marble can be seen in galleries, gardens, public spaces and private collections throughout the UK and as far afield as Beijing – as well as here at home in Robinson College gardens, and his silverwork in the Chapel.

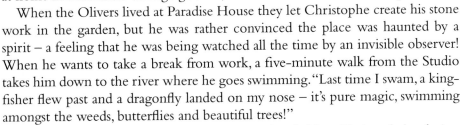

Sculpture called "Little Creature".

When the Olivers lived at Paradise House they let Christophe create his stone work in the garden, but he was rather convinced the place was haunted by a spirit – a feeling that he was being watched all the time by an invisible observer! When he wants to take a break from work, a five-minute walk from the Studio takes him down to the river where he goes swimming. "Last time I swam, a kingfisher flew past and a dragonfly landed on my nose – it's pure magic, swimming amongst the weeds, butterflies and beautiful trees!"

Concerned about the traffic congestion in Cambridge, Christophe's solution to the jams and parking problems is to clear the streets of cars, and bring in lots of colour coded trams running every few minutes in various directions throughout the city, rather like the London Underground, but using trams instead. Park and ride on a tram then? There used to be trams in Cambridge, I remind him.

Christophe shares the Studio with the jeweller, Lottie Farman. Lottie makes beautiful pieces of jewellery. She describes her work as "chunky yet feminine". Bold rings are set with rich garnets and amethysts. Her more delicate "cow parsley" pieces combine silver and gold, and, she says, are inspired by the foliage in nearby Grantchester Meadows.

At the time of writing, Newnham was runner-up in the *Sunday Times*' 101 Best Places to Live in Britain survey, published in March 2014. (The winner was Skipton in Yorkshire.) Newnham earned plaudits for offering "country living in the heart of Cambridge", with a "genuine village atmosphere", wide range of shops, and good schools, plus nearby beauty spots such as Sheep's Green and Coe Fen. What more can I say …

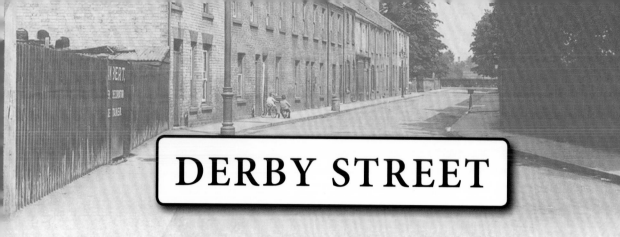

DERBY STREET

11 December 1981

At 6 a.m. when most of us are asleep, a figure in a baggy sweater, mug of tea in hand, opens his door and exchanges greetings with one of the few open-eyed creatures of that dim hour, a linnet hanging in a cage among leaves and flowers. A step or two across a passage and Basil Sargeant is in his kitchen, beginning a routine he has followed almost singlehanded since 1960.

After checking a delicate wall clock and turning on a ten-foot by eight-foot oven, he inspects the results of last evening's labours: fresh-smelling mounds of dough that have risen in darkness in 140 loaf pans. On a shelf by the oven, his tea stays warm as he dips into deep flour bins to start a new batch for the late-morning baking.

The walls around him are white tiles; pans and trays are black as the oven door, but as the sun comes out he can glimpse through his window a hanging garden. About 7.45 he takes from a ceiling hook a ten-foot paddle or "peel" with which he arranges 16 trays in the oven. The day's first white, brown and granary loaves are on their way.

(from "A hint of Basil", an article by Judy Smith)

This extract about Basil's bakery at No. 7 Derby Street captures some of the special atmosphere of the once rural outpost of Cambridge that used to be in the parish of Grantchester. Basil, who is Grantchester born and bred – "a place of peace and quietness" – regards Newnham, which he knows so well as "a funny place – more a collection of individuals than a real community."

Whatever he thinks about Newnham, Basil would surely admit that Derby Street is a rather special little community. This time last year, the entire street was invited round to the home of Mr and Mrs Robert Hirsch at No. 17–18 Derby Street to celebrate the 80th birthday of Mrs Charlotte "Lotte" Houlton who lives further along the street at No. 23 in a nicely modernised council house. When they gave the party, the Hirsches had just won £25 in the local "best window box" competition and decided to spend their winnings on giving Lotte a memorable birthday. It was a popular gesture with the local community.

Lotte Houlton is one of the oldest residents living in the street. Born in Cross Street off Mill Road, where her parents kept The Crown, Lotte later moved with her parents to The Cross Keys pub at Brookside. She was married from there. "I have lived in Newnham for 56 years", she said. Her first home there was at No. 44 Selwyn Road – she and her husband Harry, a stoker at the engineering labs, moved there in 1925. When the children had grown up she moved to a smaller house at No. 28 Newnham Road before coming to Derby Street. Until she was 70, Lotte had her own news stand opposite Lloyds Bank in Sidney Street.

Basil Sargeant, Derby Street's baker.

Robert Hirsch is the son of Paul Hirsch the musicologist, who together with his family escaped to Cambridge from Nazi Germany with his priceless collection of music intact (see Adams Road chapter). Robert, co-founder of the glass blowing company CamLab (Glass) Ltd, was a musician himself. He was, in fact, a man of many talents. He was a good businessman and a generous, paternalistic employer, who performed at concerts on the cello and kept a classical record collection in his office. A collector of china and a lover of cars, his pride and joy apparently was an Alvis car that had belonged to Douglas Bader, the air-ace.

Once the home of well-known Newnham families like the Lamberts and the Ludmans, the Starrs and the Stanbridges, all of whom practised a variety of skills and trades in the area, Derby Street had grown up in the 1870s on pasture land that once belonged to King's College, before it was divided up into little parcels of land for building. The Ordnance Survey map of 1886 shows it all in great detail.

Two large houses dominated the entrance to the street from Barton Road: on the right with its main entrance in Hardwick Street was The Croft, a big house with an entrance into the garden from Derby Street. The carriage entrance was on Barton Road. In 1881, James S. Reid MA classics lecturer of Caius College lived there.

The other large house opposite The Croft was Maitland House, whose main entrance was in Derby Street. In 1864, Alfred Paget Humphrey MA, senior Esquire Bedell[5] in the university, Bursar of Selwyn College and executive officer of the National Rifle Association, was living there. Both houses had conservatories in their gardens, and both have been pulled down in recent years to make way for flats – Cresswell Court and Maitland House.

The traders of Newnham Croft were well established by 1886. By 1874, Mr William Wilby who lived at Hope Cottage, Derby Street (so many of the cottages in the area were given pretty names in the years before 1891 when numbering was introduced), was running a baker's and grocery business at that address. By 1884,

---

[5] a ceremonial officer of a university, usually with official duties relating to the conduct of ceremonies for the conferment of degrees.

View of Derby Street in 1925. On the left is the yard of Horace Lambert, the builder.

a sub-postmaster's trade was added to his activities and in 1890 he sold out to Mr William Ernest Ellis, who carried on these trades, along with dealing in tea. The entry in the street directory for 1894 lists William Ernest Ellis as running a bakery, grocer's and the Newnham Croft post office at Hope Cottage, No. 7 Derby Street.

By 1904, Ellis had moved the post office to Grantchester Street, to the shop next door to his own home, St Mark's Lodge, whose garden backed on to Derby Street. In 1909, The Cooperative Society Stores moved into the shop, and the post office moved to its present position further down Grantchester Street.

Mr Ellis continued to run the bakery in Derby Street until 1914, with a succession of bakers helping him. Jack Willis was the baker in 1912. Two years later it was Albert George Hoppett. Then Mr Ellis sold his bakery to a Mr Haywood, who came out of retirement. After the armistice his son J. Haywood, who came from Vancouver to serve in the forces, went into the business learning the trade from his father and establishing the businesses of J. Haywood & Son all over the city. The Haywoods owned and ran the bakery until the 1960s when Basil Sargeant, who started work as an apprentice there 39 years earlier, took over.

But back now for a moment to 1861 to see who else was living in the street with William Wilby, the grocer and baker. There was, in fact, another baker at No. 1, a William Gray, and further down the street on the west side a milkman called Henry Gray. There were also clerks, carpenters and college servants in the street and a compositor called Alfred Nobbs.

Edward Cooper, a retired college porter was living at No. 18 Derby Street. When the Hirsches were making alterations to the house the builders dug up hundreds of Cooper's marmalade pots buried outside the front door. Clearly they had been made there and not thrown away. (They also found a sandstone gargoyle made perhaps by an apprentice.) Perhaps the Edward Cooper living there 100 years ago was a member of the marmalade family and got a large consignment of the stuff at Christmas! Cooper, according to the deeds of the house, bought it from John Ebenezer Foster in 1881 and sold it to Roger Sanger in 1884.

The builder in the street then was George W. Lambert who, according to the deeds in the possession of Mr and Mrs Hirsch, bought the parcel of land in 1879 from one "A. Jones, gentleman". George Lambert had seven children. One of his daughters was called Elsie and it is presumably after her, a favourite daughter perhaps, that No. 17 was named Elsie Cottage. The story is told by John Gray in his book on Newnham (I wonder if he is related to William Gray the baker, or Henry Gray the milkman), that George Lambert was an early user of the telephone – it was installed in his Derby Street home by October 1901. Lambert was also the local undertaker for many years. There was a big carpenter's workshop and paint store over what is now the garage of No. 17. The coffins were made there, and the hearse would have stood in the stable below. For many years from 1904, Lambert's neighbour and fellow craftsman at No. 18 Derby Street, was a monumental mason called T. C. Stanbridge. In fact, they both had access to a coaching house and there were interconnecting doors between one workshop and another.

Mrs Elizabeth Hirsch remembers being told by an old man in the street one day that special mutes (funeral attendants) acted as funeral bearers and mourners at all the funerals. Their caps were kept hanging up by their hearse. One day this old man had filled the mutes' caps with apples, which interrupted the proceedings in a less than reverent way. The house has a very special atmosphere – it is incredibly peaceful and Mrs Hirsch believes that that could have something to do with the fact that it was once an undertaker's.

The Derby Stores, known originally as the Derby Arms on the corner of Derby Street and Newnham Croft is another of the Newnham institutions. Open from 9 a.m. until 9 p.m. and specialising as an off-licence and a delicatessen, it attracts people from miles around. Mr and Mrs Michael Callan have been running it for ten years. They took over from a Mr Bence who has recently died.

The stores would appear to have started when William Henry Hunt, who was in business there from before 1881 until 1886, started as a miller and general shopman. John Gray says that a Mr John Glasscock then used the premises to trade as a Fly and Hackney cab proprietor. "The name 'Derby Arms' first appears here, so it would seem likely that he obtained the first licence to sell alcohol on the premises." The Derby Arms started as a "jug and bottle".

By 1891 Mr Glasscock had gone, probably directly to premises in Newnham Road adjoining the Granta public house, says John Gray. He was succeeded by Mrs Anna Hyland. By 1894 or 1895, Mrs Sarah Lakin had taken over and added the trades of grocer and tea dealer. In 1905, writes Gray, a cupful of jam could be bought there for one penny. Alfred Challis was running the stores in 1925 and in the 1950s the proprietor was a Mrs H. Pocock. Today, one of the most popular lines at the Derby Stores, apart from the pâtés and specialist cheeses, are the homemade cakes which customers like to buy by the slice. Pam Callan is prepared to make Christmas cakes for people at £2 a pound.

There is something about these Cambridge streets that inspires poetry!

In 1975, Peter Milbank wrote the following poem in a letter to the *Cambridge Evening News*:

Derby Street, house neat
Hundred yards by thirty feet
Corner stores and baker's shop
Forty dwellings, that's the lot

After reading my article on Derby Street, a former resident of Newnham, Mr J. H. Bayord, wrote in to express his surprise that no mention was made of the Ashby family in the paragraph about past proprietors of the Derby Arms. "Our family moved into Hardwick Street from Grantchester in 1938 when I was a lad of six. Mr and Mrs Ashby were occupying the Derby Arms then and right up to the time that Mrs Pocock took over. I can well remember the first day we moved into Newnham, my father sending me round the shop to get a halfpennyworth of sweets so that I wouldn't be in the way while he made our house ready for occupation."

Mr Bayord said he also attended Newnham Croft School with the Ashby daughters and was fairly certain therefore that Mr and Mrs Ashby were proprietors of the Derby Arms for at least a decade.

"Sara Payne spoke of the Ludmans. Perhaps it is worth mentioning also that they were the caretakers of Newnham Croft School in those days, right through the war years at least, and again their children were playmates of my brother and I."

For many years J. P. Dear, a bookbinder, lived at Bloomfield Cottage, No. 19 Derby Street. Today the book publishing business is represented in the street by Cyril Carder of No. 25 Derby Street, who worked for the Cambridge University Press for 49 years first as a compositor, then as a reader. If you had a job with the Pitt Press they used to say that "you were made for life". Mr Carder worked for two renowned master printers at the Press – Walter Lewis and Brooke Crutchley.

Fred Bloy, the chief technician at the Zoology Laboratory until he retired recently, lives at No. 24 Derby Street. Fred Bloy is well known in Cambridge for his work in cricket coaching – he is the coach for the County Colts.

Dorothy Starr who lived for many years at No. 11 Derby Street with her late husband Arthur Starr, the tailor, was quite a sportswoman too. She was a keen bowls player. It was said of Mrs Starr's house that the wiring was of such a low voltage that she used to go to bed by candlelight. Another tailor's widow in Derby Street was a Mrs Paine. When the broadcaster Gilbert Harding was up at Queens' College he was in lodgings with her at No. 10 Derby Street.

Rosalind Morris, a primary school teacher, bought No. 12 Derby Street in 1972 for £10,000. Later that year she married Martin Mays, a lecturer in the Chemistry Department at Cambridge who then also lived there. Two years later they bought No. 13 for £7,500 and converted the two into a very nice five-bedroomed house with the help of a local architect, Richard Lyon. The family lived there until 1982 when they sold the property for £60,000 and moved to No. 39 Barton Road. Shortly afterwards William Heffer and his family followed the Mays from Grantchester Street round to a spot next door at No. 41 Barton Road.

DERBY STREET

Revisited

Derby Street with its two long-established shops and Victorian terrace houses, still manages to maintain, despite the parking problems and traffic congestion, some of that special village atmosphere which has traditionally made Newnham so sought after as a place to live and visit. The Newnham Bakery and the Derby Stores are still well supported by local residents and others, who make the trip to buy the granary cobs and the popular loaves at the bakery (all the bread is GMO free) and from 7 a.m., their morning paper, olives, cheeses, and Kosher food on Thursdays at the Derby Stores, which has also been the post office for the past 12 years.

A reminder here that the Newnham Bakery has been going strong in Derby Street since 1861. Jonathan and Nicky Palmer took over the business in 1998. Fourteen years ago they upgraded the gas oven, and installed an office, confectionery and preparation area. "Business is good", says Nicky, "because of local support and a wholesale round". (Basil Sergeant used to deliver on his bike!) As a customer myself, I would add that the traditional baking methods ensure fresh bread every day. To achieve that freshness, baker Jonathan works six nights a week, from 7 p.m. until 9.30 a.m. The bakery also prepares hot drinks, and sandwiches which are popular with local building workers.

Round the corner at the Derby Stores the day starts at 7 a.m. when locals pop in to buy their morning paper en route to work. Seventeen years ago, the business was taken over and has been owned and run ever since by two brothers-in-law and two sisters-in-law: Neera Saini who is married to Kartar Singh, and Manjit Kaur married to Jagtar Singh, known as Jack. Kartar is Manjit's brother. Neera has been the postmistress for about 12 years. The Derby Stores is one of those shops, like all the others in Newnham, that has learnt to diversify in order to keep going. And all the shops are very community minded in an area that is still quite a tight knit community, although perhaps less so than it was say 30 years ago.

Some locals will tell you that Newnham is less pleasant than it was. Much higher house prices – Nos. 12 and 13, the two houses made into one sold recently for £600,000, reflecting Cambridge as a hot spot – have led to wealthier inhabitants,

In the Newnham Bakery, left Jill Lister and Nicky Palmer whose husband Jonathan is the baker.

fewer academics, more loft conversions, more cars with on-street parking being the norm, and frequent congestion in the streets which get blocked at times with taxis and grocery delivery vans. But in spite of a less attractive environment than previously, there is still continuity and a rootedness about the place, which draws people to and keeps them in "the village".

Take two houses in Derby Street, Nos. 17 and 18. After the death of first Robert and then Elizabeth Hirsch, the two houses returned to their original single entities. No. 18 is divided into flats: for three years the ground floor flat was occupied by Joyce Blakemore, who moved from Birmingham to Cambridge to be near her daughter Pam Blakemore Hirsch, daughter-in-law of Robert and Elizabeth Hirsch who lives with her husband Desmond Hirsch round the corner in Grantchester Street. The flats at No. 18 are now generally lived in by visiting scholars.

So some continuity, but probably fair to say a more cosmopolitan community than it used to be, with a lot more renting by academics and visiting scholars. But on the surface, you could be tempted to think that there had been few changes. After all, Derby Street looks just about the same as it did 30 years ago!

BARTON ROAD

11 November – 9 December 1982

An Anglo-Saxon burial ground, a hidden lake and a resident kingfisher are among the secrets of Barton Road, that staunchly residential road in Newnham which has become, with the building of the bypass, one of the city's key arteries.

The Anglo-Saxon burial ground lies at the junction of Barton Road and Grange Road, while the lake – Bolton's Pit, which is about two acres in area – is to be found to the south west of the Barton Road–Grantchester Road corner. It is completely invisible to the passerby as it is surrounded by private houses on the south side of the road, and is private property, although it is home to the kingfisher. Until the late nineteenth century, there were no buildings at the country end of Barton Road on the south side. A house called "Waltham Sal" just past the Grange Road turn was the last outpost. Waltham Sal, originally called the "House in the Fields", has an interesting history. A study of the Enclosure Award of 1805 shows that the House in the Fields Close belonged to Storey's Charity, as did the Red Bull inn. The tenant of the House in the Fields then was Francis Beales. In 1809, the House in the Fields was put up for auction by Thomas Prior. It was advertised in the *Cambridge Chronicle* as "a valuable copyhold estate, most pleasantly situated in the fields at the back of the colleges".

Stephanie Orford and Tim Cole in their chapter on Barton Road in John A. Gray's booklet *Newnham*, say claims were made that a tunnel for the possible smuggling of liquor linked the House in the Fields with Grantchester, but the Preservation Society could find no entrance to such a tunnel in a detailed inspection in the autumn of 1969.

The beautiful Baker map of Cambridge in 1830 shows there were just two houses on the south side of Barton Road then – the House in the Fields and Croft Lodge. But by the 1850s, over 50 houses had been built along the Barton Road. In about 1901, an important Iron Age burial was found in the garden of Croft Lodge.

The House in the Fields is listed for the first time as Waltham Sal, in 1881, when it was occupied by Dr Bushell Anningson, the medical officer of health, who became university lecturer in medical jurisprudence and continued to live in the house until 1919. From 1920 until 1931, the house was listed in the Street directories under Nos. 49, 51 and 53 Barton Road. Three families lived there.

Herbert Thomas Hockey, the estate agent, acquired the whole property in 1931 and reconverted the whole into one house and took a great interest and pride in the gardens. In 1969, when Mr Hockey died, Waltham Sal was sold to property developers who applied for planning permission to demolish it, and replace it with a block of town houses.

Stephanie Orford and Tim Cole report that City Councillor Tony Cornell, and Mr J. M. Lennox Cook, principal of the Lennox Cook School of English at No. 75 Barton Road, led a campaign to save the house and its beautiful garden from destruction. "They were partly successful, and with the help of the then Ministry of Housing and Local Government, together with the Cambridge Preservation Society, obtained an alternative scheme from the architects, Dry Halasz and Dixon. This scheme, which has since been carried out as Archway Court, allowed for the retention of the old house, but blocks of townhouses have been built in the garden behind it."

Croft Lodge with its wonderful garden was owned in the 1960s by Francis Crick, the biologist, who together with James Watson and Maurice Wilkins, won the Nobel Prize for their work on the discovery of the double helix. The astronomer, Douglas Gough, now Professor Emeritus of Theoretical Astrophysics at Cambridge University, remembers living there as a Ph.D. student from 1963–4.

Croft Lodge on the south side of Barton Road in the 1920s.

Barton Road from opposite St Mark's Church. 1925 (circa).

"I rented the top floor of the house together with two other students. We would have liked to have stayed but when we asked Odile Crick, Francis' wife, who dealt with the business side, whether we could renew our lease, she said: 'No, we are going to pull it down!'" Well, the Cricks did pull it down, and built the Croft Lodge flats in 1965 on the extensive site. I wonder, is that how he spent his Nobel Prize money?

St Mark's Church in Barton Road, the focal point of a deep community spirit which has existed for years in Newnham village, dates from 1871. *The History of Grantchester*, written in 1875 by S. P. Widnall, gives the details of the beginnings of St Mark's: "In consequence of the population of the parish having so much increased in the part adjoining Newnham, it was decided in 1871 that an effort should be made to provide a place of worship in that neighbourhood.

"A meeting was called on the 10th of June in that year to take the necessary steps for building a temporary wooden church, a subscription was opened, and so well was the call responded to that in the six weeks a sufficient sum was collected to enable the committee to sign the builders contract, and the Church was completed and opened by the Bishop on the 10th of November following. The cost was about £400."

Cost was an important feature of the St Mark's enterprise, for when in 1873 it was recorded that a bell was purchased by subscription and fired by the end of that year, the cost is listed as £32 3s 6d.

At the time the wooden church was built, the site was leased from Corpus Christi College, the patrons of the parish of Grantchester, at a nominal rent. However, in 1876, on the proposal of Mr Vansittart of Pinehurst, the two-acre site, which would give sufficient space for a parsonage and parish room, as well as a permanent church, was purchased for £600. Mr Vansittart himself contributed £300, and the college £100. Public subscription raised the rest.

The Rev. Bill Loveless, Vicar of St Mark's Church 1967–1987.

Next, they needed a parish room and a parsonage and in 1885 an appeal was issued, which brought in £500. The Parsonage was completed in 1889 at a cost of about £1,300. The foundation stone of the permanent church was laid on 23 May 1900, following an appeal for funds by the Rev. Septimus Symonds, who started his ministry there in 1898. He was vicar of St Mark's until 1931. The church was dedicated by the Bishop of Ely on St Mark's Day, 1901. In May 1916, it was decided to take steps to make St Mark's a separate parish, no longer under the wing of Grantchester. To do this the church had to raise a capital fund of at least £626 towards the endowment of the vicar's stipend.

The church was consecrated on 20 December 1917. The formal constitution of a separate parish, bounded on the south by the then borough boundary, on the east by Church Rate Walk, and on the north by Sidgwick Avenue and Leckhampton Road, was announced at Whitsuntide, 1918. The wooden church was demolished 15 years ago.

In 1902, a year after the permanent church of St Mark's was established, a big handsome family house called Ramsey House was built next to the grounds of St Mark's. It was at the same time as Millington Road was being thought of, so the architect was asked to change the frontage to make it front onto Millington Road.

Ramsey House, now No. 1 Millington Road, was built by William Ernest Johnson, a Fellow of King's College and Sidgwick lecturer in moral sciences and psychology. His family came from Ramsey in old Huntingdonshire, hence the name of the house. The Johnson family lived in the house until 1948 when it was rented from his son, Charles Johnson, by Harold and Margaret Whitehouse, who bought it in 1951 and whose home it is today.

Rustic origins are not forgotten

Hunting breakfasts at White's Stables in Barton Road, where undergraduates used to stable their horses next to the huge apple orchard that became Croft Gardens – one of the memories of Barton Road that ensure that its rustic origins are not forgotten – are vividly recalled by many of the older residents of the road.

Later, the apple trees were cut down when Croft Gardens were developed. Croft Gardens belongs to King's College, who acquired the White Horse Riding School in January 1979 and then demolished it. This must have been rather sad, a sort of "Cherry Orchard" happening, which is clearly remembered by Dame Elizabeth Hill, Emeritus Professor of Slavonic Studies at Cambridge from

1948–68. She was born Yelizaveta Fyodorovna in Russia in 1900, but has lived in Croft Gardens since the 1930s. (Dame Elizabeth Hill died in 1996.)

No. 29 Barton Road, the kindergarten and junior departments of the Shrubbery School, has an interesting history. Built in 1885, it is called the Red House and belongs to Gonville and Caius College. In 1887, two years after it was built, it was occupied by the students of Newnham College. Miss Jane Lee was the principal at that time.

From 1910–1940 it was the home of Mrs M. A. Adam, a fellow of Girton College. The Shrubbery School took it over in 1941, moving part of the school from premises in Hills Road. The Shrubbery School opened in Station Road before moving to Hills Road. In 1942, the Rev. and Mrs J. Living-Taylor took over the school. Maria Living-Taylor, who at the time of writing is 93, was the first Baptist woman minister in the country. The Living-Taylors handed on the Shrubbery School to their daughter and son-in-law, Mr and Mrs Alfred Wainwright, who took over the running of the school in 1962.

Mr Wainwright recalls that Barbara Wootton used to live at the Red House as a girl. Mrs Wootton was Professor of Sociology at Bedford College, London University when Christine Courtney of Shelford Road Trumpington was a student there. Mrs Courtney wrote to say: "As mentioned in Mrs Wootton's autobiography *In a World I Never Made*, she was married to Captain Jack Wootton of 11th Battalion, Suffolk Regiment, for exactly one-and-a-half days. He was killed in the First World War. Barton Road is also referred to in her fascinating book."

Before the Shrubbery moved into the Red House, it was the home of Professor F. Graham Smith, the director of Jodrell Bank and formerly research Fellow at Downing College.

No. 33 Barton Road, the senior department of the Shrubbery School, is called Croft Cottage. From the 1890s until the 1930s, it was the home of Baron

The Shrubbery School speech day held in the Cambridge Guildhall in the early 1950s.

View down Barton Road in the 1920s, towards the junction with King's Road. The Hat and Feathers pub is on the corner.

Anatole von Hugel of Trinity College, the curator of the University Museum of Archaeology and Ethnology.

Among the old girls of the Shrubbery School, a school with a family atmosphere to which a lot of old pupils send their children, is Pat Taylor, daughter of Capt. Taylor, the late proprietor of the *Cambridge Evening News*. The school closed down in the late 1980s when the Wainwrights retired.

The Hat and Feathers public house, the haunt of undergraduates from Selwyn College, has been in business for more than 100 years. In 1851, William Bunker was licensee. By 1886 Joseph Thurston had become the licensee, while Hat and Feathers Lane (or Short Lane), later King's Road, beside the inn was home to eight artisan families – gardeners, bricklayers, and labourers.

Nos. 37, 39 and 41 Barton Road, three similar architect designed houses, were built in 1923 for three families who were colleagues and friends: Sydney Roberts, secretary of the University Press, Charles Seltman and Dr M. B. R. Swann. There was to have been a whole block of houses stretching right up to Waltham Sal, described earlier, but the builder apparently went bankrupt.

Mrs Marjory Ady, who moved into No. 37 Barton Road in 1939 six months before the outbreak of war, is the oldest resident in that stretch of Barton Road. She came there with her parents from India. "My father, J. F. Furnivall, was in the Indian Civil Service. He retired early, having tried to get the Burmese ready for Home Rule. My mother was Burmese. When he retired to Cambridge my father lectured in Burmese history, language and law."

The new home of William and Lesley Heffer, No. 41 Barton Road, has links with Cambridge University Press too. The Heffers bought it from David Knight, the marketing director of the Press. Before that it belonged to Richard and Nora (Lady) David. Mr David, who was Secretary to the Syndics of the Press, is an expert not only on Shakespeare, but also on sedges.

Publishers, literary figures, people from the book world and authors abound in Barton Road. Further up at No. 59 Barton Road lives Mrs Helen Walker, author of children's books, and her husband Frank, who is the Unitarian Minister in Cambridge.

Author John Lennox Cook has lived since 1962 at "Toll Bar", 75 Barton Road, a house built in 1911. He left the Bell School to set up his own language school, the Lennox Cook School of English on Barton Road. When he bought the house it was divided into two flats. For many years, Toll Bar was the home of C. Forster Cooper, a fellow of Trinity Hall and the one-time superintendent of the Museum of Zoology.

John Lennox Cook is the figurehead of the language school. He sits up in his study writing novels – his latest, *The World Before Us*, has just been published. Two joint principals, Peter Bingley and Denise Swallow, run the school.

At the time of the Queen's Silver Jubilee in 1977, when the nation was planning its street parties, residents in Barton Road, thinking of their jollifications, were uncertain where to draw the line – a mile of trestle tables through leafy Newnham did not seem feasible.

But the problem was solved for the western end of the road when James and Joy Cadbury invited everyone on both sides of Barton Road between Grantchester Road and King's, Clare and Queens' College sports grounds to a party in their garden which overlooks Bolton's Pit. The Cadburys' blueprint for a jubilee party guest list give me an ideal framework for this article on Barton Road.

A house by the lake where wildlife is thriving!

It is entirely appropriate that the Cadburys, who live at No. 93 Barton Road, should have a house by the lake. James Cadbury is head of research at the Royal Society for the Protection of Birds at Sandy, Bedfordshire, so no one is better qualified to describe the birds and other wildlife that thrive on or near Bolton's Pit than he is. The lake is home to six species of wildfowl. "More than 100 mallard rest on the pool during the day", says James Cadbury. "Then at dusk and again at dawn, they fly on to the neighbouring potato fields."

Swans and great-crested grebes and coots are attracted to the reed bed on the submerged island in the middle of the lake and when the kingfishers, which breed in Newnham, are feeding their young, Bolton Pit is a favoured feeding ground for them. A roost of 4,000 swallows and pied wagtails frequent the lake, where a colony of reed warblers build their nests. Lakeside dwellers try to cause as little disturbance as possible on the lake between March and the end of June when the birds are nesting. Sometimes when it is a hard winter, the lake, which is about 14 feet deep, freezes over, and then there is skating.

A medlar tree overhangs the lake, and when the fruits ripen they become sweet smelling. Mistletoe, a scarce plant in Cambridge, grows in some of the gardens at the Bolton's Pit end of Barton Road. There are 14 or 15 old apple trees, relics of an old orchard in the area, which have mistletoe growing on them. And for the final detail in this "nature notebook", I can report that foxes frequently come into the area, and sometimes the quiet and the beady-eyed catch sight of the cubs.

The lake, which is one hectare in size, is owned by Paul Quiggin, of No. 6 Grantchester Road. But the house owners on the north bank who have access in their own right, have formed a Lake Dwellers Association, which seems to be a gentleman's agreement to treat the environment of the lake with loving care – and not to cut down trees or disturb the birds. The lake, which has existed since the beginning of the century, is of historic interest because the land has been put to various uses in the last few hundred years.

Jack Roach, formerly the assistant secretary of the Local Examination Syndicate, who together with his wife has lived for many years at No. 77 Barton Road, has written an account of the lake (he called it Barchester Lake which was one of its many suggested names – nothing to do with Trollope, more likely a shortening of Barton and Grantchester, in which he said that it started its history as a rubbish dump!

"In the sixteenth century Cambridge citizens disposed of their household refuse, 'muck mire and filth', by scattering it outside their houses in the nearest lane or ditch, but as the result of constant visitations of plague and the condemnation of their insanitary habits by the energetic Vice-Chancellor, Andrew Perne, Master of Peterhouse, the Corporation accepted his recommendation. In 1575, rubbish pits, called 'dungells' were established just beyond the limits of the town."

Jack Roach says that the rubbish pit in Fulbrooke Field, the area which concerns us here, was not one of the earliest in Cambridge as it is not included by Cooper in his Annals. But it cannot have been much later, judging by such of the contents as can be dated. "These include numerous clay tobacco pipes from the early seventeenth century, a three-handled pot dated 1612 and various tokens. The earliest legal document relating to this piece of Fulbrooke Field is dated 1737."

In 1888, the land was bought "as a brickyard" by Edward Bolton, "contractor of Newmarket Road" for £822. Brick-making, which had started there under James Clabbon in 1825, started again and continued there for the next 10 or 20 years as, recalls Jack Roach. "Many rows of small houses of pale bricks in the neighbourhood bear witness."

Edward Bolton enclosed his land with a privet hedge on its eastern boundary and with a fence along its northern boundary and at their junction marked it with a boundary stone inscribed "EB" and "GCC". The stone is at the edge of the garden of No. 77 Barton Road. Mr Roach suggests that the Bolton diggings approached and released underground springs. For the water level gradually rose and what had been a damp swamp became a pool. "Elderly residents recall how when they were boys they had spent Saturday afternoons hunting water snakes in the reeds."

Bolton's bricklaying in the marshy field was no more financially successful than Clabbons, whose widow was declared bankrupt in 1849. For his land was soon heavily mortgaged to the Capital and Counties Bank for £2,000. Brick-making came to an end. But as a pit with water at the bottom it was leased in 1900 to the University Figure Skating Club.

In 1908, the Bank as mortgagees sold the land to Clement Hobson and a few years later, in 1911, it passed into the possession of the Smart family, the clothiers, tailors, drapers and hatters of Market Street. Apparently, it ceased to be a brick-yard and was used as a country retreat by the Smarts, who built a summerhouse and rock garden.

Local residents recall that the Smarts were kind and generous landlords and allowed their neighbours access to the lake for bathing, fishing, boating and skat-ing. Mr C. J. Smart died in 1953, while the sister to whom the land was left died in 1962. It passed to a brother Mr Kenneth Smart, an occulist in Birmingham who had no local interest in the property. Rumours about its future abounded. It was said that it was to be bought by building contractors, the lake filled in, and 39 houses built on the site. "We, who were then among the 'lakeside owners', felt that something must be done quickly", said Jack Roach.

The initiative was taken by Mr W. K. Lacey, of Fulbrooke Road, and Paul Quiggin, who enlisted the help and advice of Mr H. Carter Jonas, a local resident. He was interested in the lake because as a keen yachtsman, he had experimented unsuccessfully with sailing on it. After a number of failed bids Messrs Quiggin and Lacey were finally able to buy the land and lake for £13,500, split equally between them.

"In the following years", write Stephanie Orford and Tim Cole in their article on Barton Road in John Gray's book *Newnham*: "various parts of the lakeside were sold to house owners there, giving them access and including in the deeds of sale various conditions about retaining the tranquil nature of the area. Mr Lacey sold his share to Mr Quiggin when he emigrated to New Zealand."

One lakeside resident who has a particularly beautiful view of the lake is Mr Reuben Heffer, who built his bungalow at 89 Barton Road in 1970 to the design of the architect Peter Lord. Mr Lord also designed Heffers bookshop in Trinity Street. The morning sun pours into the drawing room. Through the large windows stretch the lawn and the lake beyond. The effect is of mid-morning on Windermere. Several houses in Cambridge are called Rydal House, or Thirlmere House, so allow me that spot of poetic licence.

His son William Heffer says of the lake: "I have swum in it, cycled round it, walked round it and rowed round it. When my father retired from running the bookshop, he was given a little boat as a retirement present.

Mr Reuben Heffer, son of Ernest Heffer who founded the books side of the Heffer business, has lived in Barton Road for many years. "My father moved over here to No. 71, called 'Weathercote' in 1921 when my sister was up at Girton. Before that we lived at No. 12."

The Heffers' new neighbour when they moved across to No. 71, a house with a big cellar was Professor O. T. Jones, the Woodwardian Professor of Geology who moved to Cambridge from Manchester University. Reuben Heffer's late wife Nesta was the daughter of Professor Jones.

On the spot overlooking the lake, where Reuben Heffer built his new home, there was an old house in a state of disrepair. The house, another bungalow, belonged to Mr A. L. Bird who developed the site in the 1920s. A university lecturer in engineering, his interests were restoring old square pianos and playing the organ.

Tim Cole and Stephanie Orford say that he installed an organ in the bungalow and distributed the pipes around the house and in the loft. In 1938, he bought an 18-inch gauge scale model railway steam locomotive and tender, and kept it on a short length of track under a tarpaulin. Mr Bird was also a keen fisherman and did his fishing from a punt, which the late W. L. Stockbridge, an antique dealer from No. 109 Barton Road had built for him in mahogany. They went out fishing together in the punt.

Near neighbours in Barton Road in the 1930s were Morley Stuart, the Editor of the *Cambridge Daily News*, who lived at No. 79, and Miss M. H. Cattley, the headmistress of the Perse Girls' School a little further up at No. 95. No. 79 Barton Road, together with its other half, No. 81, was built in the 1920s by Mr A. E. Marshall, who owned and ran the grocer's shop in Newnham Road. The houses were built to be used by the staff in the shop but no employees of his ever lived there.

Another house builder in Barton Road was Ben Hayward who started the cycle shop in Trumpington Street in 1912. The family lived over the shop until they built and moved to No. 95 Barton Road. "It was open country there then – no Gough Way, just open land belonging to Corpus Christi", said Miss Kathleen Hayward, Ben Hayward's daughter who lives in a flat built by her father on the opposite side of Barton Road.

Four years after he had built No. 95, Ben Hayward sold the house and bought a plot of land in Millington Road. "We built a house there, No. 34; it was very quiet, so when this piece of ground came up for sale, we moved up here and built No. 100 just beyond and opposite No. 95." In 1956, the year he died, Ben Hayward built No. 102 for his daughter.

Further up on the south side of the road, No. 107 was built in the 1930s by a renowned biochemist and entomologist Professor David Keilin FRS, a Fellow of Magdalene College. He died in 1963 and the house was later sold to Michael Cooper, an engineer and Fellow of St John's College.

When he and his wife, Helen, and two daughters moved to Oxford in 1978, where Helen became the first woman Fellow of University College, until then an all male college, the house was sold to another Fellow of St John's, Professor Richard Perham FRS and his wife Dr Nancy Lane Perham OBE, a cell biologist in the Zoology Department and Fellow of Girton College.

Betty Barr and her sister Marjory grew up in rural Barton Road. They have lived at Orchard Close, No. 111, since 1933 in a house built by their father on part of an extensive orchard belonging to King's College. Lawrence Bend Barr, a lawyer who studied at Selwyn College, bought the orchard and sold part of it to fund the building of the appropriately named family house. Three adjoining houses were built on the other part of the orchard. At the corner of their garden is the junction of a little stream and Bin Brook.

The sisters kept ponies in the field at the back of the house. "It was like being in the country. We used to ride the ponies across the fields to Grantchester and down Barton Road and up Grange Road without having to worry about the traffic." They also rode the ponies across town and up Downing Street to the blacksmith at the top of the street.

Their father was articled to the law firm of Whitehead and Todd, and later became a partner in the firm. Betty Barr, who left the Perse Girls' School, in 1942, studied at the London School of Economics before following in her father's footsteps when she joined the firm as a lawyer in 1960. Her sister worked as a librarian in London. The family were regular worshippers at St Marks Church where Lawrence Barr was churchwarden.

One of the oldest houses in Barton Road is Barton Cottage, No. 78. Since 1937, it has been the home of Sir Vivian and Lady Fuchs, who moved there from No. 72 Barton Road. It was built in 1810 by Charles Humphrey, the builder and architect of the "Doll's House" in Maid's Causeway. For many years the house was the home of Professor Breul, who wrote his German dictionary there. The mature three-acre garden with an avenue of limes which used to lead to a nearby farm, once backed on to open cornfields. A big clue to the occupation of the distinguished owner of the house is a topiary penguin with a yew egg between his feet, whose yew beak peeks over the front hedge and is quite the talk of Barton Road.

The penguin has been tended for the past 30 years by Antarctic explorer, and the retired director of the British Antarctic Survey, Sir Vivian Fuchs who wrote the book *Ice and Men*. Sir Vivian is President of the National Geographic Society. Lady Joyce Fuchs is as keen a gardener as her husband. "I'm hardly ever indoors", she says.

Antarctic explorer Sir Vivian Fuchs and his wife, Lady Joyce Fuchs in the garden of their home in Barton Road.

A touch of Garden City

Cambridge people who regularly drive down the A505 past Letchworth Garden City will be familiar with the distinctive architectural features of the large pseudo cottages with their square-leaded windows and pebbledash facades that characterise the housing stock of the country's first garden suburb. But how many know that tucked away in Barton Road on the north side just past the Grange Road turn is a pair of houses which are pure Letchworth? In them are incorporated many of the hallmarks of the Arts and Crafts movement with its emphasis on hand-work, quality and simple design.

The houses in question are Nos. 28 and 30 Barton Road. They were built in the 1920s to the design of Bennett and Bidwell. Robert Bennett was the assistant to Raymond Unwin, the principal architect of Letchworth Garden City.

Graham Pollard, the deputy director of the Fitzwilliam Museum, who has lived for 14 years at No. 28 with his Italian wife, Maria, says that the houses were built for a cleric at St Catherine's called Mason. He built No. 30, called "Foxleigh", for his own occupation – No. 28 was built to be let. Mason's first tenant was Miss Emily Pepper, who was secretary of the Deaf and Dumb Association. Graham Pollard remembers being told by a cabinet maker from Northumberland, Tim Swann, who lived with his family at No. 41 Barton Road, that as a child he used to go and visit Miss Pepper. "Her fire consisted of a handful of chaff and in her window was a stuffed owl."

The next person to live at No. 28, a fine house with oak mantels and period fireplaces, was Ernest Haddon, son of the great A. C. Haddon, after whom the Anthropology Library is named. Ernest Haddon, who bought the house, wrote one of the standard Swahili grammar books. He was a friend of the late Kabaka of Buganda. King Freddie used to come and stay regularly at the house.

"Our son's bedroom used to be King Freddie's royal suite", said Mrs Pollard. Ernest Haddon was known to friends and neighbours as "Uncle Packy" because of his size. He was just like a pachyderm, according to those who remember him. Ernest Haddon's sister was also a successful author. Her book, *String Games for Beginners* still brings in a regular income for the family. The chair which Mrs Haddon left in the house is now used by Graham Pollard in his study.

Professor Sir Harry Godwin, who retired as Chair of Botany eight years ago, has lived at No. 30 with his wife since the 1930s. Friends describe him as "a great man – part of that group of people who in the 1930s began placing archaeology in the context of environment". Sir Harry Godwin remembers Barton Road as a country lane. The love of nature and rural pursuits is reflected in the Godwins' garden which recalls the garden of William Morris' Kelmscott Manor. A gravel path flanked by standard roses runs between the front lawns.

When Mark and Lettice Appleby built No. 2 Barton Road on the site of an orchard by the Caius playing field in 1952, bulldozers digging up the land for them unearthed a doorstep, which suggests that another house had once stood on the site. Could this have been Newnham Villa? From the 1880s until the 1930s, Newnham Villa stood between Clare Road and the Caius playing fields. In 1887, George Barnes lived there just down the road from the Hancock's dairy farm. Mrs S. E. Barnes was still living there in 1925.

The Applebys, who just after the war had to have a licence to build their house, bought the land freehold from the publican of the Red Bull across the road.

(The man and his wife were called Chapman and they later became caretakers at The Leys School.) The architect of the Appleby's home was called Myers. He designed several houses in the vicinity of the Perse Boys' School.

No. 4 Barton Road, a Newnham College hostel called "Whitstead", the home in the 1930s of H. C. Stanford, the secretary of the University Library, was designed by T. D. Atkinson, who wrote various books on the history of architecture. The architect H. C. Hughes who, with Peter Bicknell, designed No. 2 Barton Close, was apprenticed to Atkinson.

Hughes used to bicycle out to Ely Cathedral with Atkinson who had the job of advising on the fabric of the cathedral. The trip went like this: Atkinson always arrived at 12.30 p.m. just in time for lunch, when the Dean would say that there was no time for the building and if anything needed doing they wouldn't be able to afford it.

Much further up Barton Road, No. 94 was designed by H. C. Hughes in 1923 for J. N. Landon, while Nos. 88–90 were designed for the Master and Fellows of Corpus by T. H. Lyon. Hughes left Lyon's partnership in 1926 because Lyon was party to the destruction of the cottages on the site of which the Peterhouse hostel was developed next to the Master's lodge.

Nos. 32, 34 and 36 Barton Road were designed by Spalding and Myers, while Nos 38–40 were designed in March 1938 for Henry and John Twinn of No. 286 Mill Road, who were speculative builders. In 1940, No. 38 Barton Road at the corner of Barton Close became the home of Arthur Cobb and his wife Catharine. They stayed there for ten years, while their family were young, before moving to Cromwell House in Trumpington in 1950, where Mrs Cobb teaches jewellery making. She remembers that the wartime spirit was very strong in Barton Road. "Everyone got very matey doing firewatching duties." She recalls a good deal of army traffic passing up and down the road, but Barton Close was a safe place for the children to play. She and an undergraduate did all the wartime carpentry in the Close.

A market garden once stood on the site of St Mark's Court just beyond Nos. 10 and 12 Barton Road, two stylish Edwardian houses which were built as a pair in 1907. Both houses have been home at one time to different members of the Heffer family.

The real newcomer to the north side of Barton Road is Wolfson College, the formal gates of which are opened only to Royal visitors. The college, of which Graham Pollard is librarian, has brought a new element into the neighbourhood – a large cosmopolitan population, and it owns and leases several houses in Barton Road and Barton Close.

After reading "Down Your Street – Barton Road", Harry Littlechild wrote from Cottenham, to say that the article had brought back a very happy memory to him: "Although I lived on the Huntingdon Road, many of my friends lived in the Newnham area, where in fact I was actually born. Several of us young lads were in college choirs, and during the Christmas period we occasionally went carol singing in an effort to earn an honest copper.

"We always felt that we gave good value as we always sang at least two carols before knocking on the door. I can remember one very cold night when singing outside a rather large house on Barton Road. When in response to our knock on the door a dear old lady confronted us and invited us into the house. We were ushered into a large room, which was very warm by virtue of a good fire blazing away in the grate.

"There were five of us and we were each handed a carol sheet, then the lady sat down at the piano and we spent the rest of the evening singing carols. With the carols finished the lady made us a cup of cocoa, and gave us sixpence each, which in those days was a handsome sum of money, and as far as we were concerned a very successful night."

Stephen Coteman who lived in Newnham all his life until he retired, tells me: "I well recall the 1920s when the carriers' carts came in from the neighbouring villages on Wednesdays and Saturdays, and the wide grass margins by the roadside used for hay where horses and goats were tethered during the summer months.

"Where Barton Close now stands were four and a half acres of market gardens, which my father and grandfather before him farmed – going back into the last century. My grandparents lived in a thatched cottage on Grange Road where Upton House now stands.

"I remember Mr A. L. Bird (mentioned earlier in the article) who built the first bungalow on the north side of the pit. He was a captain in the RFC during the First World War, and lived there with his old mother who was very fond of cats and kept many that could be seen around the place.

"The island in the middle of Bolton's pit was then well above water level where fruit trees grew and was a pretty sight in blossom time. In the early part of this century, Johnny Cook stood at the junction of Barton Road and Newnham Road selling his haberdashery to passersby. It is still referred to as Johnny Cook's corner by the older inhabitants of Newnham."

Paul Bedale wrote to say: "We are very interested in the article on Barton Road because more than 50 years ago we lived at No. 95 Fieldside. "Our grandparents, Mr and Mrs H. G. Whibley, also lived with us. My grandfather had been Mayor of Cambridge at the turn of the century and owned Brimley, Whibley & Sons, with a grocer's shop in Market Hill.

"I can remember some of the names you mention in the article, Mr Morley Stuart and Mr Bird particularly. The latter was, I think, considered to be somewhat eccentric. There were also Quiggins in Grantchester Road at that time. Opposite to us lived Professor Landon, Fellow of Clare. In the early 30s, he was my tutor in mechanical sciences.

"I had a number of friends and acquaintances along the road who were, like myself, day boys at King's College Choir School. Amongst them were the Forster Coopers on the corner of Grantchester Road, the Rushmores who lived a little nearer the town and the Winfields, who lived beyond Grange Road. Professor Rushmore was later Master of St Catharine's College.

"Collectively we were known to our headmaster, Mr C. R. Jelf, as the 'Barton Road Ink Club,' a reference I am afraid to the state of our fingers and our exercise books.

"I have many happy memories of Barton Road, one of them being the occasion in 1929 when I had just got my first driving licence (no test required then and I accelerated along Barton Road in the family bull-nosed Oxford and reached the exhilarating speed of 40 mph!"

Don Mackay, of Roebuck House, 28 Ferry Lane, Old Chesterton was surprised that there wasn't a mention in the articles of the very colourful character, Alfred Winship, who built and lived in the house called "Make Westings", which also has a garden backing down on to the lake.

"Alfred made and lost several fortunes during an exciting lifetime. He took part in building a heavier than air flying machine, which, although it never managed to get off the ground, at least helped to blaze the trail to eventual success for others.

"He went on to be the first manufacturer of concrete roofing tiles. Acres of Winship tiles can still be seen on roofs in Cambridge. He set up his tile making operation at Milton where he dug and graded his own sand and aggregate for the purpose, with machines designed and built by himself. He started to put up buildings for other traders at his site at Milton while continuing in his old age to contrive very clever but primitively made contraptions for handling the sand.

"The pace of modern technology overtook him but he never gave up. It must be a good ten years since he died but I am sure many of your readers will remember him pottering around Cambridge in his ancient Morris Oxford well after his 80th birthday. A remarkable man and a remarkable life."

Frances McMullan of 10 Northfield, Girton, wrote to say that she was very interested in the article on Barton Road and its lovely lake. "Professor Peter and Sheila Stern have lived at No. 83 Barton Road, by the lake, for many years. Sheila and Peter are my daughter and son-in-law, and I have been finding inspiration in this lake for years. I have painted and drawn many works of the lake and its various moods."

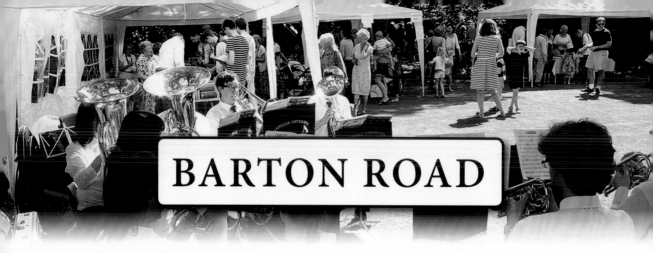

BARTON ROAD

Revisited

Nowadays, when coming into Cambridge from the open countryside to the west, the approach to the city is still relatively rural with green fields that soften the view. It is not exactly Constable country, but of the approaches into the city it is probably now one of the least jarring.

As David Jones in his book *Hideous Cambridge a city mutiliated*, published in 2013 by Thirteen Eighty One LLP, writes of this Barton Road approach: "From the bridge over the motorway, St John's Chapel tower, King's Chapel, the University Library and the Catholic church provide a modest but inviting indication of the distant city."

"The Chemistry buildings in Lensfield Road show up more than one would wish, as do the white-topped blocks of flats in the station Triangle. Further round is the inescapable sight of Addenbrooke's probably visible from Mars. But it could be much worse. This is a skyline to be preserved."

And it is still quite rural as you drive into Barton Road because the first thing you see on your left in a field next to the last house, is a herd of two dozen grazing goats, consisting of a billy goat, his harem and his daughters.

So here you are approaching one of the most famous cities in the world and in spite of the pretentious skyscrapers shooting up on the south-east side of the city, what you get here is still a touch of "rus in urbe"[6] – an appropriate image reinforced by the cows grazing on Coe Fen as you get further into the city!

The goat herd belongs to Melanie Onuorah, who lives in Thornton Close, Girton. "How did you come to be enamoured of goats?", I ask her. "I married an African. Goat meat is the staple food in Africa and Asia. Seventy-five per cent of people in the world who eat meat, eat goat."

The project was her husband's idea, but it was the Women's Institute who got her going and helped her make contact with the two ladies from whom she has been renting the field for the last five years. When the temperature drops below freezing, she looks after them by bringing them hot water. The tender loving care she gives them is reflected in their good health and beautifully soft coats.

---

[6] Latin: meaning "country in the city"

This is the only goat herd kept for its meat in the whole county. Melanie and her husband, trading as Melobi Ltd., run the Anglia Farm Shop, an online company selling frozen goat meat imported from northern Europe, as well as fresh home reared goat meat from the farm on Barton Road.

The semi-rural feel was there 30 years ago when I wrote the first series of "Down Your Street – Barton Road" articles, and it is the same today. As the report "Cambridge Suburbs and Approaches: Barton Road", prepared by The Architectural History Practice Ltd. for Cambridge City Council points out: "the rural edges to the west and to the south have been jealously preserved from development for nearly 100 years, and the area retains a strong identity and coherence." Will these edges be preserved in the 2014 Local Plan, I wonder.

Although there is much more traffic and parking congestion, there is a wide footpath shared on the north side between pedestrians and cyclists, with a sensible demarcation line between the two. The verges, lined with many different species of trees remain, as do the large detached and semi-detached houses with their front hedges and extensive rear gardens. None of the fields leading to Barton Road have been built on, and there is no bus lane scything through. Well there wouldn't be room for one!

Much of the absence of too much inappropriate or drastic change in this leafy road and its approaches, although it used to be much quieter as the Barr

"Rus in urbe" – goats grazing in the field alongside Barton Road.

Goat herd
Melanie Onuorah
with her new born
goats on Barton
Road.

sisters would point out, is due to the constant vigilance of local inhabitants, including many young people. They all work together with the local councillors to maintain the character of the area.

Councillor Sian Reid who is one of the four strong team of Lib Dem councillors in Newnham explains to me at her home in Millington Road, that they are pretty much in defensive mode when it comes to protecting this special area, part of the important West Cambridge conservation area. "Our priority is to defend the character of Barton Road, a street with its fine examples of domestic architecture. It is a very pretty road with lovely verges and trees, but the character of the road is determined by the houses. It should be seen as part of the Newnham community."

Sian Reid, daughter of the former Liberal MP Emrys Roberts, first stood as election for councillor in 2002. She says that Newnham is a wonderful place to be a councillor for. "People are so well informed, well intentioned and very active. It makes our job easy and enjoyable. Councillor Reid is clearly very community minded herself – inviting everyone in Millington Road to her house for a drinks party to meet new residents was one of her diary entries for the day after my visit.

It can't have been that easy though seeing off the massive developments proposed for north and south of Barton Road in the 2006 Local Plan. Plans to build thousands of houses were rejected by the City Council and fought through the courts. Mind you, would building on the flood plain have been such a good idea? The Bin Brook regularly causes flooding in nearby Gough Way. Geography teacher, Nigel Lucas, who lives in Barton Road and has recently retired from teaching for many years at King's College School, reckons that Gough Way, built in the 1950s would never have received planning permission today because of the flooding risk.

Professor Helen Cooper, who moved back to Cambridge from Oxford in 2004 as Professor of Mediaeval and Renaissance English and a Fellow of Magdalene College, now lives off Gough Way. She recalls: "in the Great Gough Way Drown of 1978, when we were just about to sell the house, No. 107, in preparation for the move to Oxford, we were the last house on that side of Barton Road not to be flooded, though the loo, being at a lower level, had several inches of water in it. On another (dryer) occasion, a newt turned up there, having come in through an airbrick."

One of the recent achievements of the councillors and their supporters, of which Sian Reid says she is very proud, has been the extension of the Conservation Area to include Barton Close. "There was a proposal to knock down a house at the corner of Barton Close and build a block of flats. That scheme was defeated."

But there have been changes to some of the houses in Barton Road, with several being bought up, and either converted or demolished so that the new owners can make them into even bigger mansions. No. 106, formerly the last home of Sir Vivian Fuchs who moved there from No. 78 when he retired, is one example. On Sir Vivian's death in 1999, it was sold. Later, having fallen into a state of disrepair and damaged by flooding, it was then demolished and rebuilt as "Portbridge".

The bungalow at No. 89 Barton Road overlooking the lake, built by the late Reuben Heffer who died in 1985, is being demolished as I write. The house was sold in July 2013 to a developer who has been given planning permission by Cambridge City Council to build a large house there.

Clare Hall have bought No. 102 Barton Road on the site of the ancient orchards of Corpus Christi College, and converted it into graduate student accommodation. No. 77 is another new house. The original one was flattened. And King's College wants to redevelop Croft Lodge Gardens with at least one four-storey student block close to the building line.

Wolfson College
in the spring.

Ring True

The opportunity to acquire this bell arose as a result of the donation of a set of 12 new bells to Great St Mary's to mark the University's 800th anniversary, and the old 11th bell (the second largest of the set after the Tenor bell) was saved by Wolfson from leaving Cambridge. With the College being originally founded as University College, having "Ring True" as its motto and featuring a bell in its coat of arms, this was considered an appropriate gesture in the University's anniversary year.

One of the most significant changes in Barton Road has been the expansion of Wolfson College, the major graduate college founded originally as University College in 1965 and renamed Wolfson College on 1 January 1973, in recognition of the substantial endowment from the Wolfson Foundation. Now there are more than 70 nationalities represented there. The College was originally based at Bredon House, a property built in the early twentieth century by John Stanley Gardiner a Professor of Zoology at the University from 1909–1937. He donated the house, with its long narrow garden running from Barton Road to Selwyn Gardens, to the university upon his death in 1946. The College then purchased further property on its eastern boundary.

In Barton Close, Wolfson now own Nos. 2, 3 and 5. No. 2 is named Barton House (after the village), No. 3 is named Norton House (after Frederick Norton, an early Fellow); No. 4 no longer exists (The Bursar, Christopher Lawrence suspects that the College Library is on the site of it) and No. 5 is Wolfson's President's Lodge. In Selwyn Gardens, the college owns No. 28, named Plommer House (after a founding Fellow, Dr Hugh Plommer who left his house to the college in his will). And within the college site there is a house called Selwyn Gardens House, which was once No. 26.

Though most of the College's buildings are modern, the design of the campus is similar to that of the University's older colleges, with buildings grouped around two main courts. The floor of the entrance hall to the main building is made of thin slices of granite taken from the old London Bridge (the main section of which was taken to Arizona to be rebuilt in the late 1960s).

Further acquisition of neighbouring properties continued into the 1980s, culminating in the purchase of the house and garden owned by Sir Vivian Fuchs on

Prince Albert – a forlorn figure before his statue was rescued

Some special artefacts adorn Wolfson College. Take, for example, the handsome statue of Prince Albert in the college's Chancellor Centre. Prince Albert was Chancellor of the University of Cambridge from 1847 until his death in 1861. The university, at the instigation of the next Chancellor the Duke of Devonshire, commissioned the sculptor John Henry Foley to carve the statue which was completed in 1875. It had originally stood at the entrance of the Fitzwilliam Museum, where it was unveiled in 1878 by the Prince of Wales, Albert Edward, but was moved out, or rather banished to Madingley Hall in 1956 at the say-so of the then director of the Museum, who apparently disliked Victoriana.

Here it stayed until 2004, until it was rescued by Wolfson College at the instigation of the Vice President, Dr Owen Edwards. In an article in the Wolfson College magazine 2003–2004, Dr Edwards explained how the statue "used to stand at the head of a pond beyond the outhouses of the Hall on the spacious ground, as this was the place he had last visited shortly before his death. There the statue rested, a forlorn figure covered in lichen, missing fingers due to frost damage. For many years, a visit entailed wearing stout Wellingtons and hacking one's way through nettles." Later, the pond was used for fishing so there was a path, and the plinth was a convenient ledge for bait boxes and sandwiches.

However, in 2004 the University agreed that the statue should be housed once more indoors, protected from the elements under the cupola of the new Chancellor's building at Wolfson, which was opened by the then Chancellor, HRH the Duke of Edinburgh on 17 December 2004. Prince Albert is now warm and dry and his fingers are once again intact!

the western side on the College. The acquisition of property has allowed for the building of a number of new facilities, mainly funded by donations from philanthropic foundations and individuals.

A major donation from the Singaporean businessman and philanthropist Dr Lee Seng Tee paid for the construction of two major buildings – the Lee Seng Tee Library and the Lee Seng Tee Hall. What prompted Dr Lee Seng Tee to become such a major benefactor? Dr Bill Kirkman, a Fellow of the College explains that Dr Lee whose daughter Fiona, starting in 1973, studied at the College, was a major pineapple grower in Singapore. He also had interests in rubber and investment banking. "While visiting his daughter at Wolfson and on the way to the station, he shared his concerns about disease in his pineapples with the College's senior tutor Dr Peter Lowing, a pineapple agronomist. Dr Lowing then went with a research team to Singapore, cured the pineapple disease and the College received the major benefaction!"

Barton Road's hidden lake.

St Mark's Church – focal point of Barton Road.

An article in the College magazine in 2003–2004 explains that Dr Lee also gave the college art works and other items from his extensive collections. The Betty Wu Lee Garden, which is named in honour of his wife, combines Chinese and English styles in a manner appropriate to the College.

There is neither a chapel at Wolfson, nor a High Table nor Senior Combination Room. It is an informal, warm, welcoming place with beautiful gardens.

Fuchs House named after Sir Vivian, is noted for a large topiary of a penguin with an egg (hence its other name of Penguin Palace). Sir Vivian's lead husky Blackie is buried in the grounds and a further reminder of Antarctic exploration is the design of the weathervane on the Lantern of the Western Field Building, depicting a team of huskies drawing a sleigh.

Before Wolfson College acquired Sir Vivian Fuchs' house, James Cadbury nipped across the road and dug up the cowslips growing in the Fuchs' garden, replanting them in his own garden in Barton Road. A near neighbour, Joan Wooding also went picking flowers in the Fuchs' garden. A teacher at Newnham Croft School at the time, involved in a project on wildlife conservation, she was given permission to dig up some plants, and while doing so spotted a couple of sledges in a shed. Wonder if they were used in the Commonwealth Trans-Antarctic Expedition?

Thirty years on, James and Joy Cadbury are still in their house by the lake, and their daughter Lucy and their grandson Darwin, on the opposite shore in Fulbrooke Road, but the lake has changed its ownership. "The 14 lakeshore dwellers have each contributed to the Bolton Pit Company Ltd.", James Cadbury explains. "The lake is now secure and taken care of by the committee who run the company. The lake itself has not changed, the kingfisher is still there and there are a lot of good fish – large tench, hundreds of roach and the odd large pike – but the island has eroded."

If the fish are prolific, so too is the mistletoe growing on local trees including limes and false acacia, the tree commonly known as the Black Locust. It is native to North America, in particular the states of Pennsylvania and Georgia and grows as far west as Arkansas and Oklahoma. Wonder who brought it to Newnham?

The area is not short of trees! James Cadbury recalls taking a walk up Barton Road, and noting 30 species flourishing there, including, until recently, a giant sequoia, a coastal redwood from California, growing in the garden of a house at the junction of Barton Road and Millington Road.

If the trees are thriving in Barton Road, so too is the Red Bull public house which has a popular beer garden and serves good food. The Hat and Feathers pub has fared less well, however. In fact, it has gone. Once a pub with a lot of character, and popular with students particularly from Selwyn College, it lost its way I am told, under pub company ownership and has since been converted into housing. Darwin College acquired the site in 2011 and were given planning permission, although it was in the conservation area, to convert the pub into six small self-contained flats with a communal garden, for their students. Darwin also houses students in No. 10 Barton Road.

Cambridge University Brass Band adding to the entertainment at St Mark's Church summer fête.

What goes almost without saying is that the sense of community in Barton Road, as in the rest of Newnham, is as strong as it was all those years ago. And there are many community networks linking different age groups. You only have to look at the flyers on the fence by Gonville and Caius sports ground to realise that. Here is a small sample. On offer are Pilates and yoga classes, the Newnham Runners meet every Tuesday evening in the Hardwick Social Club, there are suzuki cello lessons, Cambridge Early Music concerts as well as Cambridge eco gardening, and many more. In particular, gardening and allotments are an important part of the lives of many Newnhamites. And I have seen a notice appealing for help to find a lost tortoise.

An important focus for the community in Newnham is still St Mark's Church with its improved, and now frequently used community centre where a range of activities for all ages, from toddlers to the retired is provided by many church goers and volunteers. There is a regular session for young children called Toddles. Brownies meet there, older people play bridge, others do yoga, and some gather at the Lunch Club, to name but a few of the activities. An additional car park in the last few years has been a vital addition to the Community Centre and the Church, which also has a new glazed porch.

Drama and music (the organ is of an excellent quality) thrive at St Mark's and joint concerts with Wolfson College are held in the church. The St Mark's Church summer fête with the Cambridge University Brass Band adding to the entertainment is one of the high spots of the season. With its tombola stall, homemade cakes, plants, secondhand books and toys, as well as a bouncy castle and pink candy floss for the children, and tea served in the Church hall for the grown ups, it is one of those occasions that ranks with village cricket and picnics in the countryside, as a quintessentially English event on the summer calendar. The fête this summer was held on Midsummer's Day and the brass band played *Abide with Me* as the finale to the afternoon's entertainment.

Midsummer's Day in Cambridge this year was a specially beautiful day – hot with bright sunshine and in the parks and gardens in the city, and alongside the river people were having gentle picnics and sitting in groups, just like a Manet painting.

Mr Tom Challis manning the plant stall at the Church fête.

Alan Burgess — a dedicated Newnham campaigner

The late physicist and mathematician, Dr Alan Burgess, who was Fellow of Wolfson College, lived for many years in St Mark's Court, where he was a member of St Mark's Court Residents Society. He is remembered as one of Newnham's tireless and dedicated campaigners. His daughter, Gina Burgess Winning tells me how her father and her late mother Lore, both had a strong social conscience. "They were both concerned about the environment and for the need to preserve it."

Her parents stood up to injustice. Both were members of the Labour party in the days before Blair and New Labour. They both demonstrated at Greenham Common against cruise missiles. Alan was one of the few men there.

"Nearer home, they campaigned to preserve the village character of Newnham and they wanted to keep it as a safe, pleasant place to live and for children to go to school and play."

Lore Burgess, who escaped from Nazi Germany as a child on one of the Kindertransport trains, was an artist. "She was always very interested in history, and was a Blue Badge, tri-lingual tourist guide, with a very keen sense of the value of Cambridge historic sites and streets", her daughter recalls.

One of the biggest campaigns into which they threw themselves was the fight against the Cambridge Western Relief Road. They also campaigned successfully against a proposed car park on the old Newnham hockey ground near Newnham Croft School, and had the support, among others, of Dr J. C. Coppola of No. 26 Owlstone Road, who had come to this country from the United States to get away from the motor car. He said at the time: "In America the automobile has become a blight on the land."

Alan Burgess, his wife, Lore and son Neil cycled from Land's End to John O'Groats, camping on the way. Neil was the youngest person to have cycled that route.

As a campaigner against inappropriate roads or roads in the wrong place, Alan Burgess stuck to his principles. He always preferred to walk, cycle or use public transport, only using his car when he absolutely had to or when the alternatives were impractical. One of the things Alan Burgess loved about living in Newnham was that he could walk to work. In the last years of his life, his own car only came out of the garage perhaps once a year for its MOT test. But the family did take to the road on occasion. Gina remembers the time that her father drove the family to Leningrad for a conference. "We camped en route."

Like the Cadburys and the Coles, Professor Richard Perham and his wife Dr Nancy Lane Perham are still living at No. 107 Barton Road. Professor Perham, a molecular biologist and protein chemist, was Head of the Biochemistry Department and in 2004 became Master of St John's College until he retired in 2007.

What do they consider to have been the main changes in the last 30 years? "Fewer academics, the growth of Wolfson College and every square inch now built on. But we are lucky still to have our shops", is their verdict.

In recent years, two of their close friends who were neighbours since 1978, Mr Chris Hadley at No. 99 (a graduate of St John's College and an industrial chemist at CIBA-Geigy), and Margaret Stockbridge, a graduate of Girton College, a JP who was prominent in local life have both died.

Another person who appreciates the Newnham environment is Melanie Hey, who specialises in church conservation for the firm of architects Freeland Rees Roberts, based in City Road. She lives with her family in Barton Road in a comfortable 1930s house which, she says, has a Canadian feel to it – for several years she and her family lived in Edmonton, Alberta.

Melanie has a theory about houses. "One reason that a house is more than bricks and mortar is because of the people who have lived there. When we live somewhere we leave a trace." She believes a house feels happy when it is full of people. It is certainly true of 104 Barton Road, she says, and maybe that is because for many years it was a day nursery run by Erica Burgon. Melanie bought the house from Erica's son Paul and his wife in July 2012.

Melanie recalls that the day they moved in, her near neighbours Angi and Tim Cole called round to welcome the newcomers who were wrestling with packing cases. "Don't bother to dress up", said Angi. "We are not posh round here." At

Barton Road's public house The Red Bull is popular with the locals and visitors to Cambridge.

one time, Angi was one of five Cheltenham Ladies College girls living within a few houses of each other.

Like Sian Reid, Angi holds neighbourhood parties in her garden. The last party to be held was to mark the Queen's Diamond Jubilee in 2012. "Most people here are honourable and very caring with a strong sense of community", she says which seems to me a spot-on way of describing the good people of Barton Road. They are vigilant too!

At the time of writing, the university and some of the colleges are proposing again that the green belt land north of the Barton Road be developed. This was rejected during the preparation of the 2006 Local Plan by the council, the planning inspector and the high court.

Lib Dem city councillor for Newnham, Sian Reid says: "Ward councillors and the council are opposed to these proposals and I hope the inspector again supports our position. There are many problems with the site including that large areas are in a flood zone, it has poor access to high quality public transport, and the air quality and noise problems created by proximity to the M11. It would also have a detrimental impact on the setting of the city."

Cyclists heading across Lammas Land towards Barton Road.

Bibliography

Barker Ernest, *Age and Youth*, Oxford University Press, 1953

Betjeman John, *Summoned by Bells*, John Murray, 1989

Eden Richard, *The Origins and Development of a College for Advanced Study*, Clare Hall, 2009

Feinstein Elaine, *Ted Hughes: The Life of a Poet*, Phoenix Paperback, Weidenfeld and Nicolson, 2001

Girouard Mark, *Sweetness and Light – The Queen Anne Movement 1869–1900*. Oxford University Press, 1977

Goodman, A. W. *A little history of St Botolph's*, Cambridge

Gray John A., *Newnham*. Hanwell Publications, 1977

Guillebaud Philomena, *Cambridge's West Side Story Changes in the landscape of west Cambridge 1800–2000*. Published by Philomena Guillebaud, 2011

Henderson R. J., *A history of King's College Choir School Cambridge*, 1981.

Howarth T. E. B., *Cambridge Between Two Wars*: Collins, 1978

Jones David, *Hideous Cambridge a city mutilated*. Published 2013 by Thirteen Eighty One LLP

Keynes, Margaret, *A House by the River: Newnham Grange to Darwin College Cambridge*

Larke Helen M. and Shield S., *A short history: The Foundation of Edward Storey 1693–1980*

Nelson Owen, *The Coe Fen Road*, The Mercury Press, 1929

Raverat, Gwen, *Period Piece*, Faber & Faber Limited, 1952

Reeve, F. A., *The Cambridge Nobody Knows*, The Oleander Press, 1977

The Short History of the College by *The Master, Fellows and Scholars Selwyn College, Cambridge, 1973*

The Letters of Virginia Woolf, 6 vols. *Edited by Nigel Nicolson and Joanne Trautmann*, Harcourt Brace Jovanovich, New York, 1975

Woolf Virginia, *A Room of One's Own*, 1929

Wigham Price, A. *The Ladies of Castlebrae*, 1985

Acknowledgements

Picture credits

Images identified by page reference are either copyright to, or the property of the persons or institutions listed. Whilst every effort has been made to identify sources, the publisher will be happy to acknowledge corrections or any further information in future editions.

The publisher would like to thank the following for their kind permission to reproduce photographs:

Martin Brett, p. 97; Cambridge Antiquarian Society, pp. 3, 4
Christophe Gordon Brown, pp. 174, 175
Cambridge Archaeological Unit/Dave Webb, pp. 28, 29
Cambridgeshire Collection, pp. vix, 5, 12, 34, 36, 43, 44, 78 (bottom right), 115, 116, 119, 120, 131, 132, 135, 153, 155, 156, 178, 184, 185 and 188
Cambridge Newspapers, pp. 6, 15, 43 (left), 82, 100, 104, 117, 134, 165, 177
Churchill College Archives Centre, pp. 19, 20, 32
Eddie Collinson, p. 173
Master and Fellows of Corpus Christi College, p. 103
Darwin College/Sir Cam, p. 129, Owen M. Edwards, p. 203
Fitzwilliam College/Alison Carter, p. 25
Nigel Grimshaw, pp. 64, 65, 68
Maggie Hammond, p. 61; William Heffer, p. 163;
The Provost and Fellows of King's College Cambridge, p. 38; 60, Photography: Mike Dixon 2011 King's College Cambridge
Sara Lennox Cook, p. 66; Carol Lipton, p. 130
Neboysha Ljepojevic, p. 172; Morcom Lunt, pp. 55, 88, 98; St Marks Church, p. 186
The Principal and Fellows, Newnham College Cambridge, pp. 136, 138
Sara Payne, pp. 8, 10, 23, 24, 26, 31, 52, 54, 81, 109, 112, 113, 125, 149, 160, 168, 169, 170, 171, 182, 204, 207, 208
Tim Rawle, pp. 33, 53, 59, 126, 127; Master and Fellows of Selwyn College, p. 45
St. John's College School, pp. 57, 58; The Master and Fellows of Trinity College, pp. 22, 31 (inset), 35, 37, 70, 77, 93, 106; Tyndale House, p. 63; Alexandra Vlasto, p. 78; Peter Watson, p. 85
Julian Weigall front cover and pp. 30, 141, 142, 144, 145, 161, 181, 199, 200, 201, 202, 210
Gina Burgess Winning, p. 208; Ed Yashin, p. 128

Text permissions

Every effort has been made to reach copyright holders. The publisher would be pleased to hear from anyone whose rights they have unwittingly infringed.

We would like to thank the following for permission to use their material:

Extracts from *Age and Youth* by Sir Ernest Barker (1953). Copyright Oxford University Press. By permission of Oxford University Press

Extract from *Clare Hall, The Origins and Development of a College for Advanced Study Clare Hall 2009* by Richard Eden reproduced by kind permission of the author

Extract from *"Ted Hughes: The Life of a Poet" Phoenix PaperBack Weidenfeld and Nicolson 2001* by kind permission of the author, Elaine Feinstein

Extract from article "Looking Back" by Professor Mary Fowler in Darwin College's *50th anniversary portrait. Darwin College 2014* by kind permission of the author

Extract from *Sweetness and Light– The Queen Anne Movement 1869–1900. Oxford University Press, 1977* by Mark Girouard. By permission of Oxford University Press

Extracts from *Cambridge's West Side Story Changes in the landscape of west Cambridge 1800–2000* Published by Philomena Guillebaud 2011 reproduced by kind permission of the author

Extract from *Hideous Cambridge a city mutilated. Published 2013 by Thirteen Eighty One LLP* reproduced by kind permission of the author David Jones

Extract from *A history of King's College Choir School Cambridge 1981* reproduced by kind permission of the author Robert Henderson

Extracts from *Period Piece* by Gwen Raverat. © Estate of Gwen Raverat and reprinted by permission of Faber and Faber Ltd

Extracts from The Short History of the College *by The Master, Fellows and Scholars Selwyn College, Cambridge. 1973* by kind permission of the Master and Fellows